DATE DUE

DEMCO 38-296

Views of American
Landscapes

Thomas Nast, 'The Artist in the Mountains', 1866

Views of American Landscapes

EDITED BY

MICK GIDLEY

AND

ROBERT LAWSON-PEEBLES

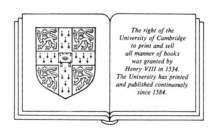

The right of the
University of Cambridge
to print and sell
all manner of books
was granted by
Henry VIII in 1534.
The University has printed
and published continuously
since 1584.

CAMBRIDGE UNIVERSITY PRESS

Cambridge
New York   Port Chester
Melbourne   Sydney

Views of American landscapes

of the University of Cambridge
n Street, Cambridge CB2 1RP
r York, NY 10011, USA
10 Stamford Road, Oakleigh, Melbourne 3166, Australia

©Cambridge University Press 1989

First published 1989

Printed in Great Britain at the University Press, Cambridge

British Library cataloguing in publication data
Views of American landscapes.
1. Arts 1750–1920. Special themes: North America. Landscape
I. Gidley, M. (Mick), *1941–*   II. Lawson-Peebles, Robert
700

Library of Congress cataloguing in publication data
Views of American landscapes/edited by Mick Gidley and Robert Lawson-Peebles.
p.   cm.
Includes bibliographical references and index.
ISBN 0-521-36435-3
1. United States in art.   2. Landscapes in art.   3. Art, American.
4. English literature – History and criticism.   5. United States in literature.
I. Gidley, M. (Mick)   II. Lawson-Peebles, Robert.
N8214.5.U6V53   1989
700 – dc20   89-7227 CIP

ISBN 0 521 36435 3

CE

Contents

Contents

Illustrations

Illustrations

Illustrations

Illustrations

Notes on contributors

CLIVE BUSH is a Senior Lecturer in English and American literature at the University of Warwick. He has published interdisciplinary articles on many aspects of American literature and culture. He is the author of *The Dream of Reason* and three books of poetry: *Clearing the Distance*, *The Range Taken* and *Shifts in Undreamt Time*.

ROBERT CLARK teaches English and American Literature at the University of East Anglia. His previous publications include *History, Ideology and Myth in American Fiction, 1823–1852* and, as editor, *James Fenimore Cooper: New Critical Essays*.

GRAHAM CLARKE is Lecturer in English and American Literature at the University of Kent, where he also teaches in the American Studies programme. His publications include essays on nineteenth-century American poetry, Poe, Hawthorne, Hemingway, Olson, and Black fiction. He is the editor of a forthcoming book of essays on the American city.

STEPHEN FENDER has taught at Edinburgh, London and various American universities, and is now Professor of American Studies at the University of Sussex. His books include *The American Long Poem*, *Plotting the Golden West: American Literature and the Rhetoric of the California Trail*, and *American Literature in Context: 1620–1830*. He is editor of the *Journal of American Studies*.

MICK GIDLEY is Director of the Centre for American and Commonwealth Arts and Studies and Senior Lecturer in American Literature at the University of Exeter. His publications include *With One Sky Above Us: Life on Indian Reservations at the Turn of the Century*, *Kopet* (on Chief

Joseph), *American Photography*, and a forthcoming book on William Faulkner.

OLAF HANSEN, former Dean of his Faculty, is Professor of American Studies at the University of Frankfurt. He has published a selection of the writings of Randolph Bourne, numerous articles on American and German literary and cultural topics, and his study of American transcendental thought will shortly be published by Princeton University Press.

ALLEN J. KOPPENHAVER is Professor of English and American Studies at Wittenberg University, Ohio. As well as writing poems, plays, and several libretti for the composer Robert J. Haskins, he has contributed articles to a variety of journals on such figures as Charles Ives, T. S. Eliot and Winslow Homer.

ROBERT LAWSON-PEEBLES has held posts at Princeton, Oxford and Aberdeen before moving to Exeter in 1988 to lecture in American and Commonwealth Arts. His publications include *Landscape and Written Expression in Revolutionary America: The World Turned Upside Down* and articles on Henry George, Poe and William Carlos Williams. He is writing books on early American literature and Ernest Hemingway.

LEO MARX is the William R. Kenan, Jr, Professor of American Cultural History in the Program in Science, Technology and Society at the Massachusetts Institute of Technology. He is the author of *The Machine in the Garden* and *The Pilot and the Passenger: Essays on Literature, Technology, and Culture in the United States*, and editor (with Susan Danly) of *The Railroad in American Art*.

BERNARD MERGEN is Professor of American Civilization at George Washington University, where he also teaches courses in American material culture in association with the Smithsonian Institution. He contributed chapters to the three-volume *Handbook of American Popular Culture* and has contributed articles on such topics as the history of labour and leisure to such journals as *American Quarterly* and *South Atlantic Quarterly*. He is Associate Editor of *American Quarterly*.

CHRISTOPHER MULVEY is Course Director of BA Honours English at King Alfred's College, Winchester. He previously taught in New York for fifteen years. He has published *Anglo-American Landscapes* and is engaged in writing *Transatlantic Manners* and editing the forthcoming *New York: City as Text*.

FRANCESCA ORESTANO teaches English and American literature at the University of Palermo, Sicily. She has published essays on such topics as Charles Dickens, Anthony Trollope, Wyndham Lewis, the American college novel in the fifties, and Mary McCarthy. She is now writing a book on John Neal and the foundations of the early American Renaissance.

PHILIP STOKES moved out of illustrative photography into educational studies, then PhD research in photography at the University of Exeter. He teaches the history and theory of photography at Trent Polytechnic, Nottingham, and has published articles on Walker Evans and other figures.

Foreword
LEO MARX

> Thus in the beginning all the world was America ...
> John Locke (1690)[1]

Ever since the transatlantic voyages of discovery, Europeans have drawn upon topographical scenes and natural objects to represent their ideas of the New World. At first, indeed, the natural environment seemed to be the only source of images capable of signifying America. Of course Europeans also depicted the unexplored continent as the domain of the 'Indians', but the native Americans, like people of color on other continents, appeared to be savages, hence their presence scarcely contradicted the Europeans' notion that in the New World, before their arrival, nature was all – or virtually all. The Indians' exotic ways merely reinforced the contrast between the wild, undeveloped continent and the built environment of Europe. All of which helps to account for the persistent habit of representing America with images of landscape.

But to what extent, it may be asked, is this habit peculiar to the representation of America? After all, don't we associate every nation with images of its characteristic terrain? We probably do, yet in the American case certain special historical circumstances enhanced the iconographic significance of topography. The most obvious of those circumstances, already mentioned, was the European tendency to disregard the indigenous culture, to think of America as little more than a huge land mass. A second, related circumstance was the unusual coming together of this astonishingly abundant, pristine, seemingly unclaimed, seemingly boundless territory and the world's most 'advanced' societies. 'A very old and a very enlightened people ... [has] fallen upon a new and unbounded country where they ... may extend themselves at pleasure,' wrote Alexis de Tocqueville: 'This state of things . . . is without a parallel in the history of the world.'[2]

Another of these special circumstances was the evolution of landscape as an aesthetic subject, and as a separate genre within the visual arts, at the time colonization was beginning. It is customary, in recounting the formation of ideas about America, to emphasize the hope of a new beginning that Europeans projected on the place, the *object* of representation (as in naming it 'the New World'); we tend to forget, however, that one *form* of representation they used – the art of landscape itself – also was new at that time. The idea of landscape as a distinct aesthetic kind had indeed just begun to seize the imagination of artists. According to the *Oxford English Dictionary*, the word 'landscape', meaning 'a picture representing natural inland scenery', first entered the language in 1603, four years before the first permanent English colony was established in Virginia. But the introduction of the word into English (it evidently was borrowed from the Dutch) did not of course mark the initial use of landscape imagery in art.[3] Incidental images of natural scenery had had a place in the visual arts since antiquity, and they had appeared with increasing frequency during the late Middle Ages and the Renaissance. Toward the end of the sixteenth century, however, a fundamental change in sensibility occurred; people took a much greater interest in the meaning and value of nature, and artists developed a new feeling for the beauty of natural scenery.[4]

In earlier periods images of the countryside had served almost exclusively as background, or as a source of adjunctive icons in ecclesiastical, mythological, or history paintings, and in portraiture. (One thinks of those tantalizingly detailed glimpses of the distant landscape we get in Renaissance portraits.) But these were subsidiary images, included chiefly for illustrative, symbolic, or allegorical purposes. In such paintings the landscape invariably represented something other than itself. The artists were not attempting to transcribe what they saw in the terrain, or to express their own feelings about it, but rather to evoke a more beautiful, divinely ordered, universal reality concealed behind the visible surface of things. To them the landscape was an embodiment of an ideal cosmos. But towards the beginning of the seventeenth century European painters, especially in Holland, began treating landscape as a subject sufficient unto itself. What requires emphasis here is that the appearance of an independent genre exclusively devoted to landscape coincided with the establishment of the first permanent European colonies in North America.[5]

The rising interest in natural scenery at this time was closely bound up with the fundamental transformation of Western culture. During the era of colonization, say between 1492 and 1776, European scientists and philosophers effected a radical change in prevailing ideas about the nature of nature, and about relations between mind and nature. To simplify greatly, before the scientific revolution associated with the discoveries of Galileo, Kepler, and Newton, and the new empirical theory of knowledge associated with Bacon, Locke, and Descartes, the reality hidden behind the surface of natural appearances had been conceived as a completed structure of unchanging universals. To get at the truth about nature, accordingly, it was necessary to grasp those timeless forms of being. But the scientific rationalists shifted the locus of reality away from abstract universals to observable, concrete particulars. They gave credence to the increasingly popular assumption that individuals could discover the truth by means of their own immediate sense perceptions.

This heightened trust in the capacity of individuals to perceive the essence of reality through direct observation also was bound up with the mentality of the merchant capitalists who then presided over the economic expansion of Europe. Mercantile success depended in large measure on each investor's judgment of the future profitability of competing ventures, including many overseas projects. In this period, indeed, their attention was being drawn to the immense profits that could be gained from prudent investments in North American real estate. The convergence of the merchant class's material and aesthetic motives in this period is suggested by the development of its taste for the contemplation of landscape, both in nature and in art. (In Holland and in Florence, where the new genre of landscape painting flourished, merchants were in fact the chief patrons of landscape painting). Like their contemporaries among the natural scientists and empirical philosophers, these men of business enjoyed the close, detailed observation of nature's visible face. They liked to think of the hard materiality of the earth's surface as an ultimate repository of order and beauty, meaning and value.

This change in sensibility was accompanied by several important technical innovations – changes in the how as well as the what – within the visual arts. Artists of the sixteenth and seventeenth centuries devised new ways of transcribing the observable particulars in the external world. The discovery of the principles of light and perspective enabled them to convey the illusion of objects existing in a defined, recessed, habitable, unified or, in a word, real space. These technical, quasi-scientific discoveries prepared the way for the creation of less abstract and symbolical, more lifelike, pictures of the landscape.

Comparable innovations in technique, in form, also enabled English writers to convey a more localized sense of place. Between the time of Shakespeare, whose settings tended to be general and vague, and the time of Defoe, landscape description in imaginative writing took on greater specificity. Implicit in the new form, 'the novel', as it developed in the period, was the culture's enhanced respect for the significance of particular characters rather than generalized types, and for *novel*, 'once only' events in specific times and places. Defoe probably was the first English writer, as Ian Watt has observed, 'who visualized the whole of his narrative as though it occurred in an actual physical environment'.[6] The rapidity and intensity with which interest in topography then seized the novelistic imagination becomes evident when we consider how brief an interval separates Defoe's work from the virtuoso performances of landscape art by Walter Scott and James Fenimore Cooper.

But the development of new, more realistic descriptive techniques does not mean, as might be supposed, that eighteenth-century writers and artists had abandoned the notion of landscape as a figuration of ideal nature. To be sure, they now could create more compelling mimetic images of the visible world, which is to say a more credible illusion of having transcribed in detail what they actually saw in – and felt about – specific locales. (It was in this period that landscape painters took to working out of doors, directly 'from nature'.) Yet most artists put these new 'realistic' techniques in the service of one or another idealizing project. Often their chief aim, as exemplified by the work of Claude Lorrain and Nicolas Poussin, the most influential landscapists of the age, was to celebrate the neoclassical concept of nature as the only locus, save for divinity, of harmony, order, and beauty. In the eighteenth century a number of theorists defined new, ostensibly universal categories – the Beautiful, the Sublime, the Picturesque – for classifying responses to external nature. Thematic and formal conventions derived from Virgil were widely used to convey an updated version of the ancient pastoral

Foreword

ideal: a harmonious way of life that reconciled the root conflict between art and nature by combining the best features of each. This vision of a 'middle landscape' was to be a fount of powerful icons for the new American republic, a nation whose citizens liked to think of themselves as inhabiting a terrain midway between the overcivilization of *l'ancien régime* and the savagery of the western frontier.[7]

All of the essays that follow are about the ways that English and American writers, painters, and photographers represented the American landscape. Looking mainly but not entirely at the century and a quarter following the Revolution, the essayists examine the preconceptions, ideological biasses, aesthetic conventions, and discursive practices that shape accounts of the North American continent. Their common subject, in other words, is the meaning of America as it was embodied in images of landscape. Although the essayists do not subscribe to any single definition of landscape, an admittedly slippery word, they initially assume, with John R. Stilgoe, that it 'means more than scenery painting' or 'a pleasant rural vista'. According to him it means

shaped land, land modified for permanent human occupation ... A landscape happens not by chance but by contrivance, by premeditation, by design; a forest or swamp or prairie no more constitutes a landscape than does a chain of mountains. Such land forms are only wilderness, the chaos from which landscapes are created by men intent on ordering and shaping space for their own ends.[8]

In treating wild, unmodified nature as landscape, many of the contributors to this volume part company with Stilgoe. They do not require, as he does, that a stretch of wilderness be materially developed, made into 'shaped land', in order to be considered a landscape. They recognize human shaping as a criterion for distinguishing landscape from mere land, but they accept a non-literal, non-physical or symbolic 'shaping', one accomplished by an act of mind or imagination, as satisfying that requirement. When an image of raw nature is embodied in a work of art – a literary account, a painting, a photograph – it thereby acquires the status of landscape. (Looking at a terrain through a 'Claude glass' – a small, portable, empty picture frame – was another, eighteenth-century means of shaping chaotic nature.) Landscape on this view is not the unmediated physical terrain itself; it must be, as Stilgoe contends, a socially constructed entity; but, in contradistinction with his view, the essayists in this volume assume that an unruly wilderness satisfies that requirement – becomes a landscape – when it is represented in words, paint, or photographic images. They regard the act of representation itself, quite apart from the specific subject, or the artist's interpretation, as imposing the requisite degree of order, value, and meaning upon the seeming chaos of the wilderness.

Having adopted this broad conception of landscape, the contributors to this volume necessarily attach great importance to those influential men for whom the American terrain was primarily an economic fact. During the colonial period, political economists and philosophers often cited the vast expanse of unused North American land to illustrate the proposition that things which exist outside the economic system have no value. According to exponents of early capitalism, marketability was the key to all value. This was John Locke's claim when he made his famous assertion, in a chapter entitled 'Of Property', that 'in the beginning all the world was America'. His often misconstrued point here is not so much the general resemblance between the American wilderness and the prehistoric state of the world, it is the function of commodity exchange as a necessary precondition of all social value. The lands of America, he is saying, are destined to remain worthless until they are included in a capitalist system.

for I ask, what would a man value ten thousand or a hundred thousand acres of excellent land, ready cultivated, and well stocked too with cattle, in the middle of the inland parts of America, where he had no hopes of commerce with other parts of the world, to draw money to him by the sale of the product? It would not be worth the enclosing, and we should see him give up again to the wild common of nature whatever was more than would supply the conveniences of life to be had there for him and his family.

Thus in the beginning all the world was America ...[9]

The predominance of this economic conception of land created many of the problems faced by artists and writers in depicting the American landscape. Some who accepted the primacy of exchange value represented the New World by mere catalogues – itemizations of potentially useful objects – as if they were adequate descriptions of place. Others attempted to reconcile the idea of land as commodity with the inherited belief, a legacy of feudalism, in the stewardship of land as the basis of community. The difference between economic and other – political, moral, aesthetic, metaphysical – meanings of land is the key to one set of

Foreword

conflicts that recurs in these essays. Another set arises, as we have seen, from the many disparities between American facts and imported preconceptions. Several focus on the peculiar difficulty of accommodating the observed details of the American scene – above all its seemingly prehistoric, scaleless character – to received aesthetic categories, or to the enhanced illusion of creating an exact transcription of reality made possible by the new nineteenth-century technology of representation, the camera.

The essays are divided into three sections. Section I contains discussions of several broad issues affecting the North American landscape and the equivocal patrimony of Old World aesthetics. The second and third sections develop the dialectic of place and idea, experience and preconception, response and convention, implicit in the first. Section II contains essays about specific aspects of Anglo-American cultural relationships, and the essays in Section III deal with the evolution of a vernacular style grounded in the particulars of American experience. If the contributors to this volume discern any large, encompassing tendency at work in the depiction of the American landscape, it is the ubiquitous aspiration for direct, original response – a response to the American terrain unmediated by inherited conventions. It is an impulse like that which inspired the innovations of Emily Dickinson, Walt Whitman, Mark Twain, Winslow Homer, and Paul Strand. It is an expression of that yearning, attributed by Wallace Stevens to the 'latest freed man', for the liberty, the self-transformative possibilities of pure being: 'to be without a description of to be'. The prospect of that kind of freedom, like having 'the ant of the self changed to an ox', was held forth by the sun (how it 'came shining into his room') or, in other words, by the American landscape.[10]

Notes

1 'An Essay Concerning the True original, Extent and End of Civil Government', in E. A. Burtt, ed., *The English Philosophers From Bacon to Mill* (New York: The Modern Library, 1939), p. 422.

2 *Democracy in America*, ed. Phillips Bradley (New York: Vintage Books, 1945), vol. 2, p. 36.

3 The use of a corrupt form of the word, 'landskip', dates from 1598, and almost certainly owes its origin to the emerging Dutch school of landscape painting. See Henry V. S. Ogden and Margaret S. Ogden, *English Taste in*

Landscape in the Seventeenth Century (Ann Arbor: University of Michigan Press, 1955), pp. 5–6.

4 For a persuasive account of that change, see Marjorie Hope Nicolson, *Mountain Gloom and Mountain Glory* (Ithaca: Cornell University Press, 1959).

5 For more comprehensive interpretations of this history, see Enzo Carli, *The Landscape in Art* (New York: William Morrow, 1980); Kenneth Clark, *Landscape into Art* (New York: Harper and Row, 1975); Peter C. Sutton, ed., *Masters of 17th-Century Dutch Landscape Painting* (Amsterdam: Rijksmuseum, 1987).

6 *The Rise of the Novel* (Berkeley: University of California Press, 1957), p. 26.

7 For an analysis of the use of the pastoral myth and its conventions in the interpretation of American experience, see Leo Marx, *The Machine in the Garden: Technology and the Pastoral Ideal in America* (New York: Oxford University Press, 1964).

8 John R. Stilgoe, *Common Landscape of America, 1580–1845* (New Haven: Yale University Press, 1982), p. 3.

9 Locke, 'Essay', p. 422.

10 Wallace Stevens, 'The Latest Freed Man,' in *The Collected Poems of Wallace Stevens* (New York: Knopf, 1957), pp. 204–5.

Acknowledgements

This book had its origins in plans for a series of workshops convened by the editors as part of the Biennial Conference of the European Association for American Studies in April 1986. The conference was held at the Hungarian Academy of Arts and Sciences, beside the Danube, in Budapest. It often seemed appropriate that between sessions of debate on American landscapes it was possible to emerge into a city of striking and seemingly endless vistas. The workshops' warmth of atmosphere – and perhaps their productivity – owed much to the hospitality of our Hungarian hosts. We were also pleased that the workshop speakers willingly agreed to revise papers in the light of discussion and further reflection. Together with some additional essays, they are presented here in amended form as, we hope, a coherent book. We would like to thank Andrew Brown of Cambridge University Press for his trust and encouragement. We are grateful to Leo Marx for his Foreword. We would like to offer formal thanks here to the many persons in a variety of institutions who provided illustrations and permissions to reproduce them; annotation of permissions is given in the list of illustrations. We would like to express gratitude to the universities of Aberdeen and Exeter for financial and other support. Patricia Dowse of American and Commonwealth Arts at Exeter was very helpful in sending out letters to keep the project moving. We would especially like to thank Sarah Moore, who wrestled successfully with the word processing of the whole script.

Mick Gidley and Robert Lawson-Peebles

1 * Introduction

MICK GIDLEY AND ROBERT LAWSON-PEEBLES

In 1852 the New York publisher G. P. Putnam pressed upon the American public a collection of essays and sketches titled *The Home Book of the Picturesque*.[1] In his prefatory 'Publisher's Notice', Putnam called it a 'home-manufactured presentation-book' (p. 7). It was a 'home book', though, in more than one sense. It was meant for the home as an 'ornamental', popular work, the equivalent to a presentday coffee table book. It was home-produced in competition with similar gift books imported from Europe. And, as its subtitle – *American Scenery, Art and Literature* – manifests, it advocated the application of predominantly European ideas of the picturesque to the home situation. With essays by Washington Irving, James Fenimore Cooper, Bayard Taylor, William Cullen Bryant and others, and steel engravings based on paintings by such figures as Thomas Cole, Asher Durand and Frederic Church, it constituted, as Putnam said, 'an experiment', a modest celebration by several hands of the pictorial possibilities of the American terrain. If its publishing history is anything to go by, the experiment was a success which led to the publication of such grand works as Bryant's two-volume, large-sized compilation of writings and engravings, *Picturesque America* (1872). Some intellectuals of the time – though not most of the contributors to *The Home Book* – thought that the indigenous people of the continent were particularly appropriate subject matter for depictions of the American scene. In 1856, for example, the editor of *The Crayon*, a pioneering and influential art journal, wrote, 'We should rejoice to see the Indian figure more often on our canvas, and the costumed European less', before going on to bemoan the fact that the Indian was too often presented as either 'a kind of savage harlequin, lost in a cloud of feathers and brilliant stuffs'

1

or too 'hung about with skulls, scalps, and half devoured fragments of the white man's carcass'.[2]

It had not always been so apparent that there was so much in the New World to celebrate or even, as *The Crayon*'s editor believed, to falsify. Charles Varlo, a Yorkshireman, was an expert on farming who owned holdings in England and Ireland and published extensively on husbandry. Yet he was not content to stay down on the farm. On the basis of extremely dubious documents he believed that he also owned the Governorship of New Jersey and, shortly after the American Revolution, he crossed the Atlantic to establish his claim. The Americans were not impressed. As a consequence Varlo travelled widely and, like so many before and since, decided on his return to Britain to turn a few pennies by publishing his experiences. But his conclusion was not what one might expect. 'After all my travels through America,' he declared, 'I saw nothing worth attention, except raising tobacco and India corn.'[3]

Varlo's is, in fact, just one of a large number of dismissive accounts of America. Although, understandably, they appeared with the greatest frequency in the years during and after the Revolution, such documents are by no means confined to that period. As soon as the New World appeared on the map of European consciousness many writers complained that they did not like what they saw, or thought they saw. The complainants found ready responses from those who were enamoured of America; hence the debate about whether or not the discovery of the continent was, as the deliberately comic reductivism of *1066 and All That* has it, a good thing for the world.

The debate, more particularly conceived, was taken up with vigour in the New World itself and has exhibited divisions of opinion at least as deep as those among its European contributors.[4] If, for instance, a significant number of people from Puritan times onwards were obeying a cultural imperative which required, in Cecelia Tichi's phrase, 'the *reform* of the New World into the utopian New Earth', others saw the continent as an Eden already, capable of sustaining life with next to no human effort.[5] If many apologists followed Tom Paine in equating America's wide spaces with freedom and opportunity, others associated them with licentiousness and violence. In one of the sourest entries in Pudd'nhead Wilson's calendar, Mark Twain commemorated Columbus's landfall with a formulation which simultaneously undercuts and exceeds the sniffiness of *1066 and All That* in its radically absurd polarization: 'October 12. – The Discovery. – It was wonderful to find America, but it would have been more wonderful to miss it.'[6]

As Leo Marx has noted in his Foreword, this collection of essays is about the ways in which America has been found in print, painting and photography. Concentrating primarily but not exclusively on the century and a quarter following the Revolution, it probes aspects of the debate over America. It examines some of the veils of preconception and prejudice which cloak the most 'balanced' accounts of the continent, or even the decision *not* to produce accounts of it. Charles Varlo's extreme conclusion that there is nothing to be seen involves, after all, a series of value judgments. 'Nothing' implies a belief in 'something'. The contributors to this volume have each asked, from their own particular area of expertise and angle of vision, what the 'something' might be in the instances they consider. In Varlo's case, it seems the landscape was viewed materialistically, as a resource. In common with many New World settlers and not a few temporary visitors, potential economic exploitation was uppermost in his mind; hence his interest in those forms of husbandry new to him. He was mistaken in the long term even in his economic calculations, but at the time his established European holdings were doubtless more attractive to him.

That 'something', whatever its components, creates a landscape – even if it is only one of vacuity punctuated by corn and tobacco plants. Peter Conrad, in the first graphic sentence of his book on British visitors to the New World, said, 'Before America could be discovered, it had to be imagined.' Similarly, in a treatment of the poetics of exploration, Stephen Bann borrowed a phrase from an André Gide novel in which Columbus is envisioned sailing ever onwards, going 'ahead, straight on. His aim was himself, and it was himself that *projected* it in front of him.'[7] Ever since 'The Discovery', as Twain called it, the 'imagination' has continued to be used in a like manner. The first contributor to *The Home Book of the Picturesque*, E. L. Magoon, aptly titled his long essay 'Scenery and Mind' in acknowledgement of the power and prescience of mental states. At one Emersonian moment he affirmed, 'Every rational inhabitant of earth is a focal point in the universe, a profoundly deep centre around which every thing beautiful and sublime is arranged, and towards which, through the exercise of admiration, every refining influence is drawn' (p. 5). According to the geographer John Brinkerhoff Jackson, 'a landscape is not a natural feature of the environment but a *synthetic*

3

space, a man-made system of spaces superimposed on the fact of the land'. As a student exclusively of the physical world, Jackson does not approve of what he calls 'the vicarious literary experience' – and he would certainly disapprove of rhetorical formulations like Magoon's – but his definition is a useful one for our purposes.[8] It makes a primary distinction between, on the one hand, 'the fact of the land' or terrain and, on the other, whatever is made of it. Even when we are considering an expanse of wilderness never worked upon by human beings (with ax, plough or, even, seed drill) that expanse, when written about, painted or photographed, becomes a synthetic space. To a Varlo the synthetic space or landscape is a resource; to a Magoon it is beneficent scenery; and to a geologist, say, it comprises data to be recorded and understood.

Whether landscape so conceived is out there, in and of the actual earth, or set in print, Jackson's distinction illuminates the way in which it lies at the intersection of 'nature' and 'culture'. As Raymond Williams has shown, 'nature' and 'culture' are amongst the most complex words in the language.[9] It follows that 'landscape' partakes of such complexity, and we have tried to reflect our awareness of its difficulties in the content and organization of the present book. The essays are so ordered as to move the reader through a narrowing focus from the general to the specific, from comprehensive cultural determinants to *some* of their effects. 'Prospects', the first section of *Views of American Landscapes*, therefore, contains contributions which discuss broad issues affecting the New World landscape and the equivocal patrimony of Old World aesthetics. The second and third sections develop the dialectic implied in the first: the second, 'Anglo-American perspectives', consists of discussions of specific aspects of Anglo-American cultural relationships; the third, 'American illustrations', deals with the evolution of a national and vernacular style.

Henry T. Tuckerman, in his contribution to *The Home Book of the Picturesque*, admitted that, despite its grandeur, the sheer scale of American scenery creates problems for the visual artist: 'The very immensity of the [mountain top] prospect renders it too vague for the limner; it inspires the imagination more frequently than it satisfies the eye' (p. 115). Clive Bush, in the opening essay in the present book, focusses on the nineteenth century but suggests that what could be called the *problematics of space* in a far more profound sense is at the root of American ideology. He draws upon a wide variety of contexts, from literary texts to aspects of city planning, to advance his speculations and make his case. Commenting on a chapter in R. W. B. Lewis's *The American Adam*, for instance, he shows that the word 'home', the ambiguities of which have already been mentioned, often sums up an important absence; American social space, in his view, is characterized by contention rather than friendly interaction.

If American ideology is rooted in the problematics of space, it may also be located in European time. Henry David Thoreau provides a good example. Although one of the most independent of Americans, constantly seeking an original relation with the universe, when he composed his account of the ascent of Mount Ktaadn, he drew upon European sources. This is one of the conclusions to be taken from the essay by Olaf Hansen. Similarly, Hansen implies that the new medium of photography took its place in a continuum which stretches back to the Pre-Socratic philosophers. Such a perspective enables us to look anew at some of the exploration photographs and at Alfred Stieglitz's celebrated cloud pictures. While Hansen deploys an American landscape in terms of sequence and circularity, Stephen Fender works initially through cracks and caesurae in tracing a 'fault line'. His essay is an analysis of a recurring trope, which he calls 'the figure of anticipation', in the work of such diverse figures as Sarah Kemble Knight, Irving, Fenimore Cooper, Cole, Bryant and, in the twentieth century, Willa Cather. Philip Stokes's essay deals with Timothy O'Sullivan and other exploration photographers who were, in two senses of the word, journeymen. He makes it clear, however, that their work was far from humble. It was at once utilitarian and introspective, densely textured and interpretively inexhaustible. Above all, we may see now that it was far from innocent. Like Hansen, but using different arguments, Stokes examines the paradox that the newest medium in the 'newest' environment should be so indelibly suffused with the tinctures of civilization.

The second group of essays, 'Anglo-American perspectives', develops one specific aspect of the paradoxes raised in the first group: the problem of assimilating American terrain to Old World modes of discourse. By the eighteenth century, English aesthetic thinkers and their landed patrons had developed extremely sophisticated methods of expressing, and therefore of appreciating, their surroundings. But when these methods were applied to America they were often found wanting – as in Tuckerman's feeling that the very immensity of American scenery 'renders it too vague for the limner'.

5

Robert Clark compares English and American writings about their respective environments and shows the relative poverty of American eighteenth-century descriptions. He accounts for it largely in economic terms, suggesting that the attitudes to the environment of figures like Thomas Jefferson was frequently utilitarian. With William Bartram offered as an exception, Clark argues that descriptions of the terrain often resembled a shopping list in which excursions into landscape aesthetics seemed out of place. Christopher Mulvey puts forward a similar case, but from a different point of view. Drawing upon the insights of Roland Barthes, Mulvey elaborates the extended textual system which allowed the English to feel that they were lords of all they surveyed. But, when in America, that aesthetics of ownership worked for them only fitfully. Certainly, they had no mediating language to understand the Mississippi River, and in consequence treated it with repugnance. This last aspect is discussed further in the essay by Robert Lawson-Peebles. In a detailed examination of the letters written by Charles Dickens during his western trip in 1842, he suggests that the great river made such a deep impression on Dickens that his reaction affected many of his later writings.

The third group of essays, 'American illustrations', both provides a response to the second and takes up matters not yet considered. Francesca Orestano, for example, shows how the undeservedly little-known writer John Neal reached back to the ancient mythological figure of Apollo in certain of his key poems and fictions. But, interestingly, according to Vanni, he did so in the context of an effort to create a new national literature. Indeed, if some Old World-oriented writers found that they were losing their voices in America, a number of Americans drew upon the vernacular to develop an appropriate syntax. The early years of the Republic saw the emergence of forms of expression related to the environment. This is the theme of essays by Graham Clarke and Bernard Mergen. Building upon work by Leo Marx and John Stilgoe,[10] Clarke shows that by the inclusion of such everyday phenomena as barns, worm fences and even particular kinds of paint, certain artists of the early Republic were able to fracture the canons of European style. In doing so, such painters as Ralph Earl and Samuel Morse turned their landscapes into ideological constructs which befitted the environment in which they found themselves. Similarly, Bernard Mergen argues that the humble almanac – the farmer's friend of the eighteenth century – played an important role in fostering the communitarian ideals of the early Republic. Through an analysis of images of snow, he reveals that the myth of Valley Forge and Emanuel Leutze's famous painting of 'Washington Crossing the Delaware' are simply the tips of a cultural iceberg, a textual system. This particular textual system, of course, excluded the South. One might almost say that the Civil War was a geopolitical inevitability.

Crèvecœur's *Letters from an American Farmer* are frequently cited in these essays, and they do sanction many different interpretations. There is, for instance, a darker side to them which anticipates the more doomladen moods of Thomas Cole. Cole was born in England and emigrated to America only to discover, like T. S. Eliot in the reverse direction a century later, that he was 'a resident alien' in an adoptive culture suffused with material values. The result, as Allen Koppenhaver affirms in his essay, was an overwhelming sense of loneliness, mitigated by his companionship with his 'kindred spirit' Bryant and granting him a grammar with which to depict certain elements of the American terrain. Indeed, Koppenhaver's essay here unites with several others in this collection to suggest that it was precisely those features of the American continent which had stripped Old World writers of their resources that now, as if in compensation, endowed New World writers, painters and photographers with fresh resources.

This point was certainly to be found in several of the contributions to *The Home Book of the Picturesque*. It is implicit in Bryant's essay on 'The Valley of the Housatonic' and Taylor's celebration of 'The Erie Railroad'. In George W. Bethune's 'Art in the United States' it was put forward with almost strident conviction: 'No artists of modern times have had such opportunities for originality, or such untrodden walks opened before them, as ours . . .' (p. 184). One such untrodden area, thought Bethune, was constituted by 'the aborigines of North America'. Mick Gidley, basing his case primarily on readings of particular examples, examines the heritage of photography's efforts to capture that particular domain. He shows that, despite the medium's much vaunted 'realism', the Indian figures in photographic landscapes are as ambiguous as the 'savage harlequin' of painting bemoaned by the editor of *The Crayon*. These representations, of course, were bound up with the actual plight of Native Americans in the culture. Also, as several of the essays in this collection hint, the situation of the Indian presents in exaggerated form the fate of the continent, forever eluding the descriptive strategies developed to portray it.[11] This perhaps accounts for the despair of several of the figures discussed here.

Here we have another example of the prescience of Crèvecœur's *Letters*. Crèvecœur, like Irving, Cooper and Cole, found himself in a land that was changing rapidly, and not necessarily for the better. His Letter XII is in consequence a study of anomie, the harrowing account of someone whose habitat is no longer intelligible to him. Similarly, Samuel Morse developed a means of expressing America, only to renounce painting in despair. Instead, he invented the telegraph, a more profitable but less fertile grammar of American space. But possibly the saddest case is that of Philip Freneau. The Revolutionary poet's last years were embittered by the absence of an audience. His last known poem (discussed by Mergen) is entitled 'Winter'. Five years later Freneau died in a blizzard. This eerie conjunction may be taken to represent the freezing that afflicts both life and language when the landscape – which lies, too, at another intersection, between the nation and its environment – has moved elsewhere. Perhaps, after all, some human beings are allowed to choose their deaths . . .

In this book we have also registered our awareness of the conceptual complexity of 'landscape' – which, as we have seen, is unlike a word such as 'terrain' in that it necessarily includes the idea of a viewer – in the choice of a doubly pluralistic title: *Views of American Landscapes*. Magoon, in *The Home Book of the Picturesque*, asserted that, 'in contemplating the relative influence of scenery on mind', we would all 'probably conclude' that 'mountains exert the greatest and most salutary power' (p. 25). Of course, as some of the essays in this book clarify, there were *cultural* reasons for coming to such a conclusion. Magoon was voicing a commonly held opinion of his time and place. On 21 July 1866 the political caricaturist and illustrator Thomas Nast contributed a full-page spread of woodcuts, 'Sketches Among the Catskill Mountains', to *Harper's Weekly*. One of these is titled 'The Artist in the Mountains' (see Frontispiece). Despite the use of the singular in his title, Nast actually depicts several artists. The mountains, indeed, are positively crowded with them. Some draw with pencils in sketch pads; some work with brushes at easels; at least one crouches under a hood to peer through a large view camera which is perched precariously on an outcropping rock; some are observed by passersby; and all of them look in different directions. Each artist sees and composes a different landscape. Each onlooker in the cartoon sees the artist's view as well as his or her own. Thomas Nast, in succession, presents his landscape of them; and we view his work.

This cartoon may serve not only to document and satirize nineteenth-century American artists' predilection for mountain scenery, but also acts as a visual parable of the difficulties of achieving a synoptic vision of anything so complicated as landscape. If we seem, from the bleakest vantage point, to have moved from Varlo's negativity only to Freneau's frozen end, this is partly because we have travelled not through America itself, but through, precisely, prospects, perspectives and illustrations: efforts to describe, understand, and come to terms with it. The essays assembled here are, in turn, views of those views, and testify to a continuing fascination.

Notes

1 *The Home Book of the Picturesque: or American Scenery, Art and Literature* (1852), rpt ed. with an Introduction by Motley F. Deakin (Gainesville, FL: Scholars' Facsimiles and Reprints, 1967). Page references hereafter will be given in the text.

2 *The Crayon*, as quoted in Robert Taft, *Artists and Illustrators of the Old West 1850–1900* (New York: Scribner's, 1953), p. 213.

3 Varlo, *Nature Display'd* (London: Printed for the Editor, 3rd edn, 1793), p. 137. A brief life of Varlo is in the *Dictionary of National Biography*.

4 The most exhaustive text on the debate over America is Antonello Gerbi, *The Dispute of the New World*, trans. Jeremy Moyle (Pittsburgh, PA: University of Pittsburgh Press, 1973).

5 Tichi, *New World, New Earth: Environmental Reform in American Literature from the Puritans through Whitman* (New Haven and London: Yale University Press, 1979), p. ix.

6 Twain, *Pudd'nhead Wilson* (1894; rpt Harmondsworth: Penguin, 1969), p. 224.

7 Conrad, *Imagining America* (London: Routledge and Kegan Paul, 1980), p. 3; and Bann, 'From Captain Cook to Neil Armstrong: Colonial Exploration and the Structure of Landscape', in J. C. Eade, ed., *Projecting the Landscape* (Canberra: Humanities Research Centre, Australian National University, 1987), p. 78.

8 Jackson, *Discovering the Vernacular Landscape* (New Haven, CT: Yale University Press, 1984), p. 8 and p. xi, author's emphasis.

9

Mick Gidley and Robert Lawson-Peebles

Williams, *Keywords: A Vocabulary of Culture and Society* (London: Fontana, 1976), pp. 76–82, 184–9.

10 Leo Marx, *The Machine in the Garden: Technology and the Pastoral Ideal in America* (Oxford: Oxford University Press, 1964) and John R. Stilgoe, *Common Landscape of America, 1580 to 1845* (New Haven, CT: Yale University Press, 1982).

11 Parallel discussion of this issue is to be found in Lee Clark Mitchell, *Witnesses to a Vanishing America: The Nineteenth Century Response* (Princeton, NJ: Princeton University Press, 1981).

Prospects

2 ✳ 'Gilded backgrounds': reflections on the perception of space and landscape in America

CLIVE BUSH

This essay is about the quality of perception, the experience of space and the particular manifestation of both in relation to outer and inner 'landscapes' in American culture. It argues that it is impossible to divide up our experience of space. In an important sense the farmlands imply the wilderness, and the wilderness the farmlands. The city implies the countryside and the countryside the city. The domestic hearth implies the public domain and the public domain the hearth. Further, we divorce the geometric from the bodily, the economic from the political and the personal from the social only at a certain risk. The landscape of any society bears the marks of the culture's struggle to mediate priorities among these possibilities, and in American culture during the nineteenth century the land had a unique history. It was not surprising, therefore, that the longest chapter in William James's *The Principles of Psychology* which appeared in 1890, the same year as the 'closing' of the 'frontier', was devoted to 'space'. In that chapter James responded in exasperation to the great German scientist, Helmholtz, who was apparently too willing to accept 'unconscious inferences' in perception. In what the American philosopher called a 'single momentous sentence', Helmholtz was over ready to entertain the quite un-American notion that 'sensations of touch' might be the 'original material of our space-percepts' which thus, from an optical point of view, 'may be assumed as given'. He went on, in a tone which is difficult to judge, 'Of course, the eye-man has the right to fall back on the skin-man for help at a pinch.'[1]

This moment from *The Principles of Psychology* represents in an abstract way some problems fundamental to American perception of space and has certain consequences, therefore, for the perception of the land itself. James, uneasy about the geometric abstraction traditionally associated with the eye, unwilling – somewhat puritanically – to make touch a *first* sensation, and possessing too much of a religious sensibility to let 'unconscious inferences' become the threshold of a secular Kantian creative act which might disturb a more metaphysically required first space, seems to us characteristically American.

Unlike *The Principles of Psychology*, this essay begins abstractly and then moves towards common experience. A few sentences from Merleau-Ponty will help to update some of the issues with which James was faced at the end of the nineteenth century:

> As far as spatiality is concerned ... one's own body is the third term, always tacitly understood, in the figure-background structure, and every figure stands out against the double horizon of external and bodily space. One must therefore reject as abstraction any analysis of bodily space which takes account only of figures and points, since these can neither be conceived nor be without horizon.[2]

Throughout the nineteenth century and for complex cultural reasons, there was a singular divorce in American culture between 'figures and points', and what Merleau-Ponty called 'bodily space'.[3] The useful phenomenological notion of 'horizon' helps to get rid of most of the difficulties of the *a priori* ideal and allows for both chance and purpose in constructing experience. For the Americans that horizon was often locked into a binary opposition of 'new earth' and 'unredeemed wilderness'. This paper will argue not only that Americans failed to take account of that double horizon of external and bodily space and that they were predisposed to abstraction of varying kinds, but that there were a number of Americans who offered a critique of the problem. This essay is divided into three parts. First we shall look at some abstract problems to do with metaphors of space, gradually moving to the more multiple analysis offered by literature. Second, the actual historical development of the 'land' with its consequent effects on the landscape will be considered. Finally, we shall look at some of the effects of the foregoing in terms of common experience.

Metaphors of space

How did Americans in the first years of the new Republic envisage space and the human figure? Was it to be measured by the hand or by the abstract figures of science? It was John Quincy Adams who pondered the relative merits of the decimal system, introduced in France under the Napoleonic code – that Cartesian 'bare idea of space', at once 'undeniable and safe' – and the British system still based on digit, span and foot. He made his much-ignored report to Congress in 1821, putting both sides of the question.[4] In spite of the fact that Americans did not go over to the decimal system, de Tocqueville noted that in spirit: 'L'Amérique est ... l'un des pays où l'on étude le moins et où l'on suit le mieux les préceptes de Descartes.' It was Kant, of course, who was to reclaim space from the religiosity of Cartesian *res extensa*:

It is therefore, solely from the human standpoint that we can speak of space, of extended things, etc. If we depart from the subjective condition under which alone we can have our intuition, namely liability to be affected by objects, the representation of space stands for nothing whatsoever.[5]

It was this same human standpoint which led Kant to his well-known and homely example of a man looking at himself in a mirror, or contemplating the possibility of fitting a left-handed glove on a right hand: 'notwithstanding all their mutual equality and similarity; the glove of the one hand cannot be used on the other'.[6] The terms of relations are identical – as for a clock moving clockwise or anti-clockwise – but the spatial properties have to be grasped by intuition. The problem still occupies contemporary physics.[7] The scientist's desire for a world of infinitely extended equivalences is brought up short against human decision intuitively given. John Quincy Adams was aware that our sense of space needed different orders of representation. Arguing against partialities for decimal arithmetic Adams pointed to the 'inflexible independence and the innumerable varieties of the forms of nature', and concluded that the ways of representing them should reflect that variety: 'gravity and extension will not walk together with the same staff'.[8]

A generation later Emerson, too, was able to grasp intuitively the difference between space and time, but his peculiar view of Reason can only be said to resemble – to borrow Jonathan Edwards's term – a kind of religious affection, albeit secularized: 'What noble emotions dilate the mortal as he enters into the counsels of the creation, and *feels by knowledge* the privilege to BE!' Emerson's employment of transcendental reason as a mode of psychological confidence laid the basis for a paean to the glorious and endless project of science itself. While he later modified this confidence, this moment stands as a monument to an extraordinarily ego-centric vision of man as master of the world. Apparently unaware of the irony, Emerson calls on the entry of Christ into Jerusalem as an analogy for the scientist's relation to nature: 'Nature is thoroughly mediate. It is made to serve. It receives the dominion of man as meekly as the ass on which the Saviour rode.'[9] One would not want to extend the image too far: scientific man on a glorious triumphal ride to his own crucifixion has no God to engineer a resurrection. Yet Emerson's figure holds a certain truth about a religious sense of space which seems pervasive in American culture. That that sense could co-exist with, indeed serve, scientific endeavour was pointed out by Lewis Mumford:

Now astrology had long before been condemned by Saint Augustine and other Christian theologians as a pagan superstition, incompatible with belief in God's exclusive providence and man's free will. With the later corrosion of Christian faith, astrology assumed a special role as a supplementary religion; and the pursuit of occult information, based on the correlation of the exact hour of a person's birth with the conjunction of the planets, demanded not merely exact time measurements but close observation of the heavens. Thus astrology fostered astronomy, as alchemy fostered chemistry. These pursuits were more important by reason of the method than for their reputed results. Copernicus and Kepler both cast horoscopes . . . [10]

That 'pursuit of occult information' within science, and more especially technology, is linked to the exigencies of power and even in the late twentieth century provides its own religious dramas. As the appallingly theatrical light of an exploding rocket, its ashes raining into the sea, recently reminded us, the propaganda of redemptive sacrifice seems as powerful as ever. Its message of 'onwards' depends on a psychology nurtured by the human figure in ecstatic decomposition in space. In his work on classic American literature, D. H. Lawrence put a question mark over Emersonian ecstatic space experience:

The root of all evil is that we all want this spiritual gratification, this flow, this apparent heightening of life, this knowledge, this valley of many-coloured grass . . . and light prismatically decomposed, giving ecstasy. We want all this without resistance. We want it continually. And this is the root of all evil in us.[11]

The multiplicity of real life is swamped by such desires. Indeed, to paraphrase Emerson's most famous essay, how bare must be the ground on which the man stands in order to have the currents of universal being circulate through him?

Reflections on the perception of space and landscape

The recovery, therefore, of the body in relation to space in a way which sets its own 'horizons' becomes urgent in our time. In the United States this 'religious' sense of space was reinforced by a number of historical factors. Even if we put to one side Puritan fears of the wilderness as unredeemed, there was a quite plausible fear of the actual land itself. The obverse side of the coin of ecstatic experience was, as Allen Koppenhaver's contribution to this book reiterates, a nightmarish sense of lostness and impotence. A work on the American Western summarizes conveniently certain aspects of this fear:

The particular relationship between the lonely man and limitless, unpopulated space is still the most impressive fact of the big country. We are continually shown Western enterprises such as the raising of telegraph poles and the laying of steel rails in terms of individual challenge. In Western drama a corporate effort is very often whittled down to a battle between one man and thousands of miles of space, with all the hazards it contains. Randolph Scott pulls Western Union through. It is one man versus big country.[12]

It was indeed simply a big country, and the need to dominate it in turn required (if the pun may be forgiven) guiding 'stars'.

A decade before the Apollo space mission, R. W. B. Lewis in his classic work, *The American Adam*, devoted a chapter to what he called 'The Hero in Space'. Speaking of James Fenimore Cooper's Leatherstocking hero Lewis said:

I call such a figure the hero in space, in two senses of the word. First the hero seems to take his start outside time, or on the very edges of it, so that his location is essentially in space alone; and, second, his initial habitat is space as spaciousness, as the unbounded, the area of total possibility.[13]

The phrases 'space alone' and 'the area of total possibility' immediately point to familiar characterizations of American space; the one reaching far back into Puritan individualism, the other drawing our attention to the epistemology of utopian vision. As the patrician Cooper's own political vision soured, and as he struggled with the actual contradictions of land use in the new democracy, the figure of the Leatherstocking in a celebrated moment shifted to an ambiguous American myth:

The sun had fallen below the crest of the nearest wave of the Prairie, leaving the usual rich and glowing train on its track. In the centre of this flood of fiery light, a human form appeared, drawn against the gilded background, as distinctly, and

17

seemingly as palpable, as though it would come within the grasp of any extended hand. The figure was colossal; the attitude musing and melancholy, and the situation directly in the route of the travellers. But embedded, as it was, in its setting of garish light, it was impossible to distinguish its just proportions or true character.

The ambivalence of Cooper's figure is manifest: the garish light stands uneasily with the rich and glowing train, and the graspable with the ungraspable, in that imagined reaching-out of another human hand. It is impossible to distinguish the 'just proportion or true character' of this huge and melancholy figure. Does this sun-bathed figure reflect the confidence of that sun-centred universe of Renaissance science, or the distortions of dehumanized form casting its shadow from the depths of Romantic hubris? Cooper brings his hero ambivalently short of an infinite universe. As the travellers approach the figure they perceive it fading into a more common light: 'a man withered but not wasted'.[14]

When the Leatherstocking finally dies his last word is 'home'. It is a familiar-enough Victorian melodramatic gesture: instinct with religious sentiment. But as Lewis pointed out, that word 'home' has a different significance for the mythic American hero: 'Oedipus, approaching the strange city-world of Thebes, was in fact coming home; the hero of the new world has no home to begin with, but he seeks one to come.'[15] These words distance Cooper from his own hero of the New World yet recapture for us the memory of the American founding experience historically and psychologically. Cooper heaps onto his hero every ecological sentiment, and relegates, through him, a simple Moravian sense of decency to the 'hunting' stage of civilization. Finally characterizing him as stoic, isolated, politically impotent and an Indian killer, he extirpates him along with the 'savages', in D. H. Lawrence's ironical appropriation from Benjamin Franklin, 'to make room for the cultivators of the earth'.[16] Whatever positive values the utopian vision of endless space as an analogue of total possibility holds, they will collapse when the first Latitudinarian and Lockean property holder digs his actual plough into the actual earth. By the end of the century the figure of the strong independent man in limitless space was not an Emersonian mystic, but a Custer needed to break the Indians' last stand.

Americans needed such a figure as imperial England needed a Gordon of Khartoum. As William Appleton Williams commented:

Reflections on the perception of space and landscape

The metaphor of space, which was once a symbol of William Blake's cosmos that awaited man's fertile and creative and transcending genius, has been transformed into a literal area in which to repeat the old frontier habit of conquering a new and virgin territory and then making it over in the image of the old society.[17]

It was, of course, neither new nor virgin, but Williams's point stands. Yet extreme individualism implicit in the American ethic combined with that 'space as spaciousness' – an abstraction of figures and points – certainly helped to produce terror on the actual frontier. Van Wyck Brooks cites R. Ross Brown's journey through the Salinas Valley of California in mid-century as evidence of what life was actually like for an individual encountering American landscape. Brown first saw a fight to the death between a bull and a grizzly bear and was then robbed at pistol point by outlaws. He took shelter for the night in a cabin filled with the bodies of a murdered immigrant family and only a little while later witnessed a bandit who had befriended him stabbed to death in a knife fight.[18]

These landscapes of terror, natural and human, help to provide historical reasons for D. H. Lawrence's comment: 'I have never been in any country where the individual has such an abject fear of his fellow-countrymen.'[19] It was Faulkner a century later who understood the deep psychology of symbolic moral geography. In *The Hamlet* (1940) a character called Houston returns to marry a woman from whom he had been unconsciously fleeing. 'You cannot,' said Faulkner, 'escape either the past or the future with nothing better than geography,' and added:

(Geography: that paucity of invention, that fatuous faith in distance of man, who can invent no better reasons than geography for escaping; himself of all, to who, so he believed, geography had never been merely something to walk upon but was the very medium which the fetterless to-and-fro-going required to breathe in.)[20]

Indeed there is a radical distinction between occupied and inhabited space (maps are for occupation), as Faulkner's 'walking on' and 'breathing in' suggest. The novelist thus confirms the phenomenologist's insight: 'We must therefore avoid saying that our body is in space, or in time. It inhabits space and time.'[21] Faulkner also, however, recorded the human tragedy of the conflict of the two views of the body's relation to the world. And it is to the actual historical manifestations of that conflict in the first half of the nineteenth century that we must now turn.

Across the continent

Accompanying the insights of the writers of the period was an actual politics and economics of development. The most concrete aspect of the psychological abstractionism of 'total possibility' was the imagining of land itself as pure money. Between 1835 and 1837, 38 million acres of public land were sold. Of these 29 million acres were bought as speculative investment, excluding costs, at a minimum of 36 million dollars. The peak years were between 1854 and 1858, when over 130 million acres of public domain were disposed of, half privately and half to states for improvement.[22] This meant in practice a large reselling into the private sector. In 1862 an English observer, D. W. Mitchell wrote:

> Speculation in real estate … has been the ruling idea and occupation of the Western mind. Clerks, labourers, farmers, store keepers, merely followed their callings for a living while they were speculating for their fortunes … The people of the West become dealers in land, rather than its cultivators.[23]

Mitchell's judgment registers a nineteenth-century Englishman's dismay at the use of land for purely speculative purposes. His picture of clerks engaged in grass-roots capitalism, is, however, a little overdrawn. It is well to remember who actually did the speculating. The following evidence is from a work largely unsympathetic to critical accounts of the history of land grants.[24] A micro-study of land speculating on the Iowa frontier estimates that in-state investors, in descending order of importance, were realtors, bankers and lawyers, farmstock raisers, merchants and manufacturers, county and town officials, physicians and attorneys. Bankers combined with specialized professionals (lawyers, surveyors, land office personnel) seem to have been the main actors in the land grant drama. Views of them differ. Some consider them smart operators of the natural market which then kept them in check, others saw them as unlicensed vampires on farmers and creditless immigrants. Whatever the actual truth (which will vary according to the details of the micro-studies and the political values of the historian), a new class of banker and professional agent came into being which posed problems of democratic regulation in a society busily making whatever profit it could while 'limitless' space lasted.

20

It is, perhaps, also important to state the obvious. On the whole, Native American peoples were not viewed as sovereign nations. They were constituted as such in law only for the purpose of swindling transactions. The spirit of original title claims on the grounds of 'discovery' and settlement was maintained. Since land was also the basis of the male suffrage, Native Americans lost political rights along with their lands. Uniquely, however, in the early Republican era, and perhaps uniquely in history, land was seen *as money* and became a primary agent of economic development. It paid off soldiers and debts. It was sold to investment companies to raise revenue and it financed local and state government. It generated working capital in land grants to canal and railroad developers who then resold to other developers. The effects of 'land as capital' can be seen even today. Land continues to be precisely 'a profitable commodity and an object of speculative interest'.[25] In the late nineteen seventies Wendell Berry commented on the problem of soil erosion in northern Kentucky:

This erosion is occurring on the cash-rented farms of farmers' widows and city farmers, absentee owners, the doctors and the businessmen who buy a farm for the tax breaks or to have 'a quiet place in the country' for the weekends. It is the direct result of economic and agricultural policy. The signs of the 'agri-dollar', big-business ... are all present: the absenteeism, the temporary and shallow interest of the land-renter, the row cropping of slopes, the lack of rotation, the plowed-out waterways, the rows running up and down the hills. Looked at from the field's edge, this is ruin, criminal folly, moral idiocy. Looked at from Washington, D.C., from inside the 'economy', it is called 'free enterprise' and 'full production'.[26]

In addition, during the nineteenth century, and especially when the legal individual holding increased from 160 to 320 acres for the settler–speculator, certain social changes were observable. With increased acreage social isolation from neighbours increased. With insufficient population concentration, fees for schooling went up, travel costs increased, institutions such as libraries came more slowly, railroads needed greater subsidies, and farmers found themselves overburdened with taxes and short of labour.[27] Even though the technological side of farming benefited, there were side-effects here too. With the development of mixed chemical fertilizers came the 'scientific sell' of industrial interests. One mid-nineteenth-century advertisement maintained, 'the rotation of crops is not the best way [of resupplying soil]; for although all crops do not remove from the soil the same proportion of its elements, yet they are removed, and the land is impoverished'.[28] The demand for 'whole food' in our time by the middle class has only minimally begun to counteract some of the excesses this kind of thinking led to. The very conception of the individual *in* space and in the utopian reduction, *out* of time, together with Faulkner's sense of 'geography' apart from the body helped to create throughout the nineteenth century a mind-set predisposed to abstraction in relation to the landscape. Against all this the somewhat pious correspondence philosophies of transcendentalist thinkers were powerless indeed.

Inhabited versus geometric space

The third part of this essay deals with a more intimate way of knowing space. It is less concerned with the actual land than with constructed space, with the inhabited more than the projected, although it will not be possible finally to separate the two. A short paragraph from Bachelard's *The Poetics of Space* (*La poétique de l'espace*, 1968) will serve to introduce three examples of interior nineteenth-century American space: the asylum, the omnibus and the domestic parlour:

Come what may the home helps us to say: I will be an inhabitant of the world, in spite of the world. The problem is not only one of being, it is also a problem of energy and, consequently, of counter energy.

In this dynamic rivalry between house and universe, we are far removed from any reference to simple geometrical forms. A house that has been experienced is not an inert box. Inhabited space transcends geometrical space.[29]

Ways of inhabiting space, as opposed to geometricizing it, seem to have been in short supply in nineteenth-century America. Throughout the country, what Mumford called the 'speculative ground plan', the notorious grid iron – developed from Baroque dreams of splendour and power – was used for city planning. The point of view of the aristocratic European court entered the democratic urban space. Mumford quotes from Palladio to give us the types of public building which sought to dominate the environs of the Prince's palace. Next to the Bank in the public square three buildings were felt to be necessary: 'one for such as were debauched or immodest ... and which we now assign to fools or mad folk; another was for Debtors ... and the third for traitors or wicked persons'.[30] The palace, the exchequer, the prison and the mad house are the buildings conceived to complement a geometricist public space. If to this impulse we add an American Puritan sensibility and Anglo-American utilitarianism, the way is prepared for the first large-scale experiment in human engineering within controlled space: the American asylum.

It is, of course, almost too fashionable a subject these days. American commentators are relatively scornful of the late Michel Foucault, but it is doubtful whether attention would have been so closely focused on this important subject were it not for his sometimes obscurantist, but always richly suggestive, work. The origins of what has become known in our own time as 'friendly fascism' can be seen in a passage (quoted from L. C. Dumon) in Foucault's *The Birth of the Clinic* (*Naissance de la clinique*, 1963). In the advice to the clinician, the psychology of the *pioneer* and *entrepreneur* is held up as an object worthy of cultivation:

seize your opportunities; calculate your chances and your risks; make yourself master of your patients and their affections; assuage their pains; calm their anxieties; anticipate their needs; bear with their whims; make the most of their characters and command their will, not as a cruel tyrant reigns over his slaves,but as a kind father who watches over the destiny of his children.[31]

In another work Foucault called the space in which this 'medical' desire for power was enacted 'the new world of the asylum', and in an important definition stated:

In the new world of the asylum, in that world of a punishing morality, madness became a fact concerning essentially the human soul, its guilt and its freedom; it was now inscribed within the dimension of interiority and by that fact, for the first time in the modern world, madness was to receive psychological status, structure and signification. But this psychologization was merely the superficial consequence of a more obscure, more deeply embedded operation – an operation by which madness was inserted in the system of moral values and repressions. It was enclosed in a punitive system in which the madman, reduced to the status of a minor, was treated in every way as a child, and in which madness was associated with guilt and wrong-doing.[32]

It is in fact that 'dimension of interiority' which the new space of the asylum was designed to construct. Increasingly political effort was directed to control minds rather than bodies and to designing space to facilitate the effort. With the democratic consent of all, the early

Republic inaugurated what D. J. Rothman called a 'cult of the asylum'. Rothman provides the figures to back up his claim. By 1850 almost every northeastern and midwestern legislature supported an asylum. By 1860 twenty-eight of the thirty-three states had public institutions for the insane. It was in these much discussed buildings that the cult of the moral individual in impersonal and absolute space was most scandalously practised. It was not so much social fear as utopian projection which turned privacy into a nightmare of self-contemplation. The buildings were so constructed as to make solitary confinement the central idea in a therapeutic system. The isolation was two fold. First, the buildings were removed from the general concourse of the community. Second, the inmates were separated from each other. In any communal activity such as labour or eating, silence was imposed. D. J. Rothman, in an acute summing up, remarks:

> The strategy for treatment flowed logically and directly from the diagnosis of the disease. Medical superintendents located its roots in the exceptionally open and fluid quality of American society. The American environment had become so particularly treacherous that insanity struck its citizens with terrifying regularity.
>
> One only had to take this dismal analysis one step further to find an antidote. Create a different type of environment, which methodically countered the deficiencies of the community, and a cure for insanity was at hand.[33]

The term 'environment' is, however, a treacherous one, coalescing physical, social, political, economic and natural factors into one determinist space. At the very moment Cooper was creating his myth of the free man in free space, and Hawthorne was meticulously charting the effects of 'isolation' in *The Scarlet Letter* (1850), the qualities of fluidity and openness were being seen medically, not as an American ideal, but as a disease in need of therapy.

Yet if the insane were hygenically regimented out of sight, Americans still had to face each other travelling across country and in the cities themselves. With no real theory of, or commitment to, public space, such public spaces as were inevitable had to be viewed with unease. Indeed, the transition from the private to the public space in our own time has all the hallmarks of a pioneering expedition. The home base must be locked, secured, insured and the neighbours alerted to detect possible attackers. Money, credit cards, a personal alarm – if not anything so melodramatic as a handgun – are carefully secured about one's person, streets reconnoitered and tested by experience to be safe are selected, the time of day checked and a companion or dog preferred. The expedition made, a return before nightfall is advised. The actor in this little drama is not a Frémont establishing a forward camp through hostile Indian territory, but a housewife on her way to a white sale.

In the mid-nineteenth century Walt Whitman exulted in the Broadway omnibus as an instance of convivial sociality which the average American could experience while moving footloose and free in a dynamic city, confidently celebrating himself while containing multitudes. However, a report from the *New York Herald* for 2 October 1864 (though it possibly contains some class-bias) nonetheless demonstrates that New Yorkers at least had other mad houses than those they had so precisely constructed:

Modern martyrdom may be succinctly defined as riding in a New York omnibus. The discomforts, inconveniences and annoyances of a trip on one of these vehicles are almost intolerable. From the beginning to the end of the journey a constant quarrel is progressing. The driver quarrels with the passengers and the passengers quarrel with the driver. There are quarrels about getting out and quarrels about the ticket swindle. The driver swears at the trap passengers and the passengers harangue the driver through the strap-hole – a position in which even Demosthenes could not be eloquent. Respectable clergymen in white chokers are obliged to listen to loud oathes. Ladies are disgusted, frightened and insulted. Children are alarmed and lift up their voices and weep. Indignant gentlemen rise to remonstrate with the irate Jehu and are suddenly bumped back into their seats twice as indignant as before, besides being involved in supplementary quarrels with those other passengers upon whose corns they have accidently trodden. Thus, the omnibus rolls along, a perfect Bedlam on wheels.[34]

The first thing that any student of the growth of the city learns is that the urban landscape is fundamentally mapped out by its transport policy. At the micro-level, the enforced intimacy of the 'Bedlam on wheels' was the noisy grouping of a population who had on the same principles of openness and fluidity decided that absolute individualism was freedom, and those incapable of withstanding its stresses should be in solitary confinement. Mumford, commenting on Emerson's dream of a new American scale of time and space, has shown how the use of faster traffic with increased range had disastrous consequences for the city: 'Rapid public transportation, instead of reducing the time required for reaching the place of work, continued to increase the distance and the cost with no gain in time whatever.' This traffic in traffic with its horizontal expansion and vertical building would eventually produce cities 'where there will be every facility for moving about the city and no possible reason for going there.'[35] The goal of safe, solitary fluidity for each individual persists in Buckminster Fuller's dream of individual 'pallets' world-routed by computers: 'Because the world around computer is continually rerouting its pallets to adjust for unexpected delays, there will be no way of planning to hijack a plane from within a pallet.'[36] With the challenge to science fiction writers and super-tec criminals Fuller once more articulates private American fears of the public space. Reflecting upon a year in the recent past (1986) in which Americans decided in large numbers not to come to Europe owing to public disturbances (hijackings and the like), one wonders what part the fantasies of the absolutely 'free' individual in utopian space, terrified of *any* threat, play alongside *actual* threat. Geometric space (or any abstraction of space) produces its own monsters coded in the semantics of dream.

Our final example in this section is that of domestic space: that 'home' which the Leatherstocking never had on earth. No one in the nineteenth century was a better presenter of it than Harriet Beecher Stowe. By combining the intimate domestic space of the American hearth with the public and political disgrace of slavery, Stowe made a forceful critique of hypocrisy, power and authority North and South. It tapped the resources of sentiment to give its many women readers an image of Eliza and her child leaping the ice-flows: a woman in action outside the home defeating the perils of nature and men, a free figure in space surviving by strength and grace. The route, however, was North not West, and the goal a political one not a vision of infinity.

Stowe herself, however, as a mother and writer of extraordinary energy, was equally capable of playing the domestic space off against those who wished to use her privacy for purposes of celebrity. A recent work looking at the relation of public stage to what is called 'literary domesticity' argues from the following anecdote that Stowe lacked the courage of her own self-image. Sarah Josepha Hale wished to compile reports on 'distinguished women' for the *Woman's Record*:

Unselfconsciously, Stowe revealed her own self-image when she wrote to Hale that she had read the request 'to my tribe of little folks assembled around the evening centre table to let them know what an unexpected honour had befallen their Mama'. And Hale's suggestion that a 'daguerreotype' of Stowe be inserted in the volume, well, that was an idea 'especially . . . quite droll'. Stowe did admit to Hale that in a moment of fantasy she had 'diverted myself somewhat with figuring the astonishment of the children should the well-known visage of their mother loom out of the pages of a book before their astonished eyes.'[37]

Perhaps it was a failure of self-image. But what is missed is the tongue-in-cheek irony of the construction of the family circle. Stowe in fact uses this diverting fantasy to protect her privacy knowing full well that her texts were freed from herself and given to the world. It was publicity not public role that Stowe felt unconfident about. The parlour of little folks was a strategy of calculated defence not submission to patriarchy. Stowe was one of the few who managed to turn the terms of enforced domestic domain and the reductive language of sentiment into a powerfully engaged political critique. For Stowe – to use Bachelard's terms – the house also helped her to claim a habitation in the world which the publicity-seeking daguerreotypist would abstract and pervert. Such a discrimination is germane to this discussion because, as Charles Dickens well knew, true privacy enables true action in the public domain to take place.[38] In the twentieth century 'publicity' would in fact be a major force shaping the landscape, with 'public' exhortations to live, act, buy, and think addressed to the private domain as messages on every highway. Even in wilderness reserves, because most people lacked the skills to inhabit an actual wilderness, a vigilant system of low-profile policing was essential. Precisely because what had once been a revolutionary ideology (free man in free space) had turned into a psychology, the American Adam in space found himself, as Lewis Mumford described the man in the space capsule, more of an 'ambulatory mummy'.[39]

In 1942 the American poet Muriel Rukeyser wrote: 'America a hundred years ago was deeply engrossed with space; it cared rather less for time.'[40] Most Americans in the nineteenth century did not realize that a truly human space is already shaped in time at the moment of inheritance. It is never empty, never silent, and never untouched. Henry Adams was to call for multiplicity against the propaganda of unitary drives. It was a multiplicity which might be placed against the progressivist psychosis with its always to-be-realized future supported by a myth of pure origin. In spite of the general argument of this essay, there were alternatives in the nineteenth century for Americans to consider as models for ways of inhabiting the world. The Shaker community offered an architecture, the Native Americans offered countless ways of living *with* nature, the New England village offered models of communality, new populations pouring into America offered multiple traditions and ways of life which might have been viewed with pride not mistrust. In our own time what is needed more than ever is a sense of *shared* space in which the earth might be allowed reciprocally to make its demands on us. The problem is not, of course, unique to America.

Notes

1 William James, *The Principles of Psychology* (New York: Henry Holt, 1890), vol. 2, p. 279.

2 M. Merleau-Ponty, *Phenomenology of Perception*, trans. Colin Smith (1962; rpt London and Henley: Routledge and Kegan Paul, 1978), p. 101.

3 See Clive Bush, *The Dream of Reason: American Consciousness and Cultural Achievement from Independence to the Civil War* (London: Edward Arnold, 1977), ch. 1.

4 H. T. Pledge, *Science since 1500: A Short History of Mathematics, Physics, Chemistry, Biology*, 2nd edn (London: Her Majesty's Stationery Office, 1966), p. 57. John Quincy Adams, *Report upon Weights and Measures* (Washington: Gales and Seaton, 1821).

5 Alexis de Tocqueville, *Oeuvres Complètes, Tome I, De la Démocratie en Amérique* (Paris: Gallimard, 1960), vol. 2, p. 11. Immanuel Kant, *Immanuel Kant's Critique of Pure Reason*, trans. Norman Kemp Smith (London: Macmillan, 1985), p. 71.

6 Immanuel Kant, *Prolegomena to Any Future Metaphysics*, trans. P. G. Lucas (Manchester: Manchester University Press,1953), section 13; quoted in J. J. C. Smart, ed., *Problems of Space and Time* (New York: Macmillan, and London: Collier Macmillan, 1964), pp. 124–5.

7 Smart, ed., *Problems of Space and Time*, pp. 6–7.

8 Adams, *Report*, p. 119.

9 Ralph Waldo Emerson, *The Collected Works of Ralph Waldo Emerson, Vol. I, Nature, Addresses, and Lectures*, introd. and notes by Robert E. Spiller (Cambridge, MA: The Belknap Press of Harvard University Press, 1971), p. 25.

10 Lewis Mumford, *The Pentagon of Power* (London: Secker and Warburg, 1971), p. 31.

11 D. H. Lawrence, *Studies in Classic American Literature* (London: Martin Secker, 1924), p. 82.

12 Jenni Calder, *There Must be a Lone Ranger* (London: Hamish Hamilton, 1974), p. 15.

Reflections on the perception of space and landscape

13 R. W. B. Lewis, *The American Adam: Innocence, Tragedy and Tradition in the Nineteenth Century* (Chicago: Chicago University Press, 1955), p. 90.

14 James Fenimore Cooper, *The Prairie, A Tale*, ed. James P. Elliott (Albany: State University of New York Press, 1985), pp. 14–16.

15 Lewis, *The American Adam*, p. 128.

16 Lawrence, *Studies*, p. 21.

17 William Appleton Williams, *The Great Evasion* (Chicago: Quadrangle Books, 1964), p. 168.

18 Van Wyck Brooks, *The Times of Melville and Whitman* (London: J. M. Dent, 1948), pp. 77–8.

19 Lawrence, *Studies*, p. 9.

20 William Faulkner, *The Hamlet* (New York: Random House, 1940), p. 242.

21 Merleau-Ponty, *The Phenomenology of Perception*, p. 138.

22 Paul W. Gates, *Landlords and Tenants on the Prairie Frontier: Studies in American Land Policy* (Ithaca and London: Cornell University Press, 1973), p. 56.

23 Quoted in Gates, *Landlords and Tenants*, p. 50.

24 Robert P. Swierenga, *Pioneers and Profits: Land Speculation on the Iowa Frontier* (Ames: Iowa State University Press, 1968).

25 Richard N. L. Andrews, 'Land in America: A brief history', in Richard N. L. Andrews, ed., *Land in America: Commodity and Natural Resource* (Lexington, MA: D. C. Heath and Co., 1979), pp. 30–8.

26 Wendell Berry, *The Unsettling of America* (San Francisco: Sierra Book Club, 1977), p. 107.

27 Quoted in Andrews, *Land in America*, p. 51.

28 Wayne D. Rasmusson, ed., *Readings in the History of American Agriculture* (Urbana: University of Illinois Press, 1960), p. 89.

29 Gaston Bachelard, *The Poetics of Space*, trans. Maria Jolas (Boston: Beacon Press, 1964), p. 47.

30 Lewis Mumford, *The City in History* (Harmondsworth: Penguin, 1961), pp. 481, 451.

31 Michel Foucault, *The Birth of the Clinic: An Archeology of Medical Perception*, trans. A. M. Sheridan Smith (New York: Vintage, 1975), p. 88.

32 Michel Foucault, *Mental Illness and Psychology*, trans. Alan Sheridan Smith (New York: Harper Colophon, 1976), p. 72.

33 D. J. Rothman, *The Discovery of the Asylum, Social Order and Disorder in the New Republic* (Boston: Little, Brown, 1971), p. 133.

34 E. L. Throm, ed., *Popular Mechanics Picture History of American Transportation* (New York: Simon and Schuster, 1952), pp. 86–7.

35 Mumford, *The City in History*, pp. 490–1.

36 Buckminster Fuller, *Critical Path* (New York: St Martin's Press, 1981), p. 341.
37 Mary Kelley, *Private Women, Public State: Literary Domesticity in Nineteenth Century America* (New York: Oxford University Press, 1984).
38 See the discussion of Dickens by Robert Lawson-Peebles in this collection.
39 Mumford, *The Pentagon of Power*, description of plate 14–15 between pp. 180 and 181.
40 Muriel Rukeyser, *Willard Gibbs, American Genius* (Garden City, New York: Doubleday, Doran, 1942), p. 75.

3 * The impermanent sublime: nature, photography and the Petrarchan tradition

OLAF HANSEN

1

Nature is a discipline of the understanding in intellectual truths. Our dealing with sensible objects is a constant exercise in the necessary lessons of difference, of likeness, of order, of being and seeming, of progressive arrangements; of ascent from particular to general; of combination to one end of manifold forces.

Ralph Waldo Emerson

the sublime (quite unlike the merely marvellous, which likewise poses the imagination with a contradiction which, however, it is not worth the effort to resolve) sets all the powers of the mind in motion in order to resolve the contradiction that threatens one's entire intellectual existence.

Friedrich v. Schelling

Almost out of Plato's cave: the question of what an image is has been raised in so many ways, just as the photographic image has evoked a large variety of comments trying to define its nature.[1] Most of these attempts to grasp the essence of the photographic image have been highly metaphorical themselves. We only have to think of Walter Benjamin's statement about the image eliminating the original, or of Susan Sontag's elaborate and somewhat obsessive reflections on the camera's aggressive qualities. Against this vast theoretical background it must seem like an undue limitation to discuss nature photography as a philosophical medium, as a kind of philosophical expression, deeply embedded in such traditional questions as those about man's place in time or his position vis-à-vis nature. If to a certain extent the genuine philosophical quality of such questions has moved out of focus, given the many answers they have provoked, the arrival of the photographic image as a fact certainly helped to create a new and acute awareness of them, and nature

31

photography more so than any other kind of photographic imagery. The photography of nature established its philosophical dignity by way of a relatively simple step of transformation: a simple step, though of great consequence. First, people used nature as an image, as a book of many images, in fact, moving through a number of different readings; the arrival of the actuality of the photographic image, this being the second step, allowed them to define the alphabet of their reading by taking an image of nature and positioning it as an object of contemplation.[2]

The photographic image of nature, in other words, created a specific kind of self-consciousness which, due to technological advancement, gave visual expression to the relationship between the readability of nature and the meaning of a reading! The emphasis here is on the *relationship* between readability and meaning, because it stresses the fundamental allegorical qualities of nature photography. Nature photography, to put it simply, always tries to express something which cannot be expressed. This paradox itself has undergone both historical and social changes; so, of course, has our view of nature, or, to be more precise, so has the allegorical reading which we apply whenever we give meaning to nature.

From its very beginning the history of photography has had to mould itself into a dialectical pattern: photography began to develop its own tradition and was, at the same time, part of an already existing tradition of visual expression. So, in a very substantial way, photography has always been at the same time both extremely practical and highly theoretical. The history of photography, in other words, has never had its period of innocence.

When the early reviewers of the daguerreotype talked about mirror-images they clearly acknowledged that the fact of the mirror, and its tradition as a metaphor, had anticipated the actual arrival and potential meanings of the photographic image.[3] I am citing this example to make a point: namely, that something as old as the idea of the sublime and a phenomenon as recent as that of photography are in a genuine philosophical sense interconnected. This becomes immediately evident if we approach the fundamental issue of time. The relationship of the photographic image to time is similar to that of the sublime to its own object of reference, in exactly the sense which Kant, in his *Critique of Judgment*, described as the provocation of limitlessness:

Nature, photography and the Petrarchan tradition

The beautiful in nature is a question of the form of the object, and this consists in limitation, whereas the sublime is to be found in an object even devoid of form, so far as it immediately involves, or else by its presence provokes a representation of *limitlessness*, yet with a super-added thought of its totality. Accordingly the beautiful seems to be regarded as a presentation of an indeterminate concept of understanding, the sublime as a presentation of an indeterminate concept of reason. Hence the delight is in the former case coupled with the representation of *Quality*, but in this case with that of *Quantity*. Moreover, the former delight is very different from the latter in kind. For the beautiful is directly attended with a feeling of the furtherance of life, and is thus compatible with charms and a playful imagination. On the other hand, the feeling of the sublime is a pleasure that only arises indirectly, being brought about by the feeling of a momentary check to the vital forces followed at once by a discharge all the more powerful, and so it is an emotion that seems to be no sport, but dead earnest in the affairs of the imagination. Hence it is irreconcilable with charms (*Reizen*); and, since the mind is not simply attracted by the object, but is also alternately repelled thereby, the delight in the sublime does not so much involve positive pleasure as admiration or respect, i.e. merits the name of a negative pleasure.[4]

'Negative pleasure' is the key term here, for our purposes, because the point in question is the fact that, among many other things, the photographic image has always represented the negation of time, an aggression against the order which time, transformed into history, imposes upon our worldly affairs. Being out of this order is the essential element in the experience of the sublime, an experience where the individual steps back to contemplate, overwhelmed at the same time by a profound sensation of terror. I need not point out here the long line of thinkers from Ralph Waldo Emerson to Walter Benjamin and André Bazin who have, like many others, associated the arrested time in the photographic image with death.

Time and timelessness, then, are the fundamental problems raised in the conjunction of nature and photography. I have mentioned the fact that the history of photography evolved as a history within a larger tradition, and in accordance with this argument we have to move away from the factual history of nature photography in order to understand those aspects of it upon which I am going to concentrate. We shall move from one date to another, from 1336 to 1871 and to 1922 and, as we go along, our movement will take us from theology to science and, finally, to aesthetics. Even if the direction of this progression seems to be linear, we shall soon discover that there is an underlying principle involved which is circular: time and timelessness as the core of nature photography are still at the center of our argument.

We should also remember that a closer look at the movement from theology to science and then to aesthetics shows how these three possible attitudes of our encounter with nature are interrelated. It also shows that they point to a common origin which the Ionian Pre-Socratic philosophers caught in the term *theoria* – theory – which first of all meant to observe the universe. Hence Aristotle's reference to the Pre-Socratic interpreters of nature as both physiologists and theologians. Thus the photographic image represents a likeness in the physical sense, as well as in the spiritual sense. *Almost* out of Plato's cave and *almost* within Aristotle's system of technical imitation, the photographic image stands somewhere in between; hardly ever, though, escaping from its specific social and historical matrix. So let us begin by taking a close look at the first point in time mentioned above, a moment of true epochē, where everything that happens becomes a threshold phenomenon, changing the consciousness of humanity.

Our *modern* experience of nature has commonly been given a definite beginning; the date 1336 has become a topos which, if we follow Jacob Burckhardt's interpretation, constitutes the re-emergence of an ancient tradition. On 26 April 1335, Petrarch set out to climb Mont Ventoux, a physical as well as a spiritual quest. From the very beginning of his climb, the effort itself is turned into a spiritual drama. Resting for a while, Petrarch reflects upon the sense of his undertaking, and he compares his physical exertions to man's earthly pilgrimage and his quest for salvation:

What shall I say? My brother laughed at me; I was indignant this happened to me three times and more within a few hours. So often was I frustrated in my hopes that at last I sat down in a valley. There I leaped in winged thoughts from things corporeal to what is incorporeal and addressed myself in words like these: 'What you have so often experienced today while climbing this mountain happens to you, you must know, and to many others who are making their way toward the blessed life. This is not easily understood by us men, because the motions of the body lie open while those of the mind are invisible and hidden. The life we call blessed is located on a high peak.' A narrow way they say leads up to it. Many hilltops intervene and we must proceed 'from virtue to virtue' with exalted steps. On the highest summit is set the end of all, the goal toward which our pilgrimage is directed. Every man wants to arrive there. However, as Naso says: 'Wanting is not enough; long and you attain it.'[5]

So from the very beginning the scene and the sense of the ascent are set: nature, a mute and therefore deceptive obstacle, makes sense only when seen within the context of self-reflection; the physical peak of the mountain is seen as the equivalent of a spiritual pilgrimage.

Indeed, at the peak of the mountain Petrarch is overwhelmed by a profound sense of awe – and he has his Augustinian moment which provides him with an explanation for a sensation which, at first, he fails to understand. Turning to St Augustine's *Confessions*, a book which he claims to have always within reach, he comes across a passage which points out that man is constantly admiring nature, in the shape of mountaintops, in the sea, in the movement of the stars, instead of being concerned about his own self:

I opened it with the intention of reading whatever might occur to me first: nothing, indeed, but pious and devout sentences could come to hand. I happened to hit upon the tenth book of the work. My brother stood beside me, intently expecting to hear something from Augustine on my mouth. I ask God to be my witness and my brother who was with me: Where I fixed my eyes first, it was written: 'And men go to admire the high mountains, the vast floods of the sea, the huge streams of the rivers, the circumference of the ocean, and the revolutions of the stars – and desert themselves.' I was stunned, I confess. I bade my brother, who wanted to hear more, not to molest me, and closed the book, angry with myself that I still admired earthly things. Long since I ought to have learned, even from pagan philosophers, that 'nothing is admirable besides the mind; compared to its greatness nothing is great'.[6]

This is Petrarch's stunning experience: looking at nature means to become engaged in a process of self-reflection, the kind of reflection which leads towards contemplation of the incomparable greatness of the soul. By using the term 'anima' for the soul and by explicitly referring to the ancient philosophers, he places his experience into a larger context, which is best described as a specific kind of movement.

The point, as Petrarch realizes, lies in the fact that the use of nature is to turn our view away from it and to direct it towards the self. Or, to put it somewhat differently, man's transformation of nature into a spiritual landscape only emphasizes the primary quality of nature. 'Physis' is the term, which in the language of the ancient philosophers preceded the term 'kosmos', and its theoretical contemplation meant to interpret the universe as both matter and spirit. As Petrarch's conclusion tells us something about the future fate of nature turned into landscape, we should briefly examine his reactions after he read the passage of the *Confessions* we mentioned.

At first he is simply angry that he didn't realize something which even the 'heathen philosophers' could have told him: that only the soul is worthy of admiration. The mountain as an object has lost its fascination. Natural height, and the height which the human soul can reach, are incomparably different. The soul will always dominate nature. We must remember, though, that Petrarch's experience, passing on an ancient tradition into modernity, came about as a part of a revived interest in the immense intellectual wealth of Neoplatonic resources. It was the Neoplatonic tradition which kept the Aristotelian idea alive that theory and theology have a shared meaning. They both transcend the sphere of utility. Petrarch's ascent of Mont Ventoux has no practical side to it; it is devoted to the sheer act of looking, and we have already seen how the desire to do just that is immediately caught up in the mind's relationship to the theological origins of its own abilities to reflect. It is quite revealing that the only justification which Petrarch gives for his desire to climb Mont Ventoux is the ancient fable of King Philip's ascent of Mount Haemus, from the peak of which the king thought he could see both the Adriatic Sea and the Black Sea. We have here once again the Christian transformation of nature into a spiritual landscape.[7]

2

Plutarch in his Morals gives a vivid account of an interview between an Egyptian priest and wise Solon, who, in the openmindedness of a truly great man searching after immemorable knowledge, had come to sit at his feet to listen. Calmly and with the few broad touches of a master, in that simple eloquence which comes of really knowing, the priest tells him of the catastrophes of submergence and upheaval which the earth's surface has suffered. What a picture!   Clarence King

This was that Earth of which we have heard, made out of Chaos and Old Night ... Man was not to be associated with it. It was matter, vast, terrific, – not his Mother Earth that we have heard of ...   Henry David Thoreau

The lesson we take from Petrarch's example is that any act of transforming nature into landscape inevitably leads to interpretation and hence to self-reflection. The experience is archetypal; it creates a kind of tradition.

Nature, photography and the Petrarchan tradition

Henry David Thoreau, for example, after having climbed Mount Ktaadn, rephrases Petrarch's experience. He feels the vicinity of another, non-human force and asks himself:

I stand in awe of my body, this matter to which I am bound has become so strange to me. I fear not spirits, ghosts, of which I am one, – *that* my body might, – but I fear bodies, I tremble to meet them. What is this Titan that has possession of me? Talk of mysteries! – Think of our life in nature, – daily to be shown matter, to come in contact with it, – rocks, trees, wind on our cheeks! the *solid* earth! the *actual* world! *where* are we?[8]

Thoreau still combines elements of scientific, mystic and even mythical approaches to nature. The mixture allows us to identify traces of the Petrarchan tradition, mainly in their Neoplatonic form of expression. It is Alexander von Humboldt who first articulates the shift from theology to science. In his *Cosmos* (1849) he makes the following statement:

It may be a rash attempt to endeavour to separate into its different elements, the magic power exercised upon our minds by the physical world, since the character of the landscape, and of every imposing scene in nature depends so materially upon the mutual relation of the ideas and sentiments simultaneously excited in the mind of the observer.[9]

Science, however, never exists as that phenomenon we call 'pure science'. The history of the construction of knowledge has repeatedly shown how, in the act of representing fundamental scientific data like time or space, the images used have always helped to preserve rudimentary elements of both myth and religion. It is not surprising, then, that the photographic image, due to its allegorical qualities, was especially suited to an ambiguity between science and theology. Which takes us to our second major ascent, that of Mount Tyndall by Clarence King in 1871.

The climbing of Mount Tyndall is, of course, presented as part of a scientific expedition, but we soon realize that the scientific account is couched in the traditional language of the quest. This is, we should remember, also the point in time when nature photography, as exemplified by Timothy O'Sullivan, joins the established tradition which we have described so far, in order to develop one of its own.

But let us first follow King on his ascent of Mount Tyndall. His report about the experience was first published in the *Atlantic Monthly* in 1871. The ruling metaphors of King's account reveal its place within the tradition. The idea of height evokes the idea of truth; the experience of the sublime is terrible at first; but it leads to the inevitable moment of self-reflection:

For a couple of months my friends had made me the target of pleasant banter about my 'highest land', which they had lost faith in. As we climbed from Thomas's Mill ... I too was becoming a trifle anxious about it; but now could not find words to describe the terribleness and grandness of the deep cañon, nor for picturing those huge crags towering in line at the east.

The 'highest land' must be found, a *must* which is first of all explained in terms of a loss of faith, *ex negativo*. Its *positive* side comes out when King graphically describes the effect which it has upon his state of self-awareness:

Rising on the other side, cliff above cliff, precipice piled upon precipice, rock over rock, up against the sky towered the most gigantic mountain wall in America, culminating in a noble pile of Gothic finished granite and enamel – like snow. How grand and inviting looked its white form, its untrodden, unknown crest, so high and pure in the clear strong blue. *I looked at it as one contemplating the purpose of his life.*[10]

This is exactly the moment where Petrarch turned to St Augustine for help. But King did not carry a book, even though, as we shall see in a moment, he metaphorically had one in mind. The most important part of his account tells us once again how the encounter with nature turns the view of the beholder towards the self. The physical confrontation becomes a spiritual one. Nature imposes upon us the task of self-awareness, of defining our place in the vast scheme of creation. For the sake of maintaining our identity, we must interpret nature, because the overwhelming sense which we feel is, as King puts it, 'desolation, desolation'.[11]

Nature, as he explains, 'impresses me as the ruins of some bygone geological period and no part of the present order – like a specimen of chaos which has defied the finishing hand of time'. Chaos is transformed into kosmos; nature into landscape. In substance, both transformations are identical. They both imply a definition of the self. Petrarch had theology to turn to, King had the book of science. He had his own theory: catastrophism, a theory which O'Sullivan would illustrate. It allowed King to replace the Christian, individual self, which was at the center of Petrarch's experience, with the idea of a national self.[12] The geological rhetoric of catastrophism provided the vocabulary of national selfhood. The scientific motif served as an answer to the question about the nature of the specific American experience vis-à-vis the sublime. We must recall here some aspects of the sublime as Kant described them in his *Critique of Judgment*. It involved terror; it led towards self-awareness; but most important, in its distinction from the beautiful, it presupposed the existence of culture and moral sense. 'Nature,' as Kant points out, 'is an object of fear, in the sublime, but yet we are not afraid of it.'

The rhetoric of geology, covering the yet uncivilized nature, presents the experience of the sublime as being essentially Gothic in character. Materiality, namely granite, has a spiritual counterpart in Gothicism as form. 'Next to this, and more pleasing to notice,' said King, is

the interest and richness of the granite forms; for the whole region, from plain to plain, is built of this dense solid rock, and is sculptured under the chisel of cold in shapes of great variety, yet all having a common spirit, which is purely Gothic. – In the much-discussed origin of this order of Building, I never remember to have seen, though it can hardly have escaped mention, any suggestion of the Gothic having been inspired by granite forms. Yet as I sat on Mount Tyndall the whole mountains shaped themselves like the ruins of cathedrals, – sharp roof ridges, pinnacled and statued; buttresses more inspired and ornamented than Milan's; receding doorways with pointed arches carved into blank facades of granite, – doors never to be opened – innumerable jutting points with here and there a single cruciform peak ...[13]

This description of nature turns it into a landscape which is a reminder of a previous age, one or two catastrophes before the emergence of mankind. The doors of those cathedrals will never open, and in consequence the whole order of the Gothic style cannot be used as an adequate expression of the American spirit. The style available to, and most adequate for, American civilization (as King would point out in another essay) had to be the style of the middle period of the Roman empire. It is a style which 'covers at once the antique and the modern', a style in tune with a system which, like the American, King judged to be a political success, but a social failure.[14]

If we want to see all that has been said so far in terms of a visual iconology, we must once more turn to King's theory of catastrophism. It is not a pessimistic view of life, but one which charges man with a task:

1 Timothy O'Sullivan, 'Karnak Region, Montezuma Range, Nevada', 1868

2 Timothy O'Sullivan, 'Hot Sulphur Spring, Ruby Valley, Nevada', 1868

3 Timothy O'Sullivan, 'Soda Lake, Carson Desert, Nevada', 1868

He who brought to bear that mysterious energy we call life upon primeval matter, bestowed at the same time a power of development by change, arranging that the interaction of energy and matter which make up environment should from time to time burst in upon the current of life and sweep it onward and upward to ever higher and better manifestations. Moments of great catastrophe, thus translated into the language of life, become moments of creation, when out of plastic organisms something newer and nobler is called into being.[15]

Clarence King was both a scientist and a Ruskinian, and to the extent that we assume that he influenced his photographer in the course of the Fortieth Parallel Expedition, we must look for the kind of iconology in O'Sullivan's photographs which reflect King's own systematic combination of geology, theology and aesthetics. These were the essential elements which King, as a founding member, brought to the Society for the Advancement of Truth in Art.[16] The *camera's work*, to borrow a phrase which would assume its most significant meaning with Alfred Stieglitz, was to document scientifically the presence of the divine in nature and to place humanity in the unfolding process of creation. Following King's version of optimistic catastrophism, O'Sullivan's images would also have to show that man was an active part in this process, that his role was that of participant rather than victim.

41

Olaf Hansen

O'Sullivan, being eminently practical, first of all asked for the construction of a custom-made large plate camera. The intrusion of the camera at work into an ambience of universal time (as opposed to human time) in the process of creation are the basic elements in the photograph of the Montezuma Range, an image showing the appropriately named Karnak region (pl. 1). The iconology emphasizes, by way of dramatization, that nature has a history to tell, which we must read by entering into it; or, to put it differently, a discourse with nature is possible if we are willing to take the risk. In the same manner O'Sullivan creates the nineteenth-century version of Petrarchan self-awareness in the image of a man looking at his own reflection in the uninviting waters of a hot sulphur spring, in Ruby Valley, Nevada (pl. 2). So the topos remains: where man encounters nature when she is, as Thoreau put it, nothing like 'mother' nature at all, the attention turns toward the self. Man, contemplating his own reflection in the water, is, of course, an archetypal image, but O'Sullivan refrains from romanticizing the meaning of the archetype. Nothing could be further from the topos of Narcissus. The familiar topos is effectively reversed: man, instead of forgetting his own self, is reminded of his solitary position, facing a hostile nature which he nevertheless must confront and eventually overcome. Nature may be uninviting, as O'Sullivan's photograph of Soda Lake, Carson Desert (pl. 3), shows, but man is caught at the threshold of intrusion. To pinpoint this exact moment, where two dimensions of time and history are about to merge, turning nature into landscape, is a kind of dramatization. We frequently find this in the photographs of O'Sullivan, when he places man or one of his artefacts into the context of nature. What we see in the photograph is work in progress, the process of a difficult reconciliation which reflects King's own version of catastrophism: 'When catastrophic change burst in upon the ages of uniformity and sounded in the ear of every living thing the words "Change or die", plasticity became the sole principle of salvation.'[17]

O'Sullivan, accordingly, tries to establish a careful balance between the history of man and the history of nature – a balance which is the prerequisite of the very idea of natural history. The actual iconography of most of O'Sullivan's images of man in nature relies on the rhetoric of natural history, which in the nineteenth century had reached its most articulate phase. We should remember Emerson's early lecture, 'The Uses of Natural History'. We must think of Thoreau's journals, of

42

Henry Adams's restless travels, of the influence of Darwin and von Humboldt. We then realize that the aim of natural history was *to place* mankind. The Romantic sublime had shown its terrible face. The post-Kantian answer, in Emerson's phrase, was the moral stoicism of man 'the naturalist'. The act of transforming nature into landscape was, once more, an act of theoretical perception. 'Oh, how alone our lives must be lived' was the outcry of Thoreau, and O'Sullivan again and again emphasized in his images the fact that nature was large and that man's perilous existence had become an essential part of his self-consciousness. If we follow this train of thought and put it into the context of nineteenth-century secularization, we cannot fail to recognize in O'Sullivan's images elements of an iconography that is both religious and secular. There is the human skull; there is man's writing carved into the rock carefully set against a ruler measuring its actual scale; there are the deserted ruins in the Cañon de Chelly; and, above all, there is the human figure introducing a factual as well as an allegorical dimension as part of the image's information.[18] If the famous photograph 'Desert Sand Hills Near Sink of Carson' (pl. 4) epitomizes the circular approach we use, and are forced to use, in our confrontation with nature, it is the camera placed visibly into the 'Karnak' of the Montezuma Range which emphasizes the use O'Sullivan made of the medium itself. It was, above all, its ability to demonstrate the act of self-reflection which allowed the unfolding drama of our perilous existence between chaos and kosmos. Implicitly O'Sullivan had already drawn the consequences from the fact that the first daguerreotype of the moon had fundamentally reversed our view of the world. Man had his own globe as his only habitat, his time and geological time had to be reconciled, just as the question about absolute time once more raised the issue about reconciling theology and science.

Placing mankind in nature, and turning nature into landscape, is always mimetic of that first act of creation, and the mimesis naturally contains the reminder that paradise has been lost. So Petrarch needed theology just as O'Sullivan relied on science. This is, of course, just another way of saying that whenever the idea or the concept of landscape becomes a serious issue, the self-definition of mankind will be at stake. O'Sullivan, more than his contemporaries in exploration photography, such as W. H. Jackson and Eadweard Muybridge, tried to express this.[19] He is therefore very much part of a transcendentalist tradition in

4 Timothy O'Sullivan, 'Desert Sand Hills Near Sink of Carson, Nevada',
1868

American cultural history. Transcendentalism has an inclination to alle-
gorize; the dominant theme of O'Sullivan's allegory was nature's fundamental and frightening indifference to the fate of mankind. Henry
Adams, a close friend of Clarence King's, summed up this experience in a
well-known passage in his *Education*, when he wrote about the death of
his sister in Italy. He realized that the sublime landscape remained uncon-
cerned; but, as he said, Mont Blanc never looked the same to him again.[20]

O'Sullivan, we should remember, had exposed himself to the cruel fact
of man-made death as a war photographer working with Matthew
Brady. His battlefield photographs strewn with dead bodies lack any
kind of glorification and heroism. All they really show is how quickly the
human body becomes part of nature again. The iconography of his
battlefield photographs is the iconography of science. His finest exploration photographs tell us something about the ways of human life, about
human life seen as its own kind of natural history.

3

Nature must be viewed humanly to be viewed at all; that is, her scenes must be associated with humane affections, such as are associated with one's native place, for instance. She is most significant to a lover. A lover of Nature is preeminently a lover of man. If I have no friend, what is Nature to me? She ceases to be morally significant. Henry David Thoreau

When a photographer presents us with what to him is an Equivalent, he is telling us in effect, 'I had a feeling about something, here is my metaphor of that feeling.' The significant difference here is that what he had a feeling about was not for the subject he photographed but for something else. He may show us a picture of a cloud, the forms of which expressively correspond to his feelings about a certain person ... The power of the equivalent, so far as the expressive-creative photographer is concerned, lies in the fact that he can convey and evoke feelings about things and situations and events which for some reason or other are not or can not be photographed. Minor White

The setting for a series of photographs taken by Alfred Stieglitz in the 1920s is so much part of the rise of the American avant-garde, that the photographs themselves may at first come as a bit of a surprise (see pl. 5). We know Stieglitz as the man who changed photographic history by resolutely defining photography as an art form when he opened the Galleries of the Photo-Secession at 291 Fifth Avenue, New York. His most famous photographs are social landscapes, street scenes in New York, images which have become classics like 'The Steerage', 'The Hand of Man' and 'The Terminal'. Stieglitz was also a gifted organizer, very much in touch with the European avant-garde. In 1911 he exhibited the first cubist painting in America, a Picasso. After the Armory Show, after the prewar years' excitement and, of course, after World War I, Stieglitz found himself in 1922 at an impasse which he tried to overcome by returning to his origins:

Thirty-five or more years ago I spent a few days in Murren (Switzerland) and I was experimenting with ortho plates. Clouds and their relationship to the rest of the world and clouds for themselves interested me ... I wanted to photograph clouds to put down my philosophy of life – to show that my photographs were not due to subject matter ... clouds were there for everyone, no tax as yet on them – free. – So I began to work with clouds ... I wanted a series of photographs which when seen by Ernest Bloch (the great composer) he would exclaim: Music! Music! Man, why that is music! ... and he would say he'd have

45

5 Alfred Stieglitz, 'Equivalent: Music No. 1, Lake George, New York',
1922

to write a symphony called 'Clouds'. Not like Debussy's, but *much, much more*.[21]

So the return to nature photography was an act of freedom. Stieglitz saw it as an escape from the confinements of a social system and the artistic dogmas which he had always tried to avoid. And yet, nature in 1922 could only serve as an approximation to what Stieglitz termed the *Truth*. He had called his cloud series *Equivalents*, and he commented upon them as 'documents of an eternal relation, perhaps even a philosophy'. In his most revealing statement he came directly to the point: 'My photographs are a picture of the chaos in the world, and of my relationship to that chaos. My prints show the world's constant upsetting of man's equilibrium, and his eternal battle to re-establish it.'[22] There is hardly anything which one needs to add. Again we have the mountain ascent, but here we are not in the realm of either theology or science. We must see Stieglitz's *Equivalents* as part of twentieth-century modernism, if simply because of the conjunction of aesthetic theory and the artefact itself. Underneath the aesthetic information we find Petrarch's experience once again: nature will only become landscape after we have gone to the extreme of questioning the full sense of our existence.

In the case of Stieglitz the sense of crisis exists before the fact, a classic symptom of modernism. The questioning of the self is a kind of given – the artistic process simply rephrases the question in a large variety of terms. If in Petrarch's case the crisis of the self was a result of a sudden shock, modernism takes this result as a beginning. The sublime has become fully integrated into the realm of aesthetics, which as a field of autonomous dignity, confronts the integrity and substance of the self by defining itself as the unmitigated negation of the established order. The sense of crisis which Stieglitz describes in the context of his explanation about the origins of his cloud series should be regarded as a symptom at best: it is the artist's question about the *relationship* of clouds to the rest of the world which is important.

The other topos which should be considered is Stieglitz's reference to music while talking about his cloud series. As an aesthetic phenomenon music is mathematically exact and at the same time a highly elusive form of expression. To be understood, music, like the *Equivalents* of Alfred Stieglitz, demands an extremely physical attention as well as an ability to think about the sensual experience in highly abstract ways. The result of Stieglitz's deliberations about his *Equivalents* can be summed up in the emphasis he places on the self. Nature in the Petrarchan tradition always provokes exactly this kind of final insight: the self, being forced to see itself in relationship to the unattainable, will always be a 'self in question'. It is this kind of programmatic process which the sublime evokes in theology, in science and in aesthetics, a process which is most adequately summed up in the terminology of Søren Kierkegaard:

Man is spirit. But what is spirit? Spirit is the self. But what is the self? The self is a relation which relates itself to its own self, or it is that in the relation (which accounts for it) that the relation relates itself to its own self; the self is not the relation but (consists in the fact) that the relation relates itself to its own self. Man is a synthesis of the infinite and the finite, of the temporal and the eternal, of freedom and necessity, in short it is a synthesis. A synthesis is a relation between two factors. So regarded, man is not yet a self.[23]

The emphasis is on the *not yet*, the correspondence, in other words, to the arrested time in nature photography. Stieglitz in his cloud images tried to express exactly, by creating an image equivalent to it, what the *not yet* was all about. This is why his photographs of clouds function as a kind of ultimate allegory: they question the self by printing out the process of self-constitution, a process which always aims at something which cannot be pinned down within the flux of human time. The act of self-constitution, like the arrested time in the photographic image, presupposes another time-frame, namely that of an anticipating memory. As Paul Strand put it, 'Photography is only a new road from a different direction but moving toward the common goal which is Life.'[24]

Notes

1 I want to thank Renate Wiegand, who so generously helped to get this essay started – and finished – by providing information from her own, vast knowledge of nineteenth-century American photography and painting.
2 See Hans Blumenberg, *Die Lesbarkeit der Welt* (Frankfurt: Suhrkamp, 1981).
3 See Herbert Grabes, *Speculum, Mirror und Looking-Glass* (Tübingen: Max Niemeyer Verlag, 1973).
4 Immanuel Kant, *Critique of Judgement*, Second Book, Analytic of The Sublime, §23.
5 Petrarch, trans. Hans Nachod, in Ernst Cassirer, ed., *The Renaissance Philosophy of Man* (Chicago: University of Chicago Press, 1948), pp. 39–40. The following is the original Latin text from which I worked: 'Quid multa? non sine fratis risu, hoc indignanti michi ter aut amplius intra paucas horas contigit. Sic sepe delusus quadam in valle consedi. Illic a corporeis ad incorporea volucri cogitatione transiliens, his aut talibus me ipsum compellabam verbis: – Quod totiens hodie in ascensu montis huius expertus es, id scito et tibi accidere et multis, accedentibus ad beatam vitam; sed idcirco tam facile ab hominibus non perpendi, quod corporis motus in aperto sunt, animorum vero invisibiles et occulti. Equidem vita, quam beatam dicilimus,

celso loco sita est; arcta, ut aiunt, ad illam ducit via. Multi quoque colles interemineant et de virtute in virtutem preclaris gradibus ambulandum est; in summo finis est omnium et vie terminus ad quem peregrinatio nostra disponitur. Eo pervenire colunt omnes, sed, ut ait Naso, *velle parur: est; cupias, ut re potiaris, oportet* (Ovidio, *Ex Ponto*, III, I, 35).' (Francesco Petrarca, *Prose*, A Cura Di G. Martellotti et al., Milan and Naples, n.d., pp. 835–6)

6 Ibid., p. 44. 'Aperio, lecturus quicquid occurreret; quid enim nisi pium et dovotum posset occurrere? Forte autem decimus illius operis liber oblatus est. Frater expectans per os meum ab Augustino aliquid audire, intentis auribus stabat. Deum testor ipsumque qui aderat, quod ubi primum defixi oculus, scriptum erat: "Et eunt homines admirari alta montium et ingentes fluctus maris et latissimos lapsus fluminum et-occeani ambitum et giros siderum, et relinquunt se ipsos." (*Conf.*, X, 8, 15). Obstupui fateor; audiendique avidum fratrem rogans ne michi molestus esset, librum clausi, iratus michimet quod nunc etiam terrestria mirarer, qui iampridem ab ipsis gentium philosophis discere debuissem nichil preter animum esse mirabile, cui magno nichil est magnum.' (Petrarca, p. 840).

7 Ibid., p. 831.

8 H. D. Thoreau, *The Maine Woods*, ed. Joseph J. Moldenhauer (Princeton: Princeton University Press, 1972), p. 71.

9 Alexander von Humboldt, *Cosmos*, 1, 5; quoted in Estelle Jussim and Elizabeth Lindquist-Cock, *Landscape as Photograph* (New Haven and London: Yale University Press, 1985), p. 41.

10 King, 'Mountaineering in the Sierra Nevada', *Atlantic Monthly*, 28 (July 1871), 64, 66, my emphasis.

11 This theme is developed in Allen Koppenhaver's contribution to this volume.

12 King, 'Catastrophism and evolution', *The American Naturalist*, 11 (Aug. 1877), 449–70.

13 King, 'Mountaineering in the Sierra Nevada', *Atlantic Monthly*, 28 (Aug. 1871), 208–9.

14 See King, 'Style and the monument', *North American Review*, 141 (Nov. 1885), 443–53. A different view is expounded in Barbara Novak, *Nature and Culture: American Landscape and Painting 1825–1875* (London: Thames and Hudson, 1980), p. 151.

15 King, 'Catastrophism', p. 470.

16 Nathan Reingold, *Science in Nineteenth Century America* (London, Melbourne, Toronto: Macmillan, 1966).

17 King, 'Catastrophism', p. 469.

18 All the photographs referred to here are reproduced in Joel Snyder, *American Frontiers: The Photographs of Timothy O'Sullivan* (Millerton: Aperture, 1981).
19 See the essays by Philip Stokes and Mick Gidley in this collection.
20 Henry Adams, *The Education of Henry Adams* (Boston and New York: Houghton Mifflin, 1918), pp. 287–9.
21 Alfred Stieglitz, 'How I Came to Photograph Clouds', in *The Amateur Photographer and Photography*, 56, No. 1819, 255; repr. in Nathan Lyons, ed., *Photographers On Photography* (Englewood Cliffs: Prentice-Hall, 1966), pp. 111–12.
22 Quoted in Dorothy Norman, *Alfred Stieglitz: An American Seer* (Millerton: Aperture, 1974), p. 161. This book reproduces all the Stieglitz photographs mentioned here, including a selection of *Equivalents*.
23 Søren Kierkegaard, *Fear and Trembling and The Sickness Unto Death* (Princeton: Princeton University Press, 1941), p. 146.
24 Paul Strand, 'Photography', *Seven Arts*, 2 (Aug. 1917), 525.

4 ∗ American landscape and the figure of anticipation: paradox and recourse

STEPHEN FENDER

Consider this excerpt from Sarah Kemble Knight's journal:

Here We found great difficulty in Travailing, the way being very narrow, and . . . it being so exceeding dark . . . Now Returned my distressed aprehensions of the place where I was: the dolesome woods, my Company next to none, Going I knew not whither, and encompassed wth Terrifying darkness . . . but being got to the Top [of a hill, I] was there amply recompensed with the friendly Appearance of the Kind Conductress of the night, Just then Advancing above the Horisontall Line . . . My tho'ts on the sight of the moon were to this purpose:

> Fair Cynthia, all the Homage that I may
> Unto a Creature, unto thee I pay;
> In Lonesome woods to meet so kind a guide,
> To Mee's more worth than all the world beside . . .

and the Tall and thick Trees at a distance, especially w^n the moon glar'd light through the branches, fill'd my Imagination wth the pleasant delusion of a Sumpteous citty, fill'd wth famous Buildings and churches, wth their spiring steeples, Balconies, Galleries and I know not what: Grandeurs wch I had heard of, and wch the stories of foreign countries had given me the Idea of.

> Here stood a Lofty church – there is a steeple,
> And there the Grand Parade – O see the people!
> That Famous Castle there, were I but nigh,
> To see the mote and Bridg and walls so high –
> They'r very fine! sais my deluded eye.

Being thus agreably entertain'd without a thou't of any thing but thoughts themselves, I on a suden was Rous'd from these pleasing Imaginations, by the Post's sounding his horn, which assured mee hee was arrived at the Stage, where we were to Lodg: . . . [1]

This is typical of a sense of dislocation which one encounters again and again in American landscape description, especially in letters and journals written by conscientious travellers of whatever degree of sophistication who are exploring territory physically and/or culturally 'westwards' of their more settled home. The dislocation takes a particular form and promotes characteristic responses that have fed into the strategies of American writing of other kinds on other subjects. Here, in Knight's journal of her 1704 journey from Boston to New York, are the three characteristic stages in the response of this kind of traveller in this situation: (1) fear and repulsion at the scaleless, unscaleable wilderness; (2) invention of a fantasy of culture, drawn not only from what was familiar to the traveller but from 'Imaginations' of 'Balconies', 'Galleries', 'Grand Parades' and 'Famous Castles' supposedly appropriate to a metropolitan society remote in time and place, set out in the most sophisticated lexical and formal expression – replete with classical allusions – of which the writer is capable; (3) realization that the project of compensatory verbal synthesis is a hopeless one, and a consequent collapse into self-mockery that has the effect of deconstructing the verbal enterprise ('Being thus entertain'd without a thou't of any thing but thoughts themselves'). The gap between the experienced nature and the imagined culture is so great that the honest writer cannot sustain allusions to the past, or to the cultural centre. The failed allusion renders absurd the formality of the language; poetic style itself becomes suspect; metonymy is broken and metaphor stretched to a point beyond which it can function as a way of expressing truth – even the truth of personal feeling.

In the early years of the Republic, it was widely agreed, even by Americans, that the new country had no literature. This didn't just mean imaginative writing, as we use the word today, but book learning of all sorts. Many reasons were advanced for this supposed deficiency, but one of the most popular was the Americans had no usable history. This proposition has assumed, from time to time, an awful credibility in the American sense of personal and national identity, from which not even modern historiography is immune.[2] In the early nineteenth century the perception seemed of a condition both endemic and immutable, insofar as it chimed with another anxiety to do with cultural displacement: that Americans, in crossing the Atlantic and establishing themselves as an independent republic, had cut themselves off from the metropolitan centre where their standards of language, fashion and custom were set. Though this essay deals with feelings of separation through time rather than space, that other, related concern must never be underestimated, especially since, at about the same time as Americans were debating the constitutional and practical wisdom of separation from the mother country, the French zoologist Buffon was publishing his 'findings' that animals and plants degenerated when transplanted to a new environment, and the Abbé Raynal was extending this rule even to human emigrants.[3]

To students of American culture, the best-known expression of this sense of the missing past comes in Washington Irving's preface to *The Sketch Book* (1819–20), 'The Author's Account of Himself', which – not incidentally – also contains a good joke at Buffon's expense. The problem is articulated in terms of contemporary associationist psychology, the idea developed by David Hume (*Treatise of Human Nature*, 1739) and David Hartley (*Observations on Man*, 1749), that certain rules governed the association of ideas in the mind, and hence that even apparently subjective standards of proportion and taste may really conform to objective descriptions of universal events. In *The Nature and Principles of Taste* (1790) Archibald Alison extended this idea into the arena of physical and social landscape perception. The contemporary polarities of sublime and beautiful, for instance, did not exist in their own right but only insofar as they aroused associations in the mind of the beholder. These associations were with events in the past – with personal or communal history. Runnymede may be nothing more than a humdrum meadow, but the scene is made powerful by the thought of what it means to our constitutional history. Similarly, an ordinary house is made special if it is where we spent a happy youth.

This is what Irving means when he writes that while 'never need an American look beyond his own country for the sublime and beautiful of natural scenery', it was Europe that 'held forth the charms of storied and poetical association'. And despite his breezy treatment of the degeneration theory, *The Sketch Book* never really escapes from under the cloud of anxiety that Americans might be radically cut off from whatever gives meaning to the ordinary events of their lives. As I have tried to show elsewhere,[4] 'Rip Van Winkle', the best known of the stories in the collection, is about a man who stands on the cusp precisely between 'the sublime and beautiful of natural scenery', but who fails to make the

53

association, falls into a stupor and awakes to a shoddy present-day America stripped of the icons of its inheritance.

Of course, not all Americans followed Irving in believing their country deficient in history to which aspiring writers might make associative allusions. Another response was simply to deny the proposition outright. There is a recurrent American appetite for 'discoveries' of cultural deposits laid down by Viking chieftains, Irish or Welsh princes, or whatever, who landed long before the Spanish and English and Dutch. In the early Republican period by far the favourite candidate for this species of cultural wish-fulfilment were the various Indian burial mounds in the Ohio River Valley and elsewhere. They were frequently mentioned by foreign and American travellers and, because the findings were archaeologically ambiguous, were encoded as the evidence of either a great, lost classical civilization, or nothing more than a heap of dead Indians. Generally speaking, the adherents of the first view were Tory travellers and their complicit reviewers in the *Quarterly Review*, who needed to argue that things had degenerated in America since Independence. The second view was put forward by the Whig *Edinburgh Review* and, perhaps most notably, by Thomas Jefferson in *Notes on Virginia* (1785), who called the mounds unremarkable.

But the need for a usable past could override the general rule contingent on the issue of degeneration, prompting even apologists for American promise to cite the Indian mounds as evidence of cultural foundations of almost classical prestige:

> I will now venture a few remarks on what has been considered a grand defect in American scenery – the want of associations, such as arise amid the scenes of the old world.
>
> We have many a spot as umbrageous as Vallombrosa, and as picturesque as the solitudes of Vaucluse; but Milton and Petrarch have not hallowed them by their footsteps and their immortal verse. He who stands on Mount Albano and looks down on ancient Rome, has his mind peopled with the gigantic associations of the storied past; but he who stands on the mounds of the West, the most venerable remains of American antiquity, *may* experience the emotion of the sublime, but it is the sublimity of a shoreless ocean un-islanded by the recorded deeds of man.

Thus Thomas Cole, in his famous 'Essay on American Scenery'.[5] But note how tentatively – the emphasis on 'may' is his – even he poses the possibility of the Indian mounds as a classical source. Bryant's 'The

Prairies' also puts the possibility in the form of a question, though by the time he has wound his rhetoric up, there is little doubt what he wants his readers to answer, and himself to believe:

> And they here –
> The dead of other days? – and did the dust
> Of these fair solitudes once stir with life
> And burn with passion? Let the mighty mounds
> That overlook the rivers, or that rise
> In the dim forest crowded with old oaks,
> Answer. A race, that long has passed away,
> Built them: a disciplined and populous race
> Heaped, with long toil, the earth, while yet the Greek
> Was hewing the Pentelicus to forms
> Of symmetry, and rearing on its rock
> The glittering Parthenon. These ample fields
> Nourished their harvests, here their herds were fed,
> When haply by their stalls the bison lowed,
> And bowed his maned shoulder to the yoke.

These puzzling and evocative deposits (perhaps evocative especially because puzzling) are reminiscent of the mysterious tracks on the prairie that so fascinate Jim Burden and the other children in Willa Cather's *My Antonia* (1918) – the circle made in the sod by Indian ponies, a faint trace which shows up only when a light dusting of snow picks it out, and which may have been a site for ceremony or just a place where Indians exercised their horses. This moves the reader, as it does the characters, because it answers a nostalgic hunger for 'history' in a featureless plain without other traces of settlement. In fact what is being evoked here is not 'history' at all but what has carelessly been called 'pre-history', as in the usage 'pre-historical', to denote early human history not narrated by the written word. And the fascination with written accounts of western exploration and settlement (and by extension the exploration and settlement of the American East when it too was 'the West') lies in how close they come to the precipice of pre-history. The further West you go, the further back in time, until you come to a border beyond which, in a sense, time itself has never been. This is why countless explorers, travellers, novelists and poets – most, but by no means all of them Americans, because the number includes European discoverers from the fifteenth century onwards, of course – have been able to turn America (and, in time, the American West) into mythical or legendary territory – into pre-lapsarian paradises, or promised lands, or other representations of 'timeless' good or evil.

But this is another way of saying that the appeal of the wilderness is not – indeed cannot be – to history. The procedure does not posit a continuum linking the present with the past in time, by which connection the past can be used by way of comparison or contrast (or to some other morally normalizing purpose) that enhances and reinforces a community's sense of itself, and against which novelty may be judged. The gap between history and pre-history is absolute. The past therefore becomes 'lost', or at best recuperated in terms of the personality imagining it, and nostalgia becomes the predominant mood in *My Antonia* as it does (even more so) in *A Lost Lady* (1923).

This is to say that pre-history cannot be used as T. S. Eliot said a 'tradition' or 'the classic' should be. Indeed it may be significant that Cather's Burden, apparently denied access to an Anglo-Saxon past to give meaning to his life and situation, has to fall back on Virgil – and then only to invoke the old trope of *translatio studii – translatio imperii* (the inevitable westward movement of culture), which he contravenes by moving to the Eastern city. Legend or myth can only reflect, in some uncertain and in no contingent way, our present reality. It cannot be used in the way the study of history has conventionally been used. And even 'legend' and 'myth' understate the difference. The Greeks, after all, believed the events of their legends and myths actually to have happened in the history of their race.

But to the supposed deficiency of history there was another answer than the blank denial – a bolder and quite irrefutable recourse. This came in on the wings of a sneer – well, actually a mild joke on the part of a generally well-disposed English emigrant to America, but turned into a sneer by the *Quarterly Review*. On his way to Illinois Territory in 1817 Morris Birkbeck paid a visit to Pittsburgh, which he had been told was 'the Birmingham of America'. Naturally he 'expected to have been enveloped in clouds of smoke, issuing from a thousand furnaces, and stunned with the din of ten thousand hammers', but instead found a modest manufacturing town:

There is a figure of rhetoric adopted by the Americans, and much used in description; it simply consists in the use of the present indicative, instead of the future subjunctive; it is called *anticipation*. By its aid, what *may* be is contemplated as though it were in actual existence. For want of being acquainted with the power and application of this figure, I confess I was much disappointed by Pittsburgh.[6]

The figure of anticipation, or modifications of it, had virtually unlimited use. To every criticism of the physical or cultural shortcomings of the new Republic, its boosters and friends could answer, in the immortal words of Henrietta Stackpole to Caspar Goodwood, 'Just you wait!' As de Tocqueville observed, 'Democratic nations care but little for what has been, but they are haunted by visions of what will be; in this direction their unbounded imagination grows and dilates beyond all measure.'[7]

Insufficient history? Thomas Cole had an excited answer to that. What does it matter if American scenery was said to lack association (though he didn't think it did), when 'American associations are not so much of the past as of the present and the future'? Look over the 'yet uncultivated scene', he advised; you will see 'no ruined tower to tell of outrage – no gorgeous temple to speak of ostentation … the mind's eye may see far into futurity. Where the wolf roams, the plough shall glisten, on the gray crag shall rise temple and tower – mighty deeds shall be done in the now pathless wilderness; and poets yet unborn shall sanctify the soil' (pp. 577–8).[8]

Yet for all its utility in the cultural debate, the figure of anticipation contained contradictions even more devastating than the appeal to the mythical pre-history of the Indian mounds. In the first place, while the imagination takes its pleasure in a meditation on the future culture of a present natural setting, what is to shut out the uglier images of the wrong sort of progress invading the very solitude which invited the reverie to begin with? To see this problem glaringly exposed there is no need to look beyond Cole's essay, where the theory of future association is set out, in the promise of the 'glistening plough' and, curiously, the erection of further (luxurious?) temples and (feudal?) towers. Earlier in the same essay, though, he admits that 'an enlightened and increasing people have broken in upon the solitude' (p. 571) – the very 'solitude' in which, perceiving the sublimity of the American wilderness, the observer might be expected to invent an American species of Romanticism.

Elsewhere in this collection Robert Clark writes of Cole's paradox as 'contradictory bathos'. Bathos or not, the contradiction is fundamental, and common to almost all 'boosters' of the present beauty and future use of the American landscape. The Cincinnati editor Timothy Flint, in the midst of a visionary projection of the coming agricultural prosperity of the West, writes of the prairies being 'vexed' with the plough, and of 'magnificent forests' along the Ohio River 'not yet despoiled' by the axe.[9] But the contradiction goes deeper than the contemporary use of the figure of anticipation in landscape description – down through a fault line in the trope itself to the bedrock on which it rests, the conceit of *translatio imperii*. For the covert tone in Bishop Berkeley's vastly popular, frequently and fancifully illustrated lines on 'Westward the course of empire takes its way'[10] (Cole himself painted a series based on the short poem) is apocalyptic – which means that, however hopeful for America's future, it also signals the end of time itself. Even those no longer picking up the allusion to the Fifth-Monarchy Men (the 'first four acts' are the Assyrian, Persian, Greek and Roman 'monarchies' and the fifth is the thousand years of peaceful rule by Christ and his Saints) could hardly miss the references to the Last Things in Berkeley's 'A fifth shall close the drama with the day' and 'Time's noblest offspring is the last'. The figure of anticipation entailed both the perfection of history in America, and its termination. Death is buried deep in the trope.

And when it comes to its utility – to the psychology of the individual in a physical and social landscape and to how he or she is to write about it – future association must fall even further short of viable figuration than the attempt to retrieve a meaningful history from the European past. For if space and time render the castle, cathedral and ruined tower inaccessible to the American meditating in and on the native environment, how much less imaginable is a culture – especially one fraught with uncertain value – not yet built? Poetic figures, after all, must not be merely fantasies; or, to put it in Coleridgian terms, there is a great difference in utility between imaginative literature which appeals to the fancy and that which works on the imagination. Metonymy depends on the real link in time; the ruin must be of the same tower. Even metaphors, however far fetched, are based on actual events compared to each other. If one term in either kind of figure is rendered indistinct, or unbelievable, or superseded by political experience, or not yet in existence, then the figure must collapse, and with it, perhaps the literary project itself.

This essay seems to be arguing itself into the curious proposition that

American literature is impossible. In fact the thesis is simply that the original pessimism about the possibility of American literature *in the forms of writing then familiar to readers and authors* was justified; that the responses to that pessimism were misconceived; and that the instability inherent in those responses produced fundamental differences between American and English literature that are still not wholly understood, or even perceived. For instance, it is possible that the characteristically deconstructive text of the classic American novel of the mid-nineteenth century – the almost incessant, frequently facetious, questioning of the fictional project that one encounters in Melville and especially Hawthorne – owes something to the feelings behind phase three of Knight's sight of the moon in the wilderness. Even more sweepingly, although the figure of association is obviously a term in that long sentence of romantic projections about the future of the American cultural enterprise – all those Phi Beta Kappa addresses[11] of which Emerson's 'The American Scholar' is the best known – one could distinguish an American Romanticism from its English counterpart, offering as evidence the use of the word 'solitude' in Cole's essay (or in Irving's 'Author's Account', for that matter, where the American sublime includes 'cataracts thundering in their solitudes')[12] as compared to Wordsworth's use of it in *The Prelude*. Solitude in Wordsworth is relative, a temporary retreat from getting and spending, a vantage point for moral judgment never far from places of human habitation. It is populated, if not by other 'solitaries' encountered by the poet's projection of himself, then by thoughts going on in the head of that figure. Cole's solitude is a wilderness, destroyed forever when settlers 'break in' on it. The feeling of loss and nostalgia in Cole's essay – and much more famously, in the autumnal setting of Cooper's *The Prairie* (1827), when the Republic was actually awakening to the early summer of the Louisiana Purchase and the opening of the West, are quite unlike anything in the literature of English Romanticism.

To speak more locally (and argue more modestly), one could claim at least that the anxiety about broken connections produced characteristic warps in the logic of American narratives. Take the odd invention in Crèvecœur's *Letters from an American Farmer* (1782), in which the author disguises himself as an English immigrant of the second generation. The narrator can't be taken – at that date – as a fully fledged character in a novel; the production certainly puzzled contemporary reviewers in this respect. He needs to emphasize the continuity of development, the orderly succession of freehold property rights from generation to generation, in a country already in a state of revolution and about to cut itself off from its parent society. When he ploughs his farm, 'various are the thoughts which crowd into my mind. I am now doing for [my son], I say, what my father did for me'.[13] The fact that he has time for these thoughts is itself remarkable, when one considers the likely daily routine of an actual small farmer of the period, but Crèvecœur puts much stress on leisure for meditation on the natural world – not only in this chapter on Farmer James's 'Situation, Feelings, and Pleasures' but more extensively in the visit to the botanist John Bartram. Bartram is also a farmer who has time now for philosophical speculation because, like the narrator's imagined father, he has completed the basic work of clearing, diking, draining and planting. Crèvecœur was trying to find a credible process by which the settler could evolve into the producer of 'literature' without running to luxury and vice. That fact that he failed – that the logic of the historical moment overrode his fictional hypotheses – produced instead the first characteristic dislocation at the end of American fiction, in which a disenchanted hero lights out for the Territory, at the same time as his author 'lights in' back to the metropolis.

Or take the case of Cooper's *The Pioneers* (1823), which is actually built around Cole's contradiction between future culture and a nature about to be lost forever, between (on the one hand) the Indians and mountain men and an older generation of feudal landlords holding title to the land by Royal patent (granted, of course, by a personage himself empowered by hereditary succession), and (on the other) a new generation of bourgeois settlers with plans to 'improve' their surroundings. The chief of those new settlers, who has given his name to the new town of Templeton, envisages the surrounding landscape in terms of anticipatory associations:

The mind of Judge Temple ... had received from his peculiar occupations a bias to look far into futurity ... To his eye, where others saw nothing but a wilderness, towns, manufactories, bridges, canals, mines, and all the other resources of an old country were constantly presenting themselves, though his good sense suppressed in some degree the exhibition of these expectations.[14]

Ranged against these ambitions (and no doubt accounting for his desire to suppress their exhibition) are the various imperatives – much insisted on by the narrative – to do with preserving the natural setting. These take two forms, themselves contradictory, within the larger opposition between culture and nature: (1) the narrow principle of conservation, of which the Judge speaks warmly in favour but which really means preserving his property and its attendant raw materials (and which Natty Bumppo contravenes by shooting a deer out of season); (2) a doomed-to-be-disappointed desire to preserve the primeval habitat for Indians, mountain men, animals, and any other being willing to live within the existing ecology. Even the Judge's more narrow concern is shot through with inconsistency, since under his jurisdiction the townspeople slaughter fish and pigeons in numbers far greater than utility demands, but it is the larger contradiction between progress and the wilderness which finally undermines the book. Chingachgook has to die, and Natty, like Crèvecœur's Farmer James, lights out for the Territory. The best Cooper can do by way of resolution is to change tracks from realistic novel to pastoral romance: the disguise of Oliver Edwards is dispensed with to reveal the 'lost', 'true' inheritor of the land (in a line of succession drawn from the original feudal grantee), and he 'resolves' the old conflict of class and generation by marrying the daughter of Judge Temple, who, at least, has shown some concern for 'environmental issues'.

Indeed, so suggestive is this line of enquiry that one has to pull oneself up from extending it into American literature of the later nineteenth century – and even the twentieth century. But of the various cases still to be considered, perhaps two could be indicated before being left for further examination by those who think it worthwhile. Look at Whitman's use of the figure of anticipation. He uses it for purposes of conventional cultural patriotism in the 'Preface' to *Leaves of Grass* (1855) and throughout *Specimen Days* (1882); but, then more originally, in the fascinating play with verb tenses and moods in 'Crossing Brooklyn Ferry', by which he first insinuates and then commands a line of continuity with his future readers. And look again at Eliot's and Pound's use of the classics. Are they allusions in the conventional sense, or are they, like Jim Burden's reference to Virgil, eclectically drawn and uncertainly applied, cited with conflicting moods not only about their content but even about the legitimacy of using them at all? Why did Pound need to insist on the mediation between Homer and Canto I, in the form of Andreas Divus's Latin translation of the Odyssey and the Anglo-Saxon 'Seafarer'? Did he sense that the gap between the myth and his text was too great to provide a useful historical analogy for the present? And does this analogical weakness explain his disastrous intellectual and moral error of trying to match Mussolini to Jefferson, when he tried to reinvent early republican America in fascist Italy? For that matter, why did American modernist poets have to go to Europe to invent modernism?

Better stop there. The point is that the deficiency of usable history in the early Republic was not just thought to be a problem; it *was* a problem – if only because so widely perceived as such. The various responses to the predicament failed to meet it, but in turn the uneasy awareness of that failure was enormously productive. The very instability resulting from recurrent disappointment led to solutions to the development of a truly original national literature: strategies for the author and powerful explanations for the critic.

Notes

1 The text used is in Perry Miller and Thomas H. Johnson, eds., *The Puritans: a Sourcebook of their Writings*, 2 vols., revised edn (New York: Harper and Row, 1963), vol. 2, pp. 429–30.

2 An example of such thinking is Louis Hartz et al., *The Founding of New Societies: Studies in the History of the United States, Latin America, South Africa, Canada and Australia* (New York: Harcourt, Brace and World, 1964).

3 Georges-Louis Leclerc, Comte Buffon, *Histoire Naturelle*, 44 vols., 1749–1804; the first edition in English appeared one year before the Declaration of Independence as *The Natural History of Animals, Vegetables and Minerals...*, trans. W. Kenrick et al., 6 vols. (London: T. Bell, 1775). Guillaume Thomas, Abbé Raynal, *Histoire ... des Européens dans les deux Indes*, 4 vols. (Amsterdam, 1770); an English translation of part of this work, *A ... History of the British Settlements and Trade in North America* (Edinburgh, 1779), modifies some of the more pessimistic predictions of the outlook for civilized development in North America.

4 *American Literature in Context, 1620–1830* (London: Methuen, 1983), pp. 165–75.

5 Thomas Cole, 'Essay on American Scenery', *The American Monthly Magazine*, 1 (1836), in John Conron, ed., *The American Landscape: a Critical Anthology of Prose and Poetry* (New York: Oxford University Press, 1974), p. 577. Subsequent references to Cole will be to this edition, and will appear in the text.

6 Morris Birkbeck, *Notes on a Journey in America . . . to the Territory of Illinois*, 5th edn (London: James Ridgway, 1819), p. 39. The sneer appears in a review of the book in the *Quarterly Review*, 19 (1818), 62.

7 *Democracy in America*, Part II, First Book, ch. 8, trans. Henry Reeve, revised edn, 2 vols. (New York: The Colonial Press, 1900), vol. 2, p. 78.

8 Variants on the theme include: [Edward Everett], 'On the Complaints in America against the British Press' (answering an essay in *The New London Monthly Magazine* for Feb. 1821), *North American Review*, 13 (1821), 40–1; [W. H. Gardiner], review of James Fenimore Cooper's *The Spy* (1821), *North American Review*, 15 (1822), 253–5; and N. P. Willis's introduction to W. H. Bartlett's sketches of *American Scenery*, 2 vols. (1840) vol. 1, p. 2. Willis follows Cole most closely.

9 Timothy Flint, *Recollections of the Last Ten Years in the Valley of the Mississippi* (1826), ed. George Brooks (Carbondale and Edwardsville: Southern Illinois University Press; London and Amsterdam: Feffer and Simons, 1966), pp. 91, 23.

10 One popular print is described in Gidley's essay in this collection.

11 For other Phi Beta Kappa addresses in this vein, see William Tudor's of 1815, *North American Review*, 2 (1815), 13–32, in Robert E. Spiller, ed. *The American Literary Revolution, 1783–1837*, 2nd edn (New York University Press, 1969), pp. 133–53; Francis Calley Gray's for the following year, *North American Review*, 3 (1816), 289–305; Spiller, pp. 163–74; and Edward Everett's 'The Peculiar Motives to Intellectual Exertion in America', Spiller, pp. 284–318.

12 See also Henry Wadsworth Longfellow's graduation oration at Bowdoin College in 1825: 'The scenery of our own country . . . so full of quiet loveliness or of sublime and solitary awe . . .' ('Our Native Writers', *Every Other Saturday*, 1, 12 April 1884; Spiller, pp. 388–9); and Francis Parkman's comment in *The Oregon Trail* that the Valley of the Platte had no 'features of grandeur, other than its vast extent, its solitude and its wildness'.

13 J. Hector St John de Crèvecœur, *Letters from an American Farmer* and *Sketches of Eighteenth Century America*, with a Foreword by Albert E. Stone (New York: New American Library, 1963), p. 49.

14 Cooper, *The Pioneers, or the Sources of the Susquehanna*, ed. James Franklin Beard, Lance Schachterle and Kenneth M. Anderson (Albany: State University of New York Press, 1980), p. 321.

5 * Trails of topographic notions: expeditionary photography in the American West

PHILIP STOKES

The topographic photography produced in the United States in the two decades after the Civil War is not only of major and enduring interest in the history of the medium, but communicates a strong physical presence. The naive perception of just one such image provides a memorable experience: witness, for example, Eadweard Muybridge's 'Valley of the Yosemite from Glacier Point, No. 33' (1872; pl. 6), with its large size, splendid hues, plentiful detail and magisterial composition. It is understandable that such work is now being reviewed and commented upon with some frequency and perspicacity.[1] We may well ask questions about the motivation for the acuity of vision and feats of craftsmanship represented by such photographs. What, indeed, is their full meaning? I hope that in the course of at least looking for answers to this question it will also prove possible to offer some thoughts as to how such meaning has been encoded, to gain an insight into what might be termed the visual language of these photographs.

It is important in the first instance to establish the photographic context which favoured this particular flowering. Photography, to a much greater extent than any more established visual medium, is bound up with the technicalities of its processes. Major evolutions in imagery have tended to be generated out of the convergences of technical opportunity with events in the world at large. In this case, when a major push of exploration westwards got under way after the cessation of Civil War hostilities, the wet plate process of photography had reached its peak, enabling vast amounts of visual data to be recorded by the expeditions. The scale of such activity is easier to sense through examples than to graph, given the extent of both geographical and temporal axes. Timothy O'Sullivan, for instance, went into the field every year between

6 Eadweard Muybridge, 'Valley of the Yosemite from Glacier Point, No. 33, California', 1872

1867 and 1874, covering ground from Idaho in the north to New Mexico, and even Panama, in the south. Much of his work was with Clarence King, on the Fortieth Parallel Surveys and elsewhere, following the general principle that material was gathered during the good months of the year, and worked up during the winter. William H. Jackson was with Ferdinand Hayden on expeditions for eight years from 1870, and it has been calculated that in the period to 1875 he obtained 2,000 negatives: a small number by today's standards, but dauntingly large when one considers what was involved in the photography of that time.

65

It was far from being the case that photographers worked only in an official context, for the growth of the trade in photographic prints had led to reasonable expectations that there would be a market for the material amongst the public at large. Indeed, elsewhere in this collection Mick Gidley points out the relationship between western expansion and the rise of photographic entrepreneurs.[2] Nevertheless, the number of serious practitioners was not sufficient to give rise to the extremes of competition which later led to a fall from the high visual seriousness and quality of production which marks the period now being considered.

Such was the potential of their process, that photographers felt justified in looking with equanimity upon the logistics of packing cameras and darkroom kits sufficient to handle plates larger than most modern photographers can imagine. It would be more than enough for most of us to work in the field with O'Sullivan's 9″ x 12″ and 8″ × 10″ plates, but we hear of mammoth sizes, like 17″ × 21″, 20″ × 24″ and even 20″ × 27″. Plates of this size – and, hence, extreme weight – had to be coated and sensitized on the spot, in special dark tents, using for the coating stage a mixture based on collodion, which is made by dissolving guncotton in ether and has the property of pouring like treacle in cold weather, while in the summer it evaporates so fast that the photographer has good reason to fear anaesthesia. Coating is achieved as the photographer holds, or in the case of large sizes, balances the plate in one hand, rocking it while steadily pouring exactly the right amount of mixture to cover the rectangular surface completely and evenly, an operation as difficult as it sounds. The plate is then sensitized in a silver nitrate bath, loaded into a dark slide (a wooden case allowing it to be taken into the light), put in the camera, exposed and brought back for development, all while it is still wet; hence the name, wet collodion process. It then remains merely to fix, wash and dry it, and get the negative safely back to base, very likely on a mule's back.

The motivation required to drive these photographers through to success, across the debris of the inevitable failures and breakages, is hardly compatible with ordinary commercial activity, even combined with a liking for adventure, especially when it is remembered that so far as the practice of photography was concerned (apart, that is, from any skills of leadership or conversational talents they possessed) they were as they still largely are, journeymen engaged to execute others' wishes. Rather, the photographic potential was recognizable as a mirror of the full range of motivations perceived as fuelling the frontier push, and it was that congruence, however fortuitous, which drove the photographers to their attainments.

On the surface it was logical, if not entirely prosaic, to employ survey teams to discover the potential of unexplored territory. Their objectives were framed in largely concrete terms; for example, in the case of King's Fortieth Parallel Survey which set out, beginning in 1867, to explore a stretch of land lying for the most part just north of the fortieth parallel, from Virginia City, a mining town in Nevada, eastwards via the Great Salt Lake to Denver City in the east, the objectives were centred upon geology, and extended to studying the 'flora and the fauna of the country and its agricultural capacity'.[3] George Wheeler's expeditions, commencing in 1871, dealt from a military standpoint with the topography of the land between Nevada and New Mexico. In no instance were they remote from thoughts of settlement, trade and industry.

Yet for all their mundane preoccupations, including rivalries between civilian and military expeditions, it was quite the done thing for leaders to take with them artists whose work and status pointed to the abstract, philosophical considerations which transcended, justified – and which might even conceal – both the minutiae of topographic records and their social and economic consequences. King, for instance, took Albert Bierstadt on his 1872 expedition when O'Sullivan was the photographer, and Bierstadt worked on the Pacific coast at the same time as Muybridge. Thomas Moran accompanied Hayden to Yellowstone in 1871, and John Wesley Powell on his Grand Cañon expedition in 1873, both times in parties which included photographers.

The intellectually least demanding aspect of an expeditionary photographer's work, that of gathering hard data of the land and its life, was catered to by the sheer size of plates and the quality of optics then available. Given the strength and persistence of a Hercules, one would have no trouble in presenting the world with a visual inventory every bit as specific and exhaustive in its way as were the scientist's or the soldier's log in others; and in terms of visual data, superior to any painting or drawing. (Unfortunately the truth of this statement cannot fully emerge from the study of an average reproduction, but a direct encounter with a large topographic photograph in fine condition would demonstrate the modesty of my claim.)

A painter would, however, legitimately claim advantage when it came

Philip Stokes

to minimizing the difference between his first-hand *experience* and the record of it. Moran called this truth to pictorial nature, even though it might involve the repositioning of natural features, and he hoped the attainment of it would cause every member of the expedition to declare that he knew the exact spot which had been represented.[4] The photographer's options are different and more limited. There is no way for the camera to compensate for the difference between human binocular vision and the lens's single point perspective, but an ingenious photographer could and did take advantage of the conventions of the Picturesque. These might permit him to tilt the frame, so as to change a slope, or dramatize an overhang. O'Sullivan in particular was aware of the advantages to be had from such machinations, as Rick Dingus discovered in the case of certain of his Witch's Rocks images.[5] Similarly, Joel Snyder observed a slight tilt of the frame (which becomes intrusive once it has been noticed) in O'Sullivan's horizontal shot of the Cañon de Chelly.[6] This causes some massive columnar formations on the right of the cañon floor to appear as if they were leaning over, threatening a flat and relatively verdant area where tiny, fragile tents are pitched, a move which significantly modifies the reading permitted by the image with its verticals corrected. Other photographers, like Muybridge, remained content to rely upon less radical accommodations of painterly composition – such as the importation of cloudy skies or decisions on framing (as in 'Valley of the Yosemite', with its subtle near balancing of masses either side of the valley) – to bring their records into accord with prevailing artistic proprieties. In all such cases the objective was to reconcile the differences between the empirical and the experiential.

Photographers, as these examples imply, had fewer problems meeting the conventions of what was considered beautiful than they encountered trying to match painters' claims for truth. Some, like Muybridge, saw both truth and beauty located towards the Sublime, as evoked in comparable work by Bierstadt. O'Sullivan, on the other hand, in the plainness and clarity of his skies, indeed in the generally austere lucidity and stillness of his images, moves one's perceptions towards the quiet cast of the Luminist mind, concerned as it was with a precisely controlled account of visible form, the description of state and place rather than narrative or activity.[7] That his truth tended to have less of the conventions of beauty within it is appropriate for the photographer who accompanied King, the disciple of catastrophism, with its tenets of life destroyed and regenerating in repeated cycles of geological disaster and stability.

The massive inventories of data, so valuable to the materialist uses of photography, were also ideal substance for symbolic readings, as exemplified by Ruskin's sense of affinity between human life and the rest of natural creation, between the human mind and all visible things. The small human figures, indices of scale to practical spectators, and emphasizing sublimity to the Romantics, provided such viewers with exemplary contemplators of the Good. Could the very fact of contemplation have been seen as a sign that the Good was even better than mere appearances proposed; or did it act to confirm the virtue of the contemplator's presence in the landscape?

Probably both are true, and the perceiver of the image would sense a vicarious sharing of the virtue of the contemplator within it, for instance, in the presence of W. H. Jackson's photograph, 'View on the Sweetwater, Wyoming' (1870). There the tiny figure in the midground is looking out from a dark, scrubby, alluvial area, across a stretch of water, past a camp, to distant mountains backed by the open, unclouded infinite sky; and, like such a figure in O'Sullivan's 'Soda Lake' (1868; pl. 3), he is not only a convenient index of scale but the signifier of the complex of ideas around the contemplation of nature so important for American landscape art.[8]

Moreover, if, as has been intimated, the exploration of America was a working out of the Manifest Destiny to pastoralize the wilderness, then those who recorded this exploration were not insensate mercenaries of expansionism, but worked in the context of a system in which Nature was a manifestation of God, perceived as immanent in its sublimity, and where the life and structure of every part, great or small, symbolized the operation of divine law. It was a ready convenience that the gentle, harmonious qualities held to constitute beauty were thought of as feminine, and that within the nineteenth-century pantheon, Nature was enthroned in the feminine gender: already infused by God, awaiting the penetration of Man, which would bring her to a state of submissive, wifely fertility. If there was to be a little rape along the way, then that was more a necessary part of Nature's schooling than a sign of philosophical confusion.[9]

In other words, each of the characteristics of these photographs, whether singly, in concert, or in conjunction with a wider context, fulfilled several different – and in terms of some current thinking, sometimes incompatible – requirements of meaning. This is remarkable. It proposes a multiplicity of interpretation, of the kind pointed to by opponents of the notion of a photographic language. William Ivins, for instance, claimed that in photography 'man had discovered a way to make visual reports in printer's ink without syntax, and without the distorting analysis of form that syntax necessitated'. Purely photographic images, he said, 'were not subject to the omissions, the distortions and the subjective difficulties that are inherent in all ... hand-made pictures'.[10] My own view is that without a syntax, even allowing for the felicitous constellation of technical characteristics of the medium at that time, the expeditionary photographers would not have succeeded as they did in embodying many levels and dimensions of meaning for their viewers to reconstruct.

To this it will be objected that the photograph is a mere transparent record of external realities, virginally innocent of its maker's intent. It is, we are sometimes told, as by Ivins, less than a translation. It is appearance pure and simple, a one-to-one correspondence with its subject, a sort of optical–chemical transcription of the scene before it. Nevertheless, even if one follows the received, process-centred line from Ivins, through Marshall McLuhan to Roland Barthes, one ends up, maybe ruefully, after reading his late work in *Camera Lucida*, noting that there remains in Barthes's mind a sense of essences witheld.[11] Even though Barthes proposes the notion of the 'analogon', the photograph as virtual copy of its subject, this is so. And indeed there *are* essences witheld, for what Barthes has vaguely, reluctantly apprehended, is that the photographer's act is a translation from world to image, which proceeds, under the photographer's control, via encodings which include perspective, tone, resolution, colour and image size in subtle, precise relationships which work as factors powerfully determining the signification of a photograph. Certainly, photography has filled the world with analogues, but the analogon, the special, unclad beast courted by so many philosophers, will only ever be, at best, a creature of the looking glass.

Even the photographer's compositional choices, less separable from the encodings of process than might casually be supposed, are vehicles for intentions towards meaning. We have already noted the significances of human figures. These are of course to be found, like peaks and lambent skies, in the paintings; but the real-life basis of the photograph warns against taking the presence of such figures as perhaps no more than a consequence of the image maker's conceit. Indeed, it is one of the effects of the geometrical absolutes of framing and perspective to discipline and draw attention to relative dispositions and scales of objects within the image.

We are exposed to the paradox that while the external world is being recorded through a mechanical system, the photographer, included in neither, selects from the one and controls the other in ways such that codes of process play against codes of selection. In topographic photography this leads the viewer to pursue the significations to be derived out of single objects, and from conjunctions between objects, or from conjunctions between the whole image and the context of its presentation.

When speaking of the process of generating metaphor out of visual images, I like to include a reminder of its association with ideas of rhetoric by using *trope* relative to derivation from a single object, and *parataxis* in the case of metaphor derived from the conjunctions of objects. Such terms help to explain *how* the multiplicity of interpretations we have noted is possible. As an example, let us look at A. J. Russell's photograph, 'The Temporary and Permanent Bridges and Citadel Rock, Green River, Wyoming' (1867–8).[12] We are shown an austere, near-desert landscape, where topping a conical, barren, snow-dusted hill, a granite mass looms above the railway, its works and its workers; the railroad and its workers together proceed from a narrow focus in the right midground to dominance of the whole foreground of the image. In terms of traditional readings, the landscape constitutes a trope for the primaeval, a truly awful sublimity; the tracks and the train together signify paratactically the powers of determination and exploitation uppermost in the minds of those days. In sum, especially as the railroad is, as it were, superimposed on the natural world, and itself conjoint with some confident-seeming figures of those who made and operate it, the viewer is afforded a visual exposition of the wilderness civilized, if not yet pastoralized. Further elaborations are derivable from the evidence of progress despite snow, the signs that the temporary is being rapidly made permanent, and by implication, the frontier advanced.

It is inappropriate here to pursue arguments reaching beyond syntax into questions bearing upon the existence of a photographic syntagm, or chain of elements analogous to the sequence of a verbal utterance, but enough has already been said to indicate that I am inclined to propose certain linguistic affinities for photographic communication. And yet, paradoxically, the very multiplicity of signification of the topographic photographs would seem to contradict such a view. Where is the articulation, the control, which turns utterance into message?

The first part of the answer is general to photography, irrespective of its kind. Whereas a painting, a novel, or a piece of music is instantly recognized as dependent for its very existence upon the cultural context out of which it grew, and thus as pointing to at least a basic set of criteria against which it may be judged, there is nothing intrinsic to photography which ascribes its roots. However unlikely, there is no reason why the camera should not have been triggered by the now overworked, hypothetical passing monkey of photographic legend who could have reached out its skinny arm to release our shutter without a picture-making thought in its simian head, and produced an image which resounded to our credit for ever after. So context free is the photograph, that perhaps it will take root anywhere, acquire chameleonlike the colours of whatever proposition it settles down with. One has only to look at the public uses of photography to see how readily this occurs; as when the year-old stock photograph of a politician takes on a grim or angry air according to whether it is paired with today's story of a run on the dollar, or a government scandal, and the photograph of a happy child becomes instantly disadvantaged when used to head an account of social deprivation.

And yet various roles, as we have seen, are fulfilled by the topographic photographs without the least anomaly or gap in their completed specificity. The Citadel Rock photograph by A. J. Russell, mentioned above, combines the roles of mundane record and expression of an aspect of what one might call frontier metaphysics. Many of O'Sullivan's images, such as his 'Karnak Region' (pl. 1), present geological records which can yet be held to exemplify the tenets of catastrophism. Within his 'Black Cañon, Colorado River, from Camp 8' (1871; pl. 7), though taken for Wheeler rather than King, there is in the cliff forms the presence of quite literally the hardest of evidence, yet its composition – which emphasizes the majestic sweep of the river and the frailty of the incongruous boat – also generates awe as it contributes to the body of empirical knowledge.

7 Timothy O'Sullivan, 'Black Cañon, Colorado River, from Camp 8,
California', 1871

The completion of our answer arises out of the phenomenon whereby
a single set of complex data may be perceived as fitting various, perhaps
mutually exclusive, hypotheses. This is commonly seen in fields such as
economics, politics, astrology and even archaeology. Indeed, Richard
Gregory offers a succinct and clear demonstration from the latter
discipline by showing how the plan of a set of post holes found during an
archaeological dig may be used to adduce the previous existence of two
quite different sets of structures upon the site.[13] Given sufficient levels
of imprecision or redundancy in the data, combined with a certain
tolerance or indeterminancy in the hypothesis, it is easy to understand
how such a situation may occur.

If we think of photography as sharing in this phenomenon, especially

73

when our concern is with a large topographic image, the quantity and density of information available, both as straight inventory and as relationships proposed between objects within the picture, is truly astronomic. Thus, there will be sufficient evidence and potential for its patterning to corroborate a whole range of notions. Indeed we can see from their use on all levels, from the governmental and scientific, through commercial to the artistic and philosophical, that the exploration photographs had an immense scope for signification. (I would propose, as already implied, that this indicates their makers' skills of multiple ordering much more strongly than it points to the variety of readings available from large masses of undifferentiated data.)

Let us turn from principle to process: a viewer at the first level of perceiving the concrete might attend to practical contexts and questions of photographic use – what is here? – how high is that? – could crops grow there? After the viewer has dealt with as much data as may be dealt with, there is a second level, and ultimately further levels of perception of ideas induced by the repeated identification of things similar and different, until we no longer wonder what they are, so much as what they mean. And the same photograph as satisfied George Wheeler's military brief or the needs of a railroad company might fit the philosophies motivating a Clarence King. (That is not to say that we may go so far as to believe any image capable of meeting any proposition, just provided it contains enough data. Put one of Russell's railroad pictures alongside the European-based Romanticism of Muybridge and a geological/ Luminist image from O'Sullivan, and their incompatibilities will probably come to the fore before their shared qualities.) The informational density, the intensity of denotation of these topographic photographs has the paradoxical effect of at the one moment seeming to confine them in the realm of concrete fact, precluding any metaphoric flights, and at the next, under pressure of all the conjunctions, the sheer clamour of the objects, to boil out language in great clouds. They demand, for their fullest appreciation, a rapid switching of the viewer's perceptual mode between the concrete and the abstract.[14]

Structurally, this is akin to the effects of the realist novel. Henry James's extreme reaction to *L'Education sentimentale*, which he said was 'like masticating ashes and sawdust . . . elaborately and massively dreary', epitomizes the view of literary realism as merely denotative.[15] It parallels the hostile view of topographic photographs as nothing more than inventories of useful data. Flaubert's gift for inducing his readers to move from the mundane specific to the general and abstract corresponds closely to the historically evident properties of large-format topographic photography, with its wide range of legitimately available significations. To summarize briefly, I believe that in a study of the foregoing phenomena, the effects of a plenitude of data, syntactically formed and complementing an extreme contextual flexibility, there lies a route to understanding the powerful, classical communication derivable from images of the type represented by the topographic photographs of the American West, from the time of their making to the present day. That the process so matched its historical moment may be partly fortune: the outcome is patently fortunate.

Notes

1 I would like to record my gratitude to Dr Adrian Thatcher of Plymouth for illuminating my ideas from a different direction. Useful studies of exploration photography and related matters include: Weston Naef, with James Wood, *Era of Exploration* (Boston: New York Graphic Society, 1974); Max Kozloff, 'The Box in the Wilderness', *Artforum*, 14, part 2 (1975), 54–9; and Estelle Jussim and Elizabeth Lindquist-Cock, *Landscape as Photograph* (New Haven and London: Yale University Press, 1985). Helpful studies of individual photographers not cited elsewhere in this essay include: Beaumont Newhall and Diane Edkins, *William H. Jackson* (Hastings on Hudson: Morgan and Morgan, 1974); Howard Bossen, 'A Tall Tale Retold: The Influence of the Photographs of William Henry Jackson on the Passage of the Yellowstone Park Act of 1872', *Studies in Visual Communication*, 8, no. 1 (1982), 98–109; C. H. Campbell, 'Albert Bierstadt and the White Mountains', *Archives of American Art*, 21, no. 3 (1981), 14–23 ; and J. Coplans, 'C. E. Watkins at Yosemite', *Art in America*, 66, no. 6 (1978), 100–6. Interesting contextual information on ideas of landscape in America is to be found in the works of Barbara Novak, cited below, and in John Wilmerding, ed., *American Light* (Washington, DC: National Gallery of Art, 1980).

2 See Gidley's essay in this volume. Also, with reference to Watkins, P. E. Palmquist, in his *Carleton Watkins* (Albuquerque: University of New Mexico Press, 1983), put the issue succinctly: '[his] early work suggests ... that litigious real estate claimants and ambitious businessmen played an ... important role in the promotion of western photography' (p. xi).

3 *New York Times* article of 8 May 1867, quoted in Naef and Wood, *Era of Exploration*, p. 127.

Philip Stokes

4 Quoted in Rick Dingus, *The Photographic Artifacts of Timothy O'Sullivan*. (Albuquerque: University of New Mexico Press, 1982), p. 51.
5 For a detailed discussion of O'Sullivan's employment of viewpoint, see ibid., pp. 31–64.
6 See Joel Snyder, *American Frontiers: The Photographs of Timothy O'Sullivan 1867–74* (Millerton, NY: Aperture, 1981), pp. 48, 93.
7 Another way of looking at this, in broad conceptual terms, is to propose European-based Romanticism as concerning itself with becoming, with movement, whether as heavenward ascension or as the fall into the abyss, whereas, perhaps via Caspar David Friedrich on the cusp, American Luminism deals with being and stasis. For his views on the Sublime and related issues, see also the essay by Olaf Hansen in this collection.
8 See Barbara Novak, *American Painting of the Nineteenth Century* (New York: Harper and Row, 1979), especially pp. 62–3, and *Nature and Culture: American Landscape Painting 1825–1875* (London: Thames and Hudson, 1980) in which also Jackson's 'View on the Sweetwater' is reproduced (p. 196).
9 This paragraph is an amalgam of ideas of nature that infused Western thought during the early industrial period. A small selection of examples might run from the Nature Philosophers in Germany, from whom Novalis spoke in his *Hymns to Night* about the dreamer entering the very womb of Nature, to bathe in the matrix of being (vide Roger Cardinal, *German Romantics in Context* (London: Studio Vista, 1975), p. 32), through the Romantic poets in England with their general application of the female gender to nature; and Ruskin who said, 'Let us go forth to contemplate Nature where she abides yet undisfigured by man.' Emerson follows in general terms, but one of the most complete expressions must be that of Louis B. Noble, who describes how Thomas Cole 'had walked with nature in her maidenhood, her fair proportions veiled in virgin robes, affianced indeed to human associations, but unpolluted, unwasted by human passion'. (*The Course of Empire, Voyage of Life and Other Pictures of Thomas Cole*, 1853, as quoted by Barbara Novak in *Nature and Culture*, p. 206). A pertinent reading in this connection is Annette Kolodny, *The Lay of the Land: Metaphor as Experience and History in American Life and Letters* (Chapel Hill: University of North Carolina Press, 1975).
10 Ivins, *Prints and Visual Communications* (Cambridge, MA: Harvard University Press, 1953), pp. 123, 128.
11 See ibid.; McLuhan, *Understanding Media* (London: Sphere, 1967), p. 202; for Barthes original position, see the essays 'The Photographic Message' and 'Rhetoric of the Image', in *Image–Music–Text*, trans. Stephen Heath (London: Fontana, 1977), especially pp. 17–18, 36; Barthes, *Camera Lucida*, trans. Richard Howard (London: Cape, 1982).

76

12 Reproduced, among other places, in Naef, *Era of Exploration*, p. 98.
13 Richard Gregory, 'The Confounded Eye', in Gregory and E. H. Gombrich, eds. *Illusion in Nature and Art* (London: Duckworth, 1973), p. 83.
14 Such rapid switching of perceptual mode, whether from the concrete to the abstract or from regard of microdetail to overall form might be partly accounted for by E. C. Zeeman's formulation of catastrophe theory, of which Zeeman offered a detailed non-numerical synopsis in *The Times Literary Supplement* of 10 Dec. 1971.
15 Henry James, *French Poets and Novelists* (London: Macmillan, 1983), p. 209–10. We are close here to Damian Grant's formulation of 'conscientious realism', by which he refers to the accumulative form of realism practised by Zola and, more sophisticatedly, by Flaubert, where ideas are found to appear out of an overbearingly heavy accumulation of objects (*Realism* (London: Methuen, 1970), ch. 2).

Anglo-American perspectives

6 * The absent landscape of America's eighteenth century

ROBERT CLARK

> Jones . . . with the stranger . . . mounted Mazard Hill; of which they had no sooner gained the summit, than one of the noblest prospects in the world presented itself to their view, and which we would present to the reader, but for two reasons. *First*, we despair of making those who have seen this prospect admire the description. *Secondly*, we very much doubt whether those who have not seen it would understand it.
>
> Henry Fielding, *Tom Jones*, Book 9, chapter 2

Henry Fielding's ironic refusal to represent the prospect from Mazard Hill may stand as a caution to all who would describe landscape in words: if you have seen it, the quality of the experience may beggar description, if you haven't seen it words may be inadequate. At this moment in *Tom Jones* (1745) the implicit claim that the evidence of the senses is beyond the expressive powers of the writer is questioned by the author's despair that he cannot produce an admirable description; evidently there is already in place a convention against which the author's performance can be measured, one which will provide both sign of his writerly skill and sign of the writing's experiential truth. To have seen is only credible if the seeing translates into the appropriate discourse.

Fielding is of course joking. His refusal is consistent with his habit of parodying existing conventions in order to construct his new province of writing; but animating the joke there is a profound unease about how convention expresses experience and it is an unease that proves instructive when we read Fielding's North American contemporaries for, despite what may be thought the obvious imperatives of traveller's accounts, prospects are rarely represented. This lack of representation and the reasons why it is filled only after the War of Independence is the subject of this essay.

The word landscape enters English from the Dutch in 1598, signifying a genre of painting, and around one hundred years later begins to enter wider use to signify a prospect or sight, a mental or verbal impression. During the eighteenth century we begin to find such beautiful descriptions as the following, taken from Dr Brown's famous Letter to Lord Lyttelton of 1756.

At Keswick you will, on one side of the lake, see a rich and beautiful landskip of cultivated fields, rising to the eye in fine inequalities, with noble groves of oak happily dispersed; and clinging to the adjacent hills, shade above shade, in the most various and picturesque forms. On the opposite shore, you will find rocks and cliffs of stupendous height, hanging broken over the lake in horrible grandeur, some of them a thousand feet high, the woods climbing up their steep and shaggy sides ... A variety of waterfalls are seen pouring from their summits, and tumbling in vast sheets from rock to rock, in rude and terrible magnificence, while on all sides of this mimic amphitheatre the lofty mountains rise around, piercing the clouds.[1]

This letter was not published until 1768, twenty-three years after the publication of *Tom Jones*, and we can deduce that its polish is not the fortuitous result of genius but rather the perfection of a thriving literary practice, the devotion of many amateur pens to the creation of such impressions. Brown's 'horrible grandeur' and 'terrible magnificence' evidence his indebtedness to Burke's recent and powerful theorization of the sublime, and it is only a little later that the heroines of many a ladies' novel will, like their readers, begin to sit down at such places as Derwent Water, glance at the view, then open their volume of Gray or Thomson to find out how to see what is before their eyes.[2] They will thus confirm the new relationship to nature of the leisured classes of the increasingly capitalist West: through transformations in the agricultural economy, urbanization, industrialization, the material world has become either an image of order and freedom or an alien entity that provokes profound and mysterious responses.

In the philosophical apparatus produced by Addison, refined by Burke and then revised by Gilpin and Price, we find the essence of these conventions: nature is either rounded, varied and discretely ordered, therefore beautiful, or it is rough and wild, therefore either sublime or picturesque, depending upon how much horror it inspires. In Addison, as Leo Marx has pointed out, the equation between order, commodity and beauty is quite explicit, for 'we take delight in a prospect which is well laid out ... in anything that hath such a variety or regularity as may seem the effect of design, in what we call the works of chance.'[3] More explicitly still, Addison asks

> But why may not a whole estate be thrown into a kind of garden by frequent plantations, that may turn as much to the profit, as the pleasure of the owner? A marsh overgrown with willows, or a mountain shaded with oaks, are not only more beautiful but more beneficial, than when they lie bared and unadorned. Fields of corn make a pleasant prospect, and if the walks were a little taken care of that lie between them, if the natural embroidery of the meadows were a little helped and improved by some small additions of art ... a man might make a pretty landscape of his own possessions.[4]

Even as these lines were written, Addison's suggestions were being put in practice at Castle Howard where, as at many later estates, belvederes and points of view were constructed so that the landowner and his guests could look out not just upon landscaped lakes and woods but equally upon a scene of rationalized agricultural labour.[5] The discovery of aesthetic value in the landscape is fundamentally linked to the transformation of the earth into an investment whose profitability must be constantly assessed, a commodity whose utility as the supporter of the once-feudal community is now in antagonistic relationship with its exchange value in money. The oak and willows that Addison plants for ornamental purposes are expensive investments that transform waste into a productive asset. His praise of aesthetic values, of order, reason and harmony, in effect offers to heal the wounds of an intensely disruptive moment – the divorce of peasant from his land, of aristocrat from feudal bonds, and the opening out of that perpetually irresolute divorce at the heart of the commodity, between use and exchange. The very categories that for Addison lead to visual pleasure, greatness of scale, openness of prospect, and uncommonness, indicate a sensibility that is expansive and dominating, eager for differentiation. Open country, vast deserts, wide expanses are pleasing for 'the rude magnificence which appears in many of these stupendous works of nature' and for the sense of liberty they inspire, whereas the uncommon grants an agreeable surprise, 'gratifies curiosity, and gives it an idea of which it was not before possessed'.[6] The idea of nature as a field of 'stupendous works', gently secularizing Christian doctrine, returns nature to mankind as already the product of labour, therefore prepared for subsequent human transformations. The idea of nature as a field of new ideas that the mind takes into possession, translates the scientific work of the Royal Society into the aesthetic realm. The very material specificity of Addison's prospects, fundamentally allied to the spirit of improvement, distinguishes his attitude from the generalization and abstraction of Renaissance pastoral that would respond to or imagine a bower of bliss as a relatively local and exclusive instance.

The content of the categorical aesthetic division established by English eighteenth-century writers of the beautiful and orderly from the sublime and wild is evidence of the economic split between a domain that had been brought into Reason, harmony, and (agri)cultural control, and a more complicated domain which, while it reminded people of the intimate other that nature once was, set limits to Enlightenment's dreams of total empire and indicated potentials yet to be harnessed. The form of this division, like the content, was evidence of the growing power of the encyclopaedic *category*, the need to first create an abstract definition before being capable of a response. The term 'picturesque' itself enshrined the conventionalization of perception, indicating the need to legislate and systematize both the means and objects worthy of representation. Yet despite the intense literary, philosophical and artistic activity producing and refining the landscape *topos* in England, and despite the training of many eighteenth-century Americans in England, it is almost eighty years after Burke's *Philosophical Enquiry into the Sublime and the Beautiful* (1757) and the beginning of the cult of the Lakes, before we find the British-born Thomas Cole offering the sublimities of nature as an antidote both to the 'meagre utilitarianism that seems ready to absorb everyday feeling and sentiment', and to the march of improvement that 'makes us fear that the bright and tender flowers of the imagination shall be crushed beneath its iron tramp':

Rural nature is the exhaustless mine from which the poet and painter have brought such wondrous treasures – an unfailing fountain of intellectual enjoyment, where all may drink, and be awakened to a deeper feeling of the works of genius, and a keener perception of the beauty of existence ... [In] civilized Europe the primitive features of scenery have long since been destroyed or modified – the extensive forests that once overshadowed a great part of it have been felled – rugged mountains have been smoothed, and impetuous rivers turned from their course to accommodate the tastes and necessities of a dense population – the once tangled wood is now a grassy lawn ... And to this cultivated state our western world is fast approaching; but nature is still predominant, and there are those who regret that with the improvements of cultivation the sublimity of the wilderness should pass away; for those scenes of solitude from which the hand of nature has never been lifted, affect the mind with a more deep toned emotion than aught which the hand of man has touched. Amid them the consequent associations are of God the creator – they are his undefiled works, and mind is cast into the contemplation of eternal things.[7]

Cole's application to the American scene of ideas that had already degenerated to cliché in Europe condenses its contradictions in the two words 'exhaustless mine', an industrial metaphor paradoxically made to speak a Cornucopian idyll. His essay makes apparent that the utilitarian exploitation which is destroying nature also gives rise to a cult of its re-creational use: nostalgia for nature's vanishing otherness is a way of defining the present within an historical process that depends upon the alienating re-creation of humanity and its environment. The process that turns nature conceptually and literally into an object of taste and consumption – 'grassy lawns' and 'wondrous treasures' – also provides a livelihood for a painter prepared to represent nature in a commodity form that can signify culture in an urban drawing room. This contra-diction becomes apparent in the way Cole's essay declines into bathos: he ends by extolling what Graham Clarke, in his contribution to this book, terms 'domestic typology', the 'neat dwellings ... abodes of plenty, virtue, and refinement' in which his audience and patrons invest, whilst still lamenting 'the ravages of the axe' that clears the ground for and finances the building of this same civilization. His paintings, on the other hand, manage to inaugurate American landscape painting pre-cisely by stabilizing this central historical contradiction within the same frame or series of frames. Thus in 'The Oxbow' and 'View of the Falls of Munda' sublime wildness is confronted with an area of pastoral or agricultural calm that the contemporary viewer knows will soon subdue it. Those of his paintings which do not represent this tension within the pictorial space often establish it in the space between the viewer and the work, offering nature as an elegiac and primeval other, pleasantly foreign to the urbanite who commissions and regards the work.

Cole's essay, with Emerson's 'Nature' of the following year, indicates the arrival in dominance of a paradigm questioningly shared by Melville, Thoreau and Hawthorne: nature is both the secular sublime and the great book of God to which civilized man must go in order to reconstruct his soul. Nature is the national past, the basis of the national identity, an infinite source of moral regeneration and guarantee of the democratic constitution. In producing this paradigm the nationalist painters, writers and thinkers of the new nation (predominantly men living in the Eastern seaboard states which were in the 1830s converting to industrial production) adapt discourses that had been formed in response to England's earlier agricultural and industrial revolutions.[8] In the eighteenth century, however, it is apparent that landscape description in America does not derive from and reproduce a nationalist myth of redemptory nature. If anything, it is distinguished by its absence.

Howard Mumford Jones has noted this absence in the sixteenth and seventeenth centuries and suggested it results from the lack of developed conventions for landscape description, and from the concern of pioneers with survival rather than aesthetic response.[9] When Columbus first described America on 11 October 1492 he did not compose the world into either a pleasing or informative landscape. He wrote in his diary 'On landing they saw green trees and much water and fruit of various kinds.' His next reference to landscape two days later is almost as meagre: 'This island is fairly large and very flat. It has green trees and much water. It has a very large lake in the middle and no mountains and all is delightfully green. The people are very gentle and anxious to have the things we bring.' Even when he returns home and makes a more formal report intended to excite interest in the discoveries he produces what seems to modern eyes a haphazard and over-generalized account:

All these islands are extremely fertile and this one [Cuba] is particularly so. It has many large harbours finer than any I know in Christian lands, and many large rivers. All this is marvellous. The land is high and has many ranges of hills, and mountains incomparably finer than Tenerife. All are most beautiful and various in shape, and all are accessible. They are covered with tall trees of different kinds which seem to reach the sky. I have heard that they never lose their leaves, which I can well believe, for I saw them as green and lovely as they are in Spain in May; some were flowering, some bore fruit and others were at different stages according to their nature. It was November but everywhere I went the nightingale and many other birds were singing. There are palms of six or eight different kinds – a marvellous sight because of their great variety – and the other trees, fruits and plants are equally marvellous. There are splendid pine woods and broad fertile plains, and there is honey. There are many kinds of birds and varieties of fruit. In the interior are mines and a very large population.[10]

Columbus's episteme varies between that of the geographer who generalizes features of the lands with a keen eye for saleable goods, and that of the individual who experiences the land as excess, a store for exploitation, a fertile ground for raising an endless supply of cash-crops. His eye directs attention to a foreground that can be exploited immediately, and leaves the more distant topography to vague generalizations and later conquests. His aesthetic sense is confined to marvelling at nature's superabundance.

There are differences between Columbus's descriptions and those of explorers and settlers in the sixteenth and seventeenth centuries but they have in common a categorizing gaze that represents the whole by fragmenting it into recognizable groups, a simple comparison of New and Old World properties, and a concern for economic utility. Howard Mumford Jones sees this tradition of travel writing as being slowly transformed and quotes John Lederer's account of his exploration of the Piedmont and Blue Ridge in *The Discoveries* (1672) as evidence of the beginnings of a more adequate way of describing the American continent:

The eighteenth of *March*, after I had in vain assayed to ride up, I alighted, and left my horse with one of the Indians, whilst with the other two I climbed up the Rocks, which were so incumbered with bushes and brambles, that the ascent proved very difficult: besides, the first precipice was so steep, that if I lookt down, I was immediately taken with a swimming in my head; though afterwards the way was more easie. The height of this Mountain was very extraordinary: for notwithstanding I set out with the first appearance of light, it was late in the evening before I gained the top, from whence the next morning I had a beautiful prospect of the *Atlantick*-Ocean washing the *Virginian* shore; but to the North and West, my sight was suddenly bounded by Mountains higher than that I stood upon. Here did I wander in snow, for the most part, till the Four and twentieth day of *March*, hoping to finde some passage through the Mountains; but the coldness of the Air and Earth together, seizing my Hands and Feet with numbness, put me to a *ne plus ultra*.

Jones suggests that this passage inaugurates the 'panoramic technique that was necessary in dealing with American scenery';[11] but in fact Lederer, like other seventeenth- and eighteenth-century American writers, gives a graphic account of his struggle against the obstacles of the wilderness but when he reaches a vantage point tells us 'the next morning I had a beautiful prospect of the *Atlantick*-Ocean washing the *Virginian* shore'. The use of the word 'prospect' indicates that the writer understands that an aesthetic response is possible at such vantage points, but his failure to represent the prospect indicates lack of ability or interest in translating a visual and painterly response into verbal form. This lack of interest is not peculiar to Lederer but shared by such writers as William Byrd, John Long, the Reverend Charlevoix, Jonathan Carver, and even, as we shall see shortly, Thomas Jefferson. Byrd, for example, in his *History of the Dividing Line*, frustrates devotees of landscape by saying 'In the evening we quartered in a charming situation near the angle of the river, from whence our eyes were carried down both reaches, which kept a straight course for a great way together. This prospect was so beautiful that we were perpetually climbing up to a neighbouring eminence that we might enjoy it in more perfection.' Only once in the entire work does he actually describe one of the prospects he finds so charming.[12] Charlevoix similarly mentions the prospects around Montreal without describing them, and when he visits Niagara passes up the chance of creating a visual image, preferring to estimate the physical dimensions of the Falls and to offer some conventional natural philosophic hypotheses about how the falling waters are eroding the rocks.[13] John Long, describing a lake where he spent the winter of 1778, tells us only that 'it is about five day's journey by water; the width in some parts about thirty miles. There are a number of small islands in it which abound with hares, partridges, and wild fowl.'[14] Carver offers many similar passages and in one characteristically shows more concern for the mineral wealth a waterfall reveals than for its spectacular appearance: 'a considerable river falls into the lake [Superior], the head of which is composed of a great assembly of small streams. The river is remarkable for the abundance of virgin copper to be found on and near its banks.'[15] In this preference for utility over aesthetics Long and Carver are in direct company with Raleigh nearly two hundred years earlier: 'This island of Trinidad has the form of a sheep hook and is but narrow, the north part is very mountainous, the soil is excellent and will bear sugar, ginger, or any other commodity that the Indies yield. It hath store of deer, wild pork, fruits, fish and fowl.'[16]

Such exceptions as there are to this language of utility are remarkable in that their lack of textual integration makes them seem like the quotation of an imported tongue, the performance of a conventional task rather than the articulation of a deeper social need. In Carver's *Travels*, for example, we are treated to a description of Lake Pepin that begins with a vantage point on the river, moves through a conventionalizing association of pyramids of rock with old ruined towers, then lifts the viewer up to a mountain top and offers a vision of Edenic plenty:

The Mississippi below this lake [Pepin] flows with a gentle current but the breadth is very uncertain, in some places being upward of a mile, in others not more than a quarter. This River has a range of mountains on each side throughout the whole of the way, which in particular parts approach near to it, in others lie at a great distance. The land betwixt the mountains and their sides, is generally covered with grass with a few groves of trees interspersed, near which large droves of deer and elk are frequently seen feeding. In many places pyramids of rocks appeared, resembling old ruined towers; at others amazing precipices: and what is very remarkable, whilst this scene presented itself on one side, the opposite side of the same mountain was covered with the finest herbage which ascended to its summit. From thence the most beautiful and extensive prospect that imagination can form opens to your view. Verdant plains, fruitful meadows, numerous islands, and all these abounding with a variety of trees that yield amazing quantities of fruit, without care or cultivation, such as the nut tree, the maple which produces sugar, vines loaded with rich grapes, and plum trees bending under their blooming burdens, but above all the fine River flowing gently beneath and reaching as far as the eye can extend, by turns attract your admiration and excite your wonder.

The Lake is about twenty miles long and near six in breadth; in some places it is very deep, and abounds in various kinds of fish.[17]

Taken in isolation this passage seems a convincing example of the topos of Edenic promise allied to picturesque, and to that extent unremarkable; however, in a text composed almost exclusively in factual geographical sentences like the last quoted above, the sudden concern with harmonious visual organization, with rhythms and pleasing epithets, and the construction of the reader as a seeker of prospects can only seem the intrusion of another way of writing. In producing this description Carver violates the conventions of his travel account – that the author only describes immediate events and sensations and generalized fact – and collapses several discrete instants of time into a rapid traverse of the mountain that gives way to a timeless vision of natural fecundity. The rapid and uncertain shifts from particular experience – 'pyramids of rocks appeared' – to timeless and impersonal generalization – 'the most beautiful ... prospect opens to your view' – evidence a disjuncture between the author and this moment of his discourse. Similar features are evident at other moments in Carver's work.[18]

The writer most frequently quoted as inaugurating a developed aesthetic response is Thomas Jefferson, but even here qualifications are necessary, Leo Marx for example admitting that 'at first glance Jefferson's *Notes on the State of Virginia* looks like a cross between a geography text book and a statistical abstract ... [It] has a dense, dry, fact-laden surface.'[19]

These admissions having been made, Marx, like Howard Mumford Jones and others, plumps for an analysis of the two set-piece descriptions that Jefferson does offer. We will come to these in a moment, but before doing so let us take a brief comparative glance at the differences between Jefferson's description of nature and those of his British contemporaries.

When Jefferson visited the gardens of Stowe during his tour of 1786, he had in his hand Whately's *Observations on Modern Gardening* which offers a thorough description of the gardens to illustrate the general point that 'the peculiar merit of that species of garden, which occupies the whole enclosure, consists in the larger scenes ... it can make room for.' His description of these scenes, as Jefferson observes, combines aesthetic and scientific analysis into splendid evocation:

The house stands on the brow of a gentle ascent; part of the gardens lie on the declivity, and spread over the bottom beyond it; this eminence is separated by a broad winding valley from another which is higher and steeper; and the descents of both are broken by large dips and hollows, sloping down the sides of the hills. The whole space is divided into a number of scenes, each distinguished with taste and fancy; and the changes are so frequent, so sudden and complete, the transitions so artfully conducted, that the same ideas are never continued or repeated to satiety ... In front of the house is a considerable lawn, open to the water, beyond which are two elegant Doric pavillions, placed in the boundary of the garden, but not marking it, though they correspond to each other; for still further back, on the brow of some rising grounds without the enclosure, stands a novel Corinthian arch, by which the principal approach is conducted, and from which all the gardens are seen, reclining back against the hills; they are rich with plantations, full of objects, and lying on both sides of the house almost equally, every part is within a moderate distance, notwithstanding the extent of the whole.[20]

The absent landscape of America's eighteenth century

Whately's prose offers the perspective and artful transitions 'never continued or repeated to satiety' capable of revealing the harmonious logic of the grounds. Jefferson notes:

Stowe. Belongs to the Marquis of Buckingham, son of George Grenville, and who takes it from Lord Temple. Fifteen men and eighteen boys employed in keeping pleasure grounds. Within the walk are considerable portions separated by inclosures and used for pastures ... There are four levels of water, receiving it one from the other. The basin contains seven acres, the lake below ten acres. Kent's building is called the temple of Venus. They are seen the one from the other, the line of sight passing, not through the garden, but through the country parallel to the line of the garden. This has a good effect. In the approach to Stowe, you are brought a mile through a straight avenue, pointing to the Corinthian arch and to the house, till you get to the arch, then you turn short to the right. The straight approach is very ill. The Corinthian arch has a very useless appearance, inasmuch as it has no pretension to any destination. Instead of being an object from the house, it is an obstacle to a very pleasing prospect. The Grecian valley being clear of trees, while the hill on each side is covered with them, is much deepened in appearance.[21]

Jefferson's *Notes* have proved useful to historians of the English garden because they tell us what Whately leaves out – the number of men employed, the surface area of the lakes, the economics of use. Beyond this, however, although his account indicates that Jefferson has an eye for the ensemble, and a rather republican one, his sense of aesthetic harmony does not give rise to verbal pictures. Rather what is presented is the verdict of the judge and assayor.

The obvious explanation of this lack is that Jefferson's text and Whately's do not have the same rhetorical function: Jefferson's notes come after Whately's and are not, at least ostensibly, intended for publication. If, however, we compare like with like, the difference will appear to be constant. Here is Jefferson in *Notes on the State of Virginia*:

The *Ohio* is the most beautiful river on earth, its current gentle, waters clear, and bosom smooth and unbroken by rocks and rapids, a single instance only excepted.
It is 1/4 mile wide at Fort Pitt:
500 yards at the mouth of the Great Kanhaway:
1 mile and 25 poles at Louisville:
. . .
[I omit here half a page of similar tabulation of widths and distances.]
. . .

91

In common winter and spring tides it affords 15 feet water to Louisville, 10 feet to La Tarte's rapids, 40 miles above the mouth of the great Kanhaway, and a sufficiency at all times for light batteaux and canoes to Fort Pitt. The rapids are in latitude 30°8′. The inundations begin about the last of March, and subside in July ... [and so on].[22]

The brief superlative aesthetic judgment and feminizing metaphor with which this description opens are scarcely borne out by the representation of *la belle rivière* as a sequence of depths, widths and distances. Moreover they are in themselves rare risks in Jefferson's *Notes on the State of Virginia*, the matter of which is mainly the notation of means of communication, geological, botanical and zoological catalogues, a simple grasping at the continent by way of categories. The feeling for ensemble, perspective and interest in subjectivity that characterize contemporary European responses is absent. It is notable that Arthur Young, Jefferson's contemporary and as much if not more given to scientific notation in his *Tours of England and Wales*, shifts effortlessly and continually between the same dry, dense matter as Jefferson and charming landscape descriptions that rival those of Whately:

To Woodbridge by Playford, etc. (not the high road, which is much inferior in pleasantness.) Passed a finely cultivated country, abounding uncommonly with turneps, the preparation of which seemed to be very compleat. A vale and lanskip to the left as beautiful as I remember anywhere to have seen. There is no water; but all the parts that compose the view are happily proportioned: the lighter tints of corn and scattered trees, with the verdure of new-mown meadows: the darker shades of wood, where the groves unite for the contrast, but not enough to affect the character of the scene, which is chearfulness: the churches rising where the happiest taste would place them; the villages, farms, and cottages, in exact union with the scene: the slope of the country bold enough to be interesting, without any abruptness to give sublimity where beauty alone should prevail; altogether unite into a perfect harmony of disposition, calculated to promote the impression which this charming lanskip must raise in the mind of every spectator that can admire a scene where art has done nothing.

Or even as in this splendid application of the aesthetics of the sublime to an industrial situation:

The coal mines are from 20 yards to 120 deep, and the coal in general dips to the south east: in sinking the pits they generally find the following strata.
    1. Brick clay 3 feet deep

2. Potters do. 15 feet
3. Smuts an imperfect coaly substance 1 foot
. . .
12. Flint coal 4
13. Iron stone 3
There may be about 1000 acres of coal on the Benthal side of the river, and 2000 on the Dale side.
These iron works are in a very flourishing situation, rising rather than the contrary.
Colebrook Dale itself is a very romantic spot, it is a winding glen between two immense hills which break into various forms, and all thickly covered with wood, forming the most beautiful sheets of hanging wood. Indeed too beautiful to be much in unison with that variety of horrors art has spread at the bottom: the noise of the forges, mills, etc. with all their vast machinery, the flames bursting from the furnaces with the burning of the coal and the smoak of the lime kilns, are altogether sublime, and would unite well with craggy and bare rocks, like St. Vincent's at Bristol.[23]

On the infrequent but much studied occasions when Jefferson's *Notes* reach for similar sense, the description needs to buttress itself by weaving sensation into geological deduction:

The passage of the Patowmac through the Blue ridge is perhaps one of the most stupendous scenes in nature. You stand on a very high point of land. On your right comes up the Shenandoah, having ranged along the foot of the mountain a hundred miles to seek a vent. On your left approaches the Patowmac, in quest of a passage also. In the moment of their junction they rush together against the mountain, rend it asunder, and pass off to the sea.

This exciting animistic account collapses millennia of evolution into an eternal present in which the rivers conspire to overthrow the mountain, but its energy is then restrained by a more diachronic view, one which opens with a traditional sublime response involving the loss of control over the senses and leads directly into a geological deduction:

The first glance of this scene hurries our sense into the opinion, that this earth has been created in time, that the mountains were formed first, that the rivers began to flow afterwards, that in this place particularly they have been dammed up by the Blue ridge of mountains and have formed an ocean which filled the whole valley; that continuing to rise they have at length broken over at this spot, and have torn the mountain down from its summit to its base. The piles of rock on each hand, but particularly on the Shenandoah, the evident marks of their

93

Robert Clark

disrupture and avulsion from their beds by the most powerful agents of nature, corroborate the impression.

Several sentences in the picturesque style give a sense of the view and reintroduce hints of the hurry and turbulence of the sublime, but then lead into a resumption of the concern with the geography of communications:

But the distant finishing which nature has given to the picture is of very different character. It is a true contrast to the foreground. It is as placid and delightful, as that is wild and tremendous. For the mountain being cloven asunder, she presents to your eye, through the cleft, a small catch of blue horizon, at an infinite distance in the plain country, inciting you, as it were, from the riot and tumult roaring around, to pass through the breach and participate in that calm below. Here the eye ultimately composes itself; and that way too the road happens to actually lead. You cross the Patowmac above the junction, pass along its side through the base of the mountain for three miles, its terrible precipices hanging in fragments over you, and within 20 miles reach Frederic town and the fine country around that.[24]

Jefferson's relief at composing himself in the calm plains of Reason after the sensory disruption caused by having to recognize the potentially uncontrollable powers of nature is palpable – and incidentally constructs an image balanced between the sublime and the beautiful such as those we have already noted in Thomas Cole.

Jefferson's other famous landscape description, that of the Natural Bridge, reveals a similar nervousness about the overwhelming powers of nature. It begins with the typical American eighteenth-century response, an attempt to register and stabilize by geometrical and geographical measurement:

The *Natural bridge*, the most sublime of Nature's works . . . is on the ascent of a hill, which seems to have been cloven through its length by some great convulsion. The fissure, just at the bridge, is, by some admeasurements, 270 feet deep, by others only 205. It is about 45 feet wide at the bottom, and 90 feet at the top; this of course determines the length of the bridge, and its height from the water. Its breadth in the middle, is about 60 feet, but more at the ends, and the thickness of the mass at the summit of the arch, about 40 feet. A part of this thickness is constituted by a coat of earth, which gives growth to many large trees. The residue, with the hill on both sides, is one solid rock of limestone. The arch approaches the Semi-elliptical form; but the larger axis of the ellipsis, which would be the cord of the arch, is many times longer than the transverse.

94

It continues with a loss of reason and self control that occasions actual terror, recuperates with a dash of the sublime, and concludes on a reassuring note of utility.

Though the sides of this bridge are provided in some parts with a parapet of fixed rocks, yet few men have resolution to walk to them and look over into the abyss. You involuntarily fall on your hands and feet, creep to the parapet and peep over it. Looking down from this height about a minute, gave me a violent head ache. If the view from the top be painful and intolerable, that from below is delightful in an equal extreme. It is impossible for the emotions arising from the sublime, to be felt beyond what they are here: so beautiful an arch, so elevated, so light, and springing as it were up to heaven, the rapture of the spectator is really indescribable! The fissure continuing narrow, deep, and streight for a considerable distance above and below the bridge, opens a short but very pleasing view of the North mountain on one side, and Blue ridge on the other, at the distance each of them about five miles. This bridge is in the county of Rock bridge, to which it has given name and affords a public and commodious passage over a valley, which cannot be crossed elsewhere for a considerable distance. The stream passing under it is called Cedar creek. It is a water of James river, and sufficient in the driest seasons to turn a grist-mill, though its fountain is not more than two miles above.[25]

After all, Jefferson is able to conclude, this frightful delight of nature that makes his head ache, actually assists in the settlement of the continent.

The only writer regularly, skilfully and unashamedly to produce landscape descriptions in eighteenth-century North America was William Bartram. Near the beginning of his *Travels through North and South Carolina, East and West Florida* he offers a description that unwittingly resembles Fielding's burlesque of the classical style in Book 4, chapter 2 of *Tom Jones*:

How gently flow thy peaceful floods, O Alatamaha! How sublimely rise to view on thy elevated shores, your magnolia groves, from whose tops the surrounding expanse is perfumed, by clouds of incense, blended with the exhaling balm of the liquidamber, and odours continually arising from circumambient groves of illisium, myrica, lauras, and bignonia.

Fortunately he soon develops a style more fitted to his own abilities and, even if he frequently sounds like a writer trying to conform to conventions, he is able to move fluently from narrating his adventures to botanical descriptions and then to landscape:

The eastern coast of the river now opens, and presents to view ample plains, consisting of grass, marshes and green meadows, and affords a prospect almost unlimited and extremely pleasing. The opposite shore exhibits a sublime contrast, a high bluff bearing magnificent forests of grand magnolia, glorious palms, fruitful orange groves, live oaks, bays and other trees. This grand elevation continues four or five hundred yards, describing a gentle curve on the river, ornamented by a sublime grove of palms consisting of many hundreds of trees together ... Above and below the bluff, the grounds gradually descend to the common level swamps on the river: at the back of this eminence opens to view expansive green meadows or savannas, in which are to be seen glittering ponds of water, surrounded at a great distance by high open pine forests and hommocks, and islets of oaks and bays projecting into the savannas.[26]

The fact that this fluidity is achieved by a botanist, and by a failed planter and trader who is now funded by an English patron, seems to me of special significance. Bartram's interest in nature is clearly at a remove from that of colonizers such as Columbus and Bradford, explorers such as Long and Charlevoix, and landowners such as Jefferson. He is apparently not interested in utility. Earlier writers had worked to measure and chart nature into exchangeable commodities but they had not been able to confer upon it a unifying image other than that of wilderness or waste. Bartram constitutes the beginning of the provision of ensemble, and he does this by relating to the landscape as a tourist in lands that were already settled (albeit thinly), and indeed through which he had travelled before when he accompanied his father's earlier voyages of exploration. His relationship to this twice-seen land is not that of invasion, conquest or colonization, nor of direct proprietorship, rather that of the bourgeois man of science to a form of capital in which he has an ideological rather than financial investment. Typically this relationship is contemplative and speculative: it depends upon acquiescence and if not inaction then action that is highly mediated. And because the relationship with actual economic activity is highly mediated it is capable of generating an ideology of nature that gives coherence to the isolated utilitarian categories produced by those who actually transform nature into commodity.

There is in Jefferson's catalogues, and in the narrow focus of traveller's tales, a remorselessness that threatens narrator and reader with insignificance. The unending flow of somehow meaningful objects, all of which seem equally exchangeable, ultimately threatens to abolish the order in the name of which they are being established, and even to place humanity on the same level. It also threatens to include anything, being haunted by omission, driven to discover, seemingly incapable of censorship. The prospect, on the other hand, constructs readers by instructing them in their subjective response, placing attention on the aesthetic rather than utilitarian qualities of objects perceived. The prospect brings elements into relationship; it harmonizes, hierarchizes, stabilizes and censors, providing an image of the world that protects the interests of those in power because wherever utility appears within it, as in Bartram's botanical descriptions, it is masked, and wherever history and economy are mentioned, they appear as ancient. There is no attention in Bartram, nor in Young, despite his 'science', to the violence of recent and current depopulations. The prospect thus substitutes an aesthetic education for a knowledge of history and provides a way for the essentially estranged perceiver to conceal the rift between the self and the world.

The reasons why this substitution becomes necessary in the years after Independence must remain a topic for further work. At the moment I am able to offer only certain suggestions concerning the changes in relationship of writer, or artist, to the land and obvious need of the new Republic for a nationalist ideology which will offer nature as the national ego. I hope, however, that this essay has revealed that in the eighteenth century, and certainly until Independence, those who represented North America showed little inclination towards landscape representation. The success of such representations as do exist, and the frequent reference to 'prospects' by travel writers, indicates a correction to either the assumption that writers found it difficult to adapt European conventions to the American landscape, or that they were obsessed with 'Nature'. What they were interested in was land in a very economic and immediate sense, and they had in their own terms an entirely adequate mode of representation. It was not until a very different order of need arose that landscape description became conventional in North America.

Notes

1 Quoted in Elizabeth Manwaring, *Italian Landscape in Eighteenth Century England: A Study Chiefly of the Influence of Claude Lorrain and Salvator Rosa on English Taste, 1700–1800* (1925; rpt London: Frank Cass, 1965), p. 175.
2 Ibid., pp. 167–200.

Robert Clark

3 Leo Marx, *The Machine in the Garden: Technology and the Pastoral Ideal in America* (New York: Oxford University Press, 1964), pp. 93–4; Joseph Addison, *Critical Essays from the Spectator*, ed. Donald F. Bond (Oxford: Clarendon Press, 1970), p. 184.

4 Addison, *Critical Essays*, p. 185.

5 A point developed by John Dixon Hunt in his lecture at the IAUPE conference, York, September 1986.

6 Addison, *Critical Essays*, p. 178, p. 179.

7 Thomas Cole, 'Essay on American Scenery, 1835', rpt in J. W. McCoubrey, ed., *American Art: Sources and Documents, 1700–1960* (Englewood Cliffs, NJ: Prentice-Hall, 1965), pp. 108–9, p. 100, pp. 99–102.

8 On these changes see Rolla M. Tryon, *Household Manufactures in the United States* (1917; rpt New York: Johnson Reprint, 1966). Their consequences for Hawthorne and Melville are discussed in my *History, Ideology and Myth in American Fiction, 1823–1851* (London: Macmillan Press, 1984).

9 Howard Mumford Jones, *O Strange New World: American Culture; The Formative Years* (London: Chatto and Windus, 1965), pp. 351–3.

10 Christopher Columbus, *The Four Voyages of Christopher Columbus*, ed. and trans. J. M. Cohen (Harmondsworth: Penguin, 1969), p. 53, p. 55, p. 116.

11 Jones, *O Strange New World*, p. 358. See also John Lederer, *The Discoveries of John Lederer in three several Marches from Virginia to the West of Carolina, and other parts of the Continent: Begun March 1669, and ended in September 1670* (1672); rpt as *The Discoveries of John Lederer*, ed. William P. Cumming (Charlottesville, VA.: University of Virginia Press, 1958).

12 William Byrd, *The History of the Dividing Line*, rpt in *The Prose Works of William Bird of Westover*, ed. Louis B. Wright (Cambridge, MA: Harvard University Press, 1966), p. 250, p. 266.

13 Revd P. F. X. de Charlevoix, *Journal of a Voyage to North America*, 2 vols. (London: Dodsley, 1761), pp. 214, 353.

14 John Long, *Voyages and Travels in the Years 1768–1788* (Chicago: Donnelley, 1922), p. 80.

15 Jonathan Carver, *Travels Through the Interior Parts of North America in the Years 1761, 1767, and 1768* (London: J. Waller, 1778), p. 138.

16 Sir Walter Raleigh, 'The Discovery of Guiana', in Richard Hakluyt, ed., *The Principal Navigations, Voyages, Traffiques and Discoveries of the English Nation*, ed. Jack Beeching (Harmondsworth: Penguin, 1972), pp. 386–410, p. 386.

17 Carver, *Travels*, pp. 54–5.

18 Cf. Carver's description of the Falls of St Anthony, p. 70, which, although he visits in November are described in the Spring.

19 Marx, *The Machine in the Garden*, p. 118.

20 Thomas Whately, *Observations on Modern Gardening and Laying Out Pleasure Grounds* (1770; rpt New York: Garland, 1982), p. 213.
21 Thomas Jefferson, 'Notes on A Tour of English Gardens' (1786), rpt in *Writings* (New York: Viking, 1984), p. 625.
22 Jefferson, 'Notes on the State of Virginia' (1781, first published 1785), rpt in *Writings*, pp. 133–4.
23 Arthur Young, *Tours in England and Wales, Selected from the Annals of Agriculture* (1792–1808; rpt London: University of London, 1932), pp. 69–70, 151–2.
24 Jefferson, 'Notes', p. 143.
25 Jefferson, 'Notes', pp. 148–9. Of the many commentaries on these passages the most stimulating by far is that by Wayne Franklin, *Discoverers, Explorers, Settlers: The Diligent Writers of Early America* (Chicago: University of Chicago Press, 1979).
26 William Bartram, *Travels through North and South Carolina, Georgia, East and West Florida* (1791; rpt Dublin: Moor, Jones, McAllister and Rice, 1793), pp. 47, 138.

7 ✳ Ecriture and landscape: British writing on post-revolutionary America

CHRISTOPHER MULVEY

This essay is part of a wider discussion that takes as its starting point sixty British titles about America and seventy American titles about Britain, all written by men and women who crossed and recrossed the Atlantic, all written in the nineteenth century, travel books as such some of them, but also letters and diaries, sometimes forms very close to fiction.[1] Taken together, these create a pattern, a textual system. Immediately perhaps, we should expand the proper range of reference here, since this putative textual system suggests books on America by Americans, books on Britain by Britons. A more complete system yet would include for its consideration and analysis books on both countries by continental writers; after all, de Tocqueville wrote about both America and Britain. And another range of reference suggests itself – the interaction of related textual systems, as for example the exchange between Spanish and South American writers writing about Spain and South America.

I must limit myself, because of the context of this essay and because of the restrictions of my own reading, to the nineteenth century, indeed to the early nineteenth century, to the period of American history called the early Republic, but the discourse began two hundred years before and has continued nearly a hundred years since so that in truth we are dealing with a textual system that has extended itself through four hundred years of discourse. At least a thousand Anglo-American titles exist for the nineteenth century alone; there must be some thousands more for the full period. There must be many thousands more with just the relevant French, German, and Spanish titles included. There are delimitations possible however. Several readings produce several repetitions and more readings produce more repetitions. Certain responses to landscape were the recurrent themes of this literature and they provide a continuing development of Romantic sensibility from Wordsworth to Twain.

The history of art is said to be a history of seeing. And John Berger would have it in *Ways of Seeing* that 'Seeing comes before words.'[2] But that, the first sentence of his useful book, contains the first error. It is the primary error since it does not recognize that seeing, i.e. perception, is all about encoding experience, and encoding is all about language. We see as we are enabled to see by those processes, essentially linguistic, which permit us to organize the universe into something seeable. Before we see what is *there*, we must separate and differentiate something to be seen from the endless, infinite continuum of reality. This act of separation and differentiation is the fact which poises us to see (and then perhaps to talk). But this act is a cultural act, one which we are capable of performing in the way in which we perform it because we have been given the preforms and the preconceptions and the pretexts by which to make out forms, conceptions and texts. This act of differentiation is what Barthes after Derrida after Barthes calls *writing*. Writing, we are told, with deliberate but not arch paradox, precedes speech. Writing, *ecriture*, is the act of the mind's inscription on *reality*, the world, the continent of North America. It is an act of intellection which precedes all subsequent encodings, in thought or sight or speech. In describing this act of the intellect as *writing*, advantage is taken of the metaphorical translation to this act of intellection of the distancing effects of writing, an act which would appear so clearly to separate us from *reality*, while seeing would not appear to separate us from *reality* (while doing so just as much in fact). Writing here is that 'mode of writing', so Roland Barthes, 'whose function is no longer communication or expression, but the imposition of something beyond language which is both history and the stand we take in it'.[3] The implication of History, meaning after the Fall (but there is no meaning before the Fall), is that culture interposes before nature, that perception interprets *reality*. We are involved in a promiscuous intercourse with discourse. We *write* before we see before we speak.

The British then wrote on post-revolutionary North America before they wrote upon the pages of their variously named books about their travels in post-revolutionary North America. The British wrote on America and as they wrote on America they were able to see it, and then, and only then, could they talk about it. The English person had eventually to look to the American to guide his or her seeing of the American landscape. That was only proper since it was a return for the guidance to the seeing and presenting of the English landscape that the reading of things English had provided throughout the eighteenth century for the American traveller in England. And this reading was to continue to guide the American seeing throughout the nineteenth century. As Robert Clark and Graham Clarke show in their contributions to this book, the English landscape was in this sense a classical landscape for the American viewer.

For the English viewer, by contrast, the classical landscape was that of Italy. As the Englishman approached the city of Rome, he approached that enriched and transcendental emotional state that the American so frequently recorded as he approached the city of London; the stir that the Englishman felt as he approached the Mantuan birthplace of Vergilius Maro, this stir was that felt by the American approaching the Stratford birthplace of William Shakespeare. Claude Lorrain's landscapes of the Roman Campagna had been the models of late seventeenth-century landscape painting in England, and not only models of painting. The English landscape itself had been self-consciously rewritten in the course of the eighteenth century according to a script that had developed from Claude. Landscape art was not only a painterly genre but an art form in which the medium was the elements of nature, that was 'nature' defined as hill, valley, river, tree, stone, rock. Artists like William Kent, Humphry Repton, and Capability Brown wrote the English rural text anew.

Almost a century after the work of these men were completed, the greatest American exponent of landscape art, Frederick Law Olmsted, creator of Central Park, identified the nobility of this art as arising from a direct intercourse between artist and nature. Nature was not represented but re-presented:

What artist, so noble, has often been my thought, as he, who with far-reaching conception of beauty and designing power, sketches the outline, writes the colours, and directs the shadows of a picture so great that Nature shall be employed upon it for generations before the work he has arranged for her shall be realized.[4]

Between Frederick Law Olmsted and the eighteenth-century masters whom he so admired stood the figure of the Reverend Mr William Gilpin, the man who had between 1770 and 1804 taken the landscape art yet a stage further than it had reached in the hands of Kent and his followers. Gilpin's art did not require that mountains be razed and valleys be levelled. Gilpin had reconceived the art of landscaping so that it might become an art for the middle classes when before him it had been an art of the upper classes. Gilpin's principles of the picturesque were for the land traveller what landscape gardening was for the landowner. In 1770, William Gilpin had proposed for himself a tour of England, with, as he put it, 'a new object of pursuit, that of not barely examining the fact of the country, but of examining it by the rules of picturesque beauty.'[5]

This is not the place to elaborate the rules of picturesque beauty. Gilpin did it well enough in 1770 for the rules to have become a habitual mode of seeing by 1815. His first followers had needed Claude Lorrain glasses to aid picturesque viewing. His nineteenth-century followers laughingly discarded the glasses and mocked him as Dr Syntax, but they saw as if they were using his glasses anyway. It need here only be said that Gilpin interposed the picturesque between the Burkean duo of the Sublime and the Beautiful so that the travelling Briton could explore regions like the Lake District and the Wye Valley. Travelling Britons were enabled to respond to lake and valley with sentiments like those of landowners. They began to say that they loved the landscape and they spoke of a passion that made them possessive, even jealous, of their views. The regions that attracted most attention were, by British standards at least, wild regions but they were to be domesticated and possessed by the process of picturesque perception. Gilpin's rules were a mode of production and the consumable produce was 'landscape'. It was a new way of cultivating the land. The land so enjoyed did not have to be owned in terms of real estate. The land so enjoyed did not have to be cultivated in agricultural terms.

When Defoe wrote up his *Tour of the Whole Island of Great Britain* in the years between 1724 and 1728, a pleasing prospect was one which showed signs of fertility or was potentially fertile. Gilpin showed the way to profitable use of land that was of no use to the landowning class. In the process, he provided ways of seeing that could make the wilderness of America beautiful. By focusing on Gilpin, I provide an easy way of presenting my argument, but I do so at the expense of promoting an individual, William Gilpin, to a kind of prominence that it might be just as easy to demonstrate he does not deserve. But Gilpin

Christopher Mulvey

nonetheless helps well enough to identify a development in bourgeois taste that was, by the end of the nineteenth century, to have redrawn the visual map so that only those features which could be described as picturesque could be seen by the traveller. At the beginning of the eighteenth century, Defoe would have passed by everything that was attracting the attention of the English tourist 150 years later. And this was a phenomenon which was by no means restricted to the English.

In his essay in *Mythologies* on the handbook of the French tourist, Roland Barthes writes:

The Blue Guide hardly knows the existence of scenery except under the guise of the picturesque. The picturesque is found any time the ground is uneven. We find again here is this promoting of the mountains, this old Alpine myth (since it dates back to the nineteenth century) which Gide rightly associated with Helvetico-Protestant morality and which has always functioned as a hybrid compound, the cult of nature and puritanism (regeneration through clean air, moral ideas at the sight of mountain tops, summit-climbing as civic virtue, etc.). Among the views elevated to aesthetic existence, we rarely find plains (redeemed only when they can be described as fertile), never plateaux. Only mountains, gorges, defiles, and torrents can have access to the pantheon of travel, inasmuch, probably, as they seem to encourage a morality of effort and solitude.[6]

If we set aside the sanctimonious and dismissive judgments by which Barthes privileges his own insights above those of his fathers, we see that he confirms the notion that nature was invented just in time to make ready the wilderness of America – and it was invented just in time to reward a profitable tourist trade.

The English began to go to America as tourists in 1815 but what they were looking for in America were the effects of the more rugged kind of English countryside. And American landscapes most readily appreciated were those that were most picturesque; these were at the same time the most English. Travellers responded, as might be expected, to what was most familiar and to what was most conventional, and satisfactory landscapes were to be found in New England and New York – traditionally the most 'English' regions of the Americas. To say that a valley was English was to say that it was picturesque and very beautiful. There were to be found numerous pretty and neat farms on Long Island, in the Mohawk and the Genessee Valleys, in the Connecticut Valley and outside of Boston. And in all these places there were also to be found towns and villages where, said John Lambert in 1808, 'a remarkable neat and elegant style of architecture and decoration seems to pervade all the buildings'.[7] Americans had by labour and long cultivation been able to suggest England.

The Americans achieved such a landscape only rarely and this was in itself taken as an indication not of the economic and agricultural realities with which the American farmer had to deal, but as an indication of sluttish and slovenly habits. This was the primary conclusion of Fanny Kemble's *Journal* (of 1831 and 1832) but it was not her only conclusion. She, as did others, also took it as an indication of a general insensitivity to landscape.

The national failure of spirit was to be more remarked on when it appeared more outrageous. Fanny Kemble was so taken by the Hudson Highlands that her questions on the failure of the Americans, as it seemed to her, to respond in the proper way to what they saw, took a deeper turn: 'Is it possible,' she asked, 'that a perception of the beautiful in nature is a result of artificial cultivation? – is it that the grovelling narrowness of the usual occupations to which the majority addict themselves has driven out of them the fine spirit, which is God's altar in men's souls? – is it that they become incapable of beauty? wretched people!'[8] This is a point that supports some of Robert Clark's argument in his essay in the present volume. Also, Allen Koppenhaver takes it up when he notes Thomas Cole lamenting in 1835 the fact that no one felt as he felt about the great beauty of the American landscape. 'I feel I stand alone', Koppenhaver quotes him as saying, and it was a sentiment frequently repeated in the journal of the sensitive traveller.

But Fanny Kemble's *Journal* provided in fact good examples of the kind of fine writing, refined feeling and Romantic response that the American people were trying to emulate in their own writing about the English landscape. *Sketches of Society in Great Britain and Ireland* by C. S. Stewart, MA, of the US Navy, published in the same year as Fanny Kemble's *Journal*, showed in its descriptions of the Scottish Highlands an appreciation of the landscape that came close to matching Fanny Kemble's own. The identification of the Hudson Highlands with those of Scotland was to become a favoured trope of the Luminist school. If the English traveller on the other hand had seen the Scottish Highlands, he had anticipated these Hudson views quite satisfactorily. Or to reverse the reference, as Charles Stewart said of Loch Lomond: 'In its general features, it is not unlike some points in our principal rivers, and scarce

105

rivals in beauty the more bold and romantic sections of the Hudson.'[9] Consequently in the 1830s the Briton writing about the Hudson Highlands and the American writing about the Scottish sounded very much alike.

When the English traveller moved beyond the familiar, the pleasing, the 'English' landscape in America, the first step was always the beautiful conceived in terms of the Lake poets; for this reason the Hudson River, with its great glacier-cut valley, never failed to excite a powerful response. But when the traveller left the Hudson to move west along the Erie Canal, he or she moved towards new problems in landscape: those posed by Niagara in American sensibility and taste were already well-engaged with these. The most frequently painted subjects in the early Republic were, says Elizabeth McKinsey in *Niagara Falls: Icon of the American Sublime*, George Washington and the Niagara Falls. By 1776, the Falls had become a standard scene to which travellers were refusing to add new detail. The text was being firmly established and yet it came as a shock to each new visitor. This was a problem that faced poet and painter alike as they contemplated a scene that reached beyond the resources of their aesthetic. McKinsey argues that the picturesque was defeated by Niagara:

> If American nature was indeed grander, vaster, and more sublime than European nature, as so many Americans in the infant republic professed, then it is hardly surprising that English picturesque conventions did not prove adequate to paint the American landscape. After all, these conventions were developed after landscape gardening became widespread and inculcated a taste for unified, controlled vistas. How could such taste compass the vast extent and powerful impression of the scene at Niagara? Artists were compelled to find new techniques.[10]

It could also be argued that Niagara was the ultimate Romantic landscape; it was the landscape that all but guaranteed an encounter with the Wordsworthian divine; those who could not get in touch with this emotional reality elsewhere could by way of travelling to Niagara give themselves the awful experience. Niagara was an epic subject and it reached to the limits of poetic imagination and statement; beyond it lay, as Fanny Trollope said, nonsense, the nonsense of the laughable as well as the nonsense of the ineffable.[11]

Unlike the landscapes of the Hudson, this landscape could not easily be anticipated in Europe; there were few ways of preparing emotion and language in advance and travellers felt their deficiencies strongly, humbly turning their attention to details that could be described. They fondly imagined what the great poets would make of the scene, and, above all, indignantly turned both upon those who did not feel the profundities of the occasion and upon those who built hotel, souvenir shop, or power mill to exploit the 'great and glorious cataract'. Fanny Kemble's general disdain of the unpoetical, 'wretched' people was an emotion that in this particular place became one shared by the most pedestrian of English travellers.

Prove themselves as they might at Niagara, the English travellers became like the Americans they despised, nonplussed when they faced the landscape beyond Niagara: the valley of the Mississippi. For this there was absolutely no counterpart at all in European experience. Not even the experience of the Ocean itself, often used as a measure of the grandeur of Niagara, could help. The European traveller could not prepare himself for the impression that the Mississippi was to make on him. One result was that travellers seldom enjoyed the journey to or from New Orleans. In 1830, Thomas Hamilton was struck to the point of dumbness by 'the dreary and perpetual solitudes', 'the huge alligators', 'the trees, with long and hideous drapery of pendent moss', 'the giant river rolling onward the vast volume of its dark and turbid waters.'[12]

The Romantic sensibility, used to expect rocks and mountains in sublime landscapes, looked in vain for rocks and mountains in the first thousand miles of the Mississippi's northward course, but this deficiency could not detract from the claims of the river to some special consideration: 'Rocks and mountains are fine things undoubtedly but they could add nothing of sublimity to the Mississippi ... It could brook no rival and it finds none.' The colossal singularity of the river forced the Romantic traveller to redefine for himself the nature of aesthetic response. It caused him to make up the definition of his terms anew. The Mississippi did more than dominate the landscape. It was a horizon and foreground in one; it went beyond the limits of vision; it stretched unchanging beyond the limits of imagination.

'The imagination is perhaps susceptible,' Hamilton wrote of the view from his steamboat, 'but of a single powerful impression at a time. Sublimity is uniformly connected with unity of object.' The Falls of Niagara were sublime because Nature had arranged things in such a way that there was absolutely nothing else to be seen and yet what was to be seen could be contained in a single set of perspectives. But the Mississippi had to be seen in time as well as in space. The traveller had to travel not only to it but along it. It was in no one place and yet it was all one thing. It had to be endured as well as enjoyed. 'The prevailing character of the Mississippi,' Hamilton concluded, 'is that of solemn gloom.' Thomas Hamilton's credentials as a man of sensibility and of Romantic feeling were very sound ones, but he showed himself to be much tried by the Mississippi: 'I have trodden the passes of the Alp and Appenine, yet never felt how awful a thing is nature, till I was borne on its waters, through regions desolate and uninhabitable ... our vessel, like some huge demon of the wilderness, bearing fire in her bosom, and canopying the eternal forest, with the smoke of her nostrils.'

Hamilton, like other travellers, seemed to pass through stages of visual overloading into those of visual deprivation as the forest and stream rolled by: 'Conversation,' he wrote, 'became odious, and I passed my time in a sort of dreary contemplation.'[13] These phases were analogous to phases that Stephen Fender identifies elsewhere in the present volume as those through which Sarah Kemble Knight passed on her journey from Boston to New York in 1704. Though Hamilton certainly felt 'a fear and repulsion at the scaleless, unscaleable wilderness', as Fender puts it, he spent less time in the next phase, that of inventing 'a fantasy culture'. But this was in fact a way in which a number of British travellers did fill in their Mississippi time and scene. Hamilton's emotions, however, included a mix of anger that inhibited the kind of indulgent fantasy that marked other travellers' speculations about the future farms, villages, and cities that could one day adorn the banks of the Mississippi. Hamilton moved more rapidly to the defeated third stage of hopelessness. There was no Walter Scott or William Wordsworth to do for the Mississippi Valley what the novelist had done for the Highlands or the poet had done for the Lake District. There was no great soul from New Orleans, from Natchez or from Vicksburg to show the way – and none to be for some time to come. It was exactly this point, as Fender points out, that Thomas Cole took up for the continent in general in his 'Essay on American Scenery'. The result was that Hamilton's description of the Mississippi Valley sounded an uncertain note; sensibility was subdued. Hamilton could not yet allow himself, because he had no one to lead him, to help him seize the emotional opportunity offered by the Mississippi landscape.

Were the Wye Valley a thousand miles long, would it have attracted the attention of William Gilpin and William Wordsworth? Travellers whose sensibility had been cultivated by the smaller scale of the English landscape had to strive hard to enjoy the American scene. The Mississippi, like the forest at the beginning of the century and the prairie in the middle, overwhelmed most travellers, leaving them depressed and exhausted by what they could not see as much as by what they could. Wordsworth had set no pattern for response to Nature on this scale. The British writing on the landscape of the early Republic was at first feeble, feeble because Britons could not see that landscape until it was *written*, separated and differentiated, that is, from the great continuum of the North American continent. French geographers have used the word *ecriture* to mean exactly that mark left on the landscape by human settlement and habitation. A village is said to write its history on or in the landscape. We may accept this, if we recognize that the 'landscape' is itself a writing. The village writes its history in a writing. The British travellers to America in the early Republic took landscapes with them from Europe as textual–perceptual formulation. These they located and identified as convention directed inclination. The Hudson River Highlands and the Falls of Niagara were relatively easily situated. But the Mississippi Valley was not to be textually located until after the Civil War.

Notes

1 See my book *Anglo-American Landscapes* (Cambridge: Cambridge University Press, 1983) for another treatment of some of the texts in this system.
2 John Berger, *Ways of Seeing* (Harmondsworth: Penguin with the BBC, 1972), p. 7.
3 Roland Barthes, *Writing Degree Zero*, trans. Johnathan Culler (London: Cape, 1967), p. 7.
4 Frederick Law Olmsted, *Walks and Talks of An American Farmer* (New York: Putnam, 1852), vol. 1, p. 133.
5 William Gilpin, *Observations on the River Wye*, ed. Sutherland Lyall (London: Richmond, 1973), p. 1.
6 Roland Barthes, *Mythologies* (London: Paladin, 1976), trans. Annette Lavers, p. 7.4
7 John Lambert, *Travels through Canada and the United States* (London: Baldwin, 1816), vol. 2, pp. 306–7.

Christopher Mulvey

8 Fanny Kemble, *Journal* (London: Murray, 1835), vol. 2, p. 256.
9 Charles Stewart, *Sketches of Society in Great Britain and Ireland* (London: Carey, Lead and Blanchard, 1835), vol. 2, p. 145.
10 Elizabeth McKinsey, *Niagara Falls: Icon of the American Sublime* (Cambridge: Cambridge University Press, 1985), pp. 2, 64.
11 Fanny Trollope, *Domestic Manners of the Americans* (London: Whittaker, Treacher, 1832), p. 306.
12 Thomas Hamilton, *Men and Manners in America* (Edinburgh: Blackwoods, 1833), vol. 2, p. 191.
13 Ibid., vol. 2, pp. 192–4, 232.

8 ✳ *Dickens goes west*

ROBERT LAWSON-PEEBLES

Are you quite sure Sir, that you do not view America
through the pleasant mirage which often surrounds a
thing that has been, but not a thing that is . . . This is not
the Republic I came to see. This is not the Republic of
my imagination.

Dickens's well-known letter to his close friend, the actor W. C. Macready,
seems to mark the low-point of the novelist's relationship with America.
Dickens arrived in the United States on 21 January 1842, and initially was
delighted by the warmth of his reception. It seemed a triumphant realization of his long-held wish to visit those whom he called his 'distant
countrymen'. Within three weeks, however, a reaction began to set in and,
in that letter of 22 March, the process seemed to have been completed.[1]

Focusing on the letter to Macready, commentators have located three
reasons for Dickens's volte-face within the first few weeks of his arrival.
The first is that he was vilified by the American press for speaking out for
an international copyright law. Like many of his predecessors, Dickens
had lost large sums of money because of pirate American editions. The
American press regarded pirating as 'smart' business behaviour, and
attacked the novelist as a Royalist upstart who was trying to undermine
free American institutions. The second reason is that Dickens quickly
became oppressed by the constant claims on his attention. He could
never seem to escape into privacy. Intruders even entered his hotel room
in the small hours of the morning. The third reason is that American life
seemed degraded and dull. It appeared to Dickens to be a society of
deadening conformity and preposterous self-aggrandizement, bruta-
lized in the South by slavery and everywhere by disgusting behaviour,
particularly the habit of spitting.[2]

111

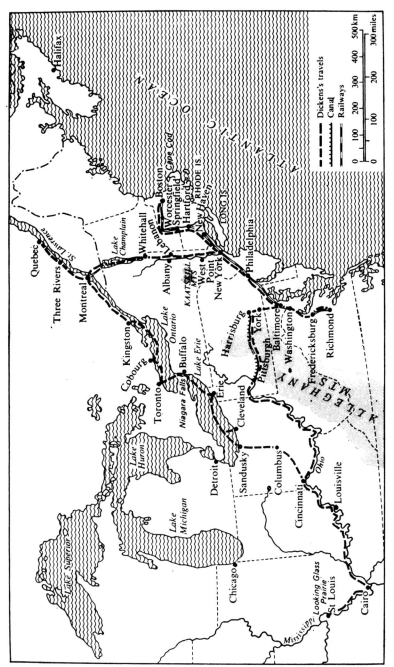

8 Map showing Dickens's travels in North America, 1842

Dickens goes west

These reasons for Dickens's negative view of America comport conveniently with disdainful accounts by other British travellers. Frances Trollope's *Domestic Manners of the Americans* (1832) remains the locus classicus of British hauteur in the face of American life, while even the urbane Rupert Brooke could maliciously repeat the remark of 'an Oxford man' that America should be called El Cuspidorado. What is unusual about the change in Dickens's attitude is its speed and violence. The editors of the new standard edition of his letters pinpoint three days in February 1842 as the time when, ill and able to reflect on his experiences in some welcome privacy, he reacted against the United States. Arnold Goldman and John Whitley take the theme of illness further. In the Penguin edition of *American Notes* (originally published in 1842), they suggest that Dickens may have undergone 'a form of psychic collapse in America' which in part accounts for the darker tone of the post-American fictions.[3]

Previous analyses of Dickens's revulsion against America, then, identify the causes either within American society or within the novelist's psyche. I would like to propose a third possible cause: the American terrain. The process of revulsion, I suggest, was reinforced as Dickens went westwards into the American hinterland. These new experiences provided him with a language which (so to speak) brought into full bloom an anti-pastoral element which had already taken root in his fiction. I will try to substantiate my argument firstly by looking in some detail at the letters Dickens wrote during the western journey; and secondly by relating those letters to *American Notes*. The conclusion, I think, is that the letter to Macready represents a way-station rather than the terminus of Dickens's first affair with America.

The map (pl. 8) summarizes Dickens's 1842 tour. After landing in Boston he travelled through New England to New York, and then to Philadelphia and Washington. He circled south to Fredericksburg, returned to Washington, and then moved to Baltimore in preparation for his sojourn westwards. In Baltimore he wrote a number/of letters, including the one to Macready. On the same day, 22 March, he advised another friend, the painter Daniel Maclise, that

As to Scenery, we really have seen very little as yet. It is the same thing over and over again. The railroads go through the low grounds and swamps, and it is all one eternal forest, with fallen trees mouldering away in stagnant water and

113

decaying vegetable matter – and heaps of timber in every aspect of decay and utter ruin.

The West would, he believed, be a great contrast to the nullity of Eastern terrain.

In this and other letters of the same date Dickens tends to portray himself as an epic hero. There is, however, a qualifying note of comedy in the manner of Fielding; hence the beginning of the letter to Maclise:

From the depths of the Far West, whither we are now going – from the heights of the Alleghanny [sic] Mountains which we are about to ascend – from the small cabin of the canal boat in which we embark – from the surface of the Lakes we have yet to traverse – and amidst the silence of the broad prairies we shall shortly cross – nay from the gloom of the Great Mammoth Cave in Kentucky, and high above the roar and spray of dread Niagara – my voice shall be heard, cursing the Academy.

The precise incident which provoked this gale of imprecation is not recorded. Perhaps Maclise's duties as a Royal Academician prevented him from writing to Dickens, who demanded frequent letters from his friends. What is plain is the epic form in which the letter is set. The style is ceremonial, indeed Miltonic. This one long sentence is created by piling up subsidiary clauses and suppressing the main clause until the end. The narrative opens in medias res. We are not told the cause of this storm in a teacup. We do know, on the other hand, that Dickens is about to renew his search for the real America after two months of unsatisfying East-coast travel. The deeds which the hero will perform are superhuman. It is here that the comedy is invoked, in the deflation after the final caesura.

There is no comedy, however, in the most forcefully presented element of epic, the amplitude of the setting. The vastness of the various components of American terrain is contrasted with the slightness of the means of travel. The vertical and horizontal dimensions are enormous. Dickens even proposes burrowing into the earth in the cave named after that beast sought by Jefferson and many others to refute Buffon's thesis about a miasmic and degenerative America. The Great Mammoth Cave had been discovered in 1809. It had a main chamber some seven miles long and 159 branches adding at least another seventy miles to its extent. It had become an important sight for the tourist. Harriet Martineau spent two nights in a coach to reach it. Dickens, as it happens, was not able to spare the time.

Nevertheless, the cave could function as a motif for Dickens's epic journey. Other letters written from Baltimore repeat, with a sense of wonder rather than comedy, the distance he has to cover – some two thousand miles – in order to reach St Louis, which he called 'my utmost Western point'. It is worth recalling that this was Dickens's first extended journey beyond the British Isles. He had previously made brief visits only to France and Belgium. It is understandable therefore that he should emphasize the change in scale as he turned westwards. The epic provided a suitable vehicle for his flight of fancy. The form would recur, but the feelings would become less fanciful.[4]

Dickens travelled by railroad and stagecoach to Harrisburg, boated up the Pennsylvania Canal, crossed the Alleghenies by another railroad, and then took a second canal-boat en route for Pittsburgh. It was at this stage of the journey that he next wrote home, on 28 March, an extensive letter to John Forster, his intimate friend and later his biographer. The letter details the hardships of travel and dwells on the horrors of expectoration. Cuspidors, it seems are nonexistent, or American aim is poor, with unpleasant results. These themes are not new. Neither is the description of the 'forlorn and miserable' appearance of the new settlements, with their dilapidated dwellings and girdled trees.

It is in the description of the trees that a new motif emerges which injects the first element of foreboding in this epic journey: 'settlers have been burning down the trees; and . . . their wounded bodies lie about, like those of murdered creatures; while here and there some charred and blackened giant rears two bare arms aloft, and seems to curse his enemies.' This is an inversion of the comic cursing episode of just six days earlier. Dickens uses one of his favourite techniques – that of animating the inanimate – to present an image of incipient threat. It is a threat which will be realized fully in *American Notes*. In this present letter, the image is counterpointed against one of the writer himself, looking down from the train crossing Blair's Gap Summit at a scene of vigorous activity. Otherwise, the terrain is given relatively little attention. The 'deep, sullen' gorges of the Pennsylvania Canal cannot compare with the Sublime 'terrors', of Glencoe; while the Susquehanna Valley, often the site of Picturesque tourism, is noted merely as being 'very beautiful'.[5]

Dickens left Pittsburgh on 1 April, travelling down the Ohio River by steamboat. Letters written on board and in Cincinnati (where he spent two nights) show that the voyage is a pleasant relief after the canal and mountain journeys. The first letter, written to Macready on the first day, talks about 'skimming down this beautiful Ohio, its wooded heights all radiant in the sunlight'. Further letters written over the next four days develop images of light and ease in a blend of epic and pastoral. The most repeated refrain is that the Ohio is nine hundred miles long and normally broader than the Thames at Greenwich. The banks are overgrown with trees, as are the islands which sometimes divide the river. Some earlier themes are continued, such as the poor facilities and the poor company. And another new one is introduced. In Pittsburgh Dickens visited a solitary confinement prison, and he conjures a nightmare out of the constant solitude. He imagines a prisoner, afflicted by this 'silence of death', unable to escape from 'some inexplicable silent figure that always sits upon his bed'.[6]

There is a hiatus in the letters, lasting from 4 to 15 April. In that period Dickens stayed overnight at Louisville, passed into the Missis-sippi and journeyed up it to St Louis. He remained in St Louis on 10 and 11 April, and on the next day visited the Looking Glass Prairie, staying overnight in Lebanon. He returned from St Louis to Cincinnati by the same route, arriving there on 19 April. During the return trip Dickens wrote a long letter to Forster which the biographer took care to print accurately in his *Life*. Much of the letter is spent denouncing slavery and describing some of the people he had met. One paragraph is devoted to the Looking Glass Prairie. The Prairie was a favoured sight of the tourist in the West. In 1836–7, for instance, Edmund Flagg had responded rapturously to it, extolling its 'wild melody of loveliness'. In stark contrast, all Dickens feels is disappointment:

The widely-famed Far West is not to be compared with even the tamest portions of Scotland or Wales. You stand upon the prairie, and see the unbroken horizon all round you. You are on a great plain, which is like a sea without water. I am exceedingly fond of wild and lonely scenery, and believe that I have the faculty of being as much impressed by it as any man living. But the prairie fell, by far, short of my preconceived idea. I felt no such emotions as I do in crossing Salisbury Plain. The excessive flatness of the scene makes it dreary, but tame. Grandeur is certainly not its characteristic.

Dickens separates from the remainder of the party 'to understand my own feelings the better', and concludes that 'to say (as the fashion is, here) that the sight is a landmark in one's existence, and awakens a new set of sensations, is sheer gammon'. Dickens's disillusion is marked, as it was on the Pennsylvania Canal, by a comparison with a well-known British sight. The result is the collapse of the Sublime, punctured by the comic 'sheer gammon', and a return to the language of nullity which marked the letter of 22 March to Maclise. There is little to write about 'the Far West'; even Dickens's 'Faculty' is frustrated. The epic journey has been a failure. The only element of epic to remain – and this emerges with greater insistence as time passes – is the pressing need to get home.

W. H. Auden seems to have had a similar experience:

> I cannot see a plain without a shudder:
> 'O God, please, please, don't ever make me live there!'

Dickens used the term 'prairie' in his later fiction as a pejorative adjective. Yet if the Looking Glass Prairie is nugatory, at least it is writable. Dickens had compared this supposed 'landmark' with British scenery and (as was quite common) with the sea. The only 'seamark' of the trip west, the Mississippi River, is, as Christopher Mulvey suggests in his essay, beyond comparison. Indeed, the following sentences from Dickens's letter to Forster indicate that it cannot be described:

The last 200 miles of the voyage from Cincinnati to St. Louis are upon the Mississippi, for you come down the Ohio to its mouth. It is well for society that this Mississippi, the renowned father of waters, had no children who take after him. It is the beastliest river in the world . . .

After this ellipsis Dickens mentions the dangers posed by 'blocks of timber' floating in the river, the use of an alarm bell to warn of an imminent collision and the succeeding 'concussion which nearly flung one out of bed . . .' This second ellipsis leads to the conclusion:

While I have been writing this account, we have shot out of that hideous river, thanks be to God; never to see it again, I hope, but in a nightmare. We are now on the smooth Ohio, and the change is like the transition from pain to perfect ease.

It is the lacunae that are notable here. There is not one word of description of the Mississippi itself, or of the sights on its banks. There is almost no account of the dangers of the river (about which more in a moment), and instead a note of the inadequate precautions taken against them. Dickens has moved into an account of his sense perceptions, which impel him into writing about the present moment. He makes no attempt to describe the environment which causes those sense perceptions. Certainly, on his return eastwards he would once again describe scenery, principally the Niagara Falls. But the accounts of the river journeys between Cincinnati and St Louis exist solely in those ellipses. They are at this stage beyond language. The means of describing them would be developed later, as Dickens suggested, in nightmare visions.[7]

The best-known nightmare is Cairo, at the confluence of the Ohio and the Mississippi. It is the 'dismal swamp' of chapter 12 of *American Notes* and the infamous Eden, 'the grim domains of Giant Despair' in *Martin Chuzzlewit* (1843–4). This aspect of Dickens's epic journey has been transformed into a New World Pilgrim's Progress. I would like, however, to look at the description of the two rivers in *American Notes*. Like many other travellers, Dickens used his letters home as a source for the subsequent book. Forster, in particular, was entrusted with the care of extensive descriptions which would be transferred into *American Notes*, in some cases verbatim.[8]

There was no material on the Mississippi to be transferred. Instead, Dickens, now safely back in England, produced a nightmare. It begins in *American Notes* with that account of Cairo, referring to 'the hateful Mississippi' as 'a slimy monster hideous to behold'. After killing off Cairo, Dickens turns his attention solely to the river:

But what words shall describe the Mississippi, great father of rivers, who (praise be to Heaven) has no children like him! An enormous ditch, sometimes two or three miles wide, running liquid mud, six miles an hour: its strong and frothy current choked and obstructed everywhere by huge logs and whole forest trees: now twining themselves together in great rafts, from the interstices of which a sedgy, lazy foam works up, to float upon the water's top; now rolling past like monstrous bodies, their tangled roots showing like matted hair; now glancing singly by like giant leeches; and now writhing round and round in the vortex of some small whirlpool, like wounded snakes.

The opening sentence draws on the letter of 15–17 April to Forster. But now the literal inexpressibility of the river has been turned into a flourish of rhetoric ('But what words'), a feigning modesty which is drawn from the classical rhetoricians and which was often used by the Picturesque tourist as a prelude to detailed description. The ellipsis has been closed into an exclamation mark, and the lacuna has been filled by a long sentence which expands the note in the letter about 'blocks of timber' into an actively aggressive riverscape. Active participles and a group of unpleasant similes animate the trees and give the scene a horrific life-in-death appearance. In its appalling mobility it is reminiscent of the work of Edgar Allan Poe.[9]

Many travellers reacted to the Mississippi with horror and disgust. Edmund Flagg was one of them. They also reacted with distaste to the Missouri, which gives the Mississippi south of St Louis much of its character. The explorer Prince Maximilian of Wied noted that when the Missouri flooded it produced 'a wild scene of devastation, to which the broken poplars not a little contributed'. The artist on his expedition, Karl Bodmer, sketched the scene several times. During another expedition the ornithologist John James Audubon remarked on the constant shifts of the river's course. In consequence 'perhaps millions of trees' were washed 'away from the spots where they may have stood and grown for centuries past'. It made him philosophize about the transience of the natural world, at the mercy of malignant forces.[10]

Such reactions were based on objective evidence. An engineer calculated that the Missouri

yearly carries into the Mississippi 550,000,000 tons of earth, which has been brought an average distance of not less than 500 miles. The work thus represented is equivalent to 275,000,000,000 mile-tons, or tons carried one mile. The railroads of the United States carried in the year 1901 141,000,000,000 mile-tons of freight.

T. S. Eliot, who knew the Mississippi well, called it 'a strong brown god – sullen, untamed and intractable ... destroyer, reminder/Of what men choose to forget'. Both rivers, then, made people revise their belief in the essential beneficence of nature. Dickens does precisely this, producing a series of morbific and cloacal images which suggest that the river is a public menace not unlike the institutional menaces that so exercised him in Britain.[11]

Dicken's retrospective account of the Mississippi, then, is not of itself unusual. Neither is the fact that he has woven the discrete letters into a flowing narrative. Many travellers, particularly those who were also novelists, employed continuous narrative rather than the epistolary method in their books. What *is* unusual is the way in which the narrative flows; for images of the Mississippi run into other sections of *American Notes*. As we have seen from the letters, Dickens responded to the Ohio

119

with pleasure. That response is almost entirely absent from the book. Travellers like Edmund Flagg recorded their enthusiasm for 'la Belle Rivière', as it was called, and even worried that the Mississippi would pollute it. None of them produced a scene like this:

The river has washed away its banks, and stately trees have fallen down into the stream. Some have been there so long, that they are mere dry, grizzly skeletons. Some have just toppled over, and having earth yet about their roots, are bathing their green heads in the river, and putting forth new shoots and branches. Some are almost sliding down, as you look at them. And some were drowned so long ago, that their bleached arms start out from the middle of the current, and seem to try to grasp the boat, and drag it under water.

This is Dickens writing about the Ohio. His remembered vision of the Mississippi was so powerful that it dislocated his recorded responses to the other river. He has discarded 'the transition from pain to perfect ease' that distinguished the two, and now depicts the Ohio as a malignant force inverting the arboretum which had been an important element in his letters about that river. The nightmare vision of the Mississippi has turned the Ohio upside down. This is reinforced by another dislocation. The image of the malevolent trees included here was originally contained in Dickens's letter of 28 March while he was travelling from Baltimore to Pittsburgh. And this second dislocation is accompanied, like the first, by an increment of horror. The trees are no longer simply passive and maledictory. They are homicidal.[12]

The Mississippi runs into other aspects of natural description in the *Notes*. The Susquehanna Valley, summed up in the letter of 28 March to Forster simply as 'very beautiful', is now appropriately treated to a sentence of Picturesque description. Yet it is modulated by a lighting effect. 'The mist, wreathing itself into a hundred fantastic shapes, moved solemnly upon the water; and the gloom of evening gave to all an air of mystery and silence which greatly enhanced its natural interest.' Picturesque tourism is not enough; it must now be shrouded with hints of solitude and decay. Reasonably, the hint of death here is transient and the tone is lighter, but the scene is sculpted so that it anticipates the horrific visions of the Ohio and Mississippi. The 'mystery and silence' here is also related to yet another dislocation. In the letter of 1–4 April the nightmare of the solitary prisoner occurred in the Pittsburgh prison. In the *Notes* it takes place in the Eastern Penitentiary in Philadelphia, before Dickens left on his western trip. It is as if, in retrospect, the whole journey was marked by moments of horror and apprehension.[13]

Let me conclude by making two points. The first is about the relationship of word and world; the second about the importance of Dickens's western journey in the context of his fiction. It would firstly be wrong to assert there is anything unusual about Dickens's general reaction against America. The literature of travel is littered with complaints about the collapse of the Republic of the Imagination. The contrast between the first and second versions of D. H. Lawrence's *Studies in Classic American Literature* is just one of the more recent memorials to the fracture of Old World projections on the rocks of the New. What is striking about Dickens's response is the extent of the dislocation. I have intentionally used this term several times. Dickens, I suggest, dislocated the Mississippi because the Mississippi disoriented him. The ellipses in that letter of 15–17 April 1842 indicate, I think, that the Mississippi along which he was (according to his account) at that moment travelling was beyond words.

We have seen that, confronted with the 'Far West', many of the techniques that Dickens used for natural description simply collapsed – another term I am forced to use frequently. The American frontier, then, became for Dickens the frontier of form. Indeed, one might even suggest that Dickens had gone beyond the frontier of form. The ellipses indicate that Dickens had been stripped of language, an intensely disturbing experience, especially for a highly articulate man whose living depends upon the written word. Dickens took his revenge accordingly.[14]

Secondly, I think it would be wrong to assert that Dickens purged himself of the Mississippi in *American Notes* and *Martin Chuzzlewit*. The Mississippi, I suggest, provided the second of two stages which persuaded him to reject decisively the simple pastoral opposition of miasmic city and restorative countryside which informs such early novels as *Oliver Twist* (1837–9). The first stage occurred in *The Old Curiosity Shop* (1841). The journey of Little Nell and her grandfather out of London is initially set in the pastoral imagery of 'the singing of the birds, the beauty of the waving grass, the deep green leaves, the wild flowers'. It ends amongst 'brown thatched roofs' and a 'stream that rippled by the distant watermill', presided over by 'the blue Welsh mountains far away'. The setting is deceptive. Nell and her grandfather die amidst the pastoral beauties of Wales. As Steven Marcus has suggested, not simply the cities but the whole of Britain has been turned into one vast Necropolis.[15]

This first rejection of the pastoral is linked with the second. Dickens was writing *The Old Curiosity Shop* while the visit to the New World was changing from a pipe-dream to a firm plan. Nell's journey involves a great spatial movement by British standards; and a great textual movement, for it covers some thirty-two chapters. It proceeds westwards in hopeful search of renewal. It could be regarded therefore as an imaginative anticipation of Dickens's journey within the next two years. For, like many others, in crossing the Atlantic he was engaging in the hopeful travelling which had always impelled people to the New World.

By the time he came to write *Martin Chuzzlewit* Dickens had enough material to pillory such speciousness. He did it, appropriately, in the American figure of General Choke. The General, it will be recalled, asserted that Queen Victoria lived in the Tower of London. When asked if he had actually visited England, he responded: 'In print I have Sir . . . not otherwise.' It may be that Dickens was pillorying himself for his earlier optimism about America. His westward journey, recorded in the letters, was marked in its optimistic moments by images similar to Nell's: green leaves, waving grass, and mountains. But it is an even greater disappointment.

It is an even greater disappointment because instead of death *in* the landscape, the West provided Dickens with a vision of the death *of* the landscape. Before he visited America Dickens realized that virtuous people could die in a pastoral landscape; after his visit he realized that the landscape itself could disintegrate. Death not only marked the failure of human hopes; it became a worldwide, all-embracing holocaust. It is in this apocalyptic mode that the image of the Mississippi survives in Dickens's fiction. It can be found in the Staggs's Gardens episode of *Dombey and Son* (1846–8) and in 'the turbid living river' imagery that Dickens develops from *Martin Chuzzlewit* into a metaphor of society in *Little Dorrit* (1855–7). It is also, I would suggest, one of the sources of the appalling deliquescence that spreads through *Bleak House* (1852–3), with the 'death-like and mysterious' waterway at its heart. In particular, the Mississippi seeps into the opening chapter of Dickens's last completed novel, *Our Mutual Friend* (1864–5). The river, as so often, is the Thames at London. But such terms as 'savage', 'matted' and 'wilderness' suggest that Dickens has another river in mind:

Allied to the bottom of the river rather than the surface, by reason of the slime and ooze with which it was covered, and its sodden state, this boat and the two figures in it obviously were doing something they often did, and were seeking what they often sought. Half savage as the man showed, with no covering on his matted head, with his brown arms bare to between the elbow and the shoulder, with the loose knot of a looser kerchief lying low on his bare breast in a wilderness of beard and whisker, with such dress as he wore seeming to be made out of the mud that begrimed his boat, still there was business-like usage in his steady gaze ... Wheresoever the strong tide met with an impediment, his gaze paused for an instant. At every mooring-chain and rope, at every stationary boat or barge that split the current into a broad-arrowhead ... at the paddles of the river steamboats as they beat the filthy water, at the floating logs of timber lashed together lying off certain wharves, his shining eyes darted a hungry look ... What he had in tow, lunged itself at him sometimes in an awful manner when the boat was checked, and sometimes seemed to try to wrench itself away, though for the most part it followed submissively. A neophyte might have fancied that the ripples passing over it were dreadfully like faint changes of expression on a sightless face; but Gaffer was no neophyte and had no fancies.

After the voyage on the Mississippi Dickens was no neophyte, but the river would haunt his fancies for the rest of his days.[16]

Notes

1 Dickens, letter 22 March 1842 to W. C. Macready, *The Letters of Charles Dickens*, ed. Madeline House, Graham Storey and Kathleen Tillotson (Oxford: Clarendon Press, 1974), vol. 3, pp. 155–6. Henceforth cited as *Letters*.

2 Dickens's reaction against America is discussed, amongst others, by Edgar Johnson, *Charles Dickens: His Tragedy and Triumph* (Boston: Little, Brown, 1952), vol. 1, pp. 443–6; Robert B. Heilman, 'The New World in Charles Dickens's Writings', *Trollopian*, 1 (Sept. 1946), 25–53 and (March 1947), 11–26; Steven Marcus, *Dickens: From Pickwick to Dombey* (London: Chatto and Windus, 1965), pp. 240–52; Helen K. Heineman, *Three Victorians in the New World* (Unpublished Ph.D. Dissertation, Cornell University, 1967), chs. 4–6; Michael Slater, 'Introduction' to *Dickens on America and the Americans* (Brighton: Harvester, 1979), pp. 18–23; and Sidney P. Moss, *Charles Dickens's Quarrel with America* (Troy, NY: Whitston, 1984). An interpretation which comes closer to mine is in Lewis Bogaty, *Dickens's America* (Unpublished Ph.D. Dissertation, Ohio State University, 1976).

3 Rupert Brooke, *Letters from America* (London: Sidgwick and Jackson, 1931), p. 46. Dickens, *Letters*, vol. 3, p. x. Arnold Goldman and John Whitley, 'Introduction' to *American Notes* (Harmondsworth: Penguin, 1972), pp. 27, 35. The secondary texts on British travel literature are too numerous to cite in full. Two recent ones which develop their discussions with much insight and sophistication are Peter Conrad, *Imagining America* (London: Routledge and Kegan Paul, 1980) and Christopher Mulvey, *Anglo-American Landscapes* (Cambridge: Cambridge University Press, 1983).

4 Letters 22 March 1942 to Maclise and Thomas Mitton, *Letters*, vol. 3, pp. 152–4, 161. See also *Letters*, vol. 3, pp. 141–50, 153 fn2, 163.

5 Letter 28 March 1842 to John Forster, *Letters* vol. 3, pp. 167–72. Many of the details of Dickens's journey west are taken from W. C. Wilkins, ed., *Charles Dickens in America* (1911: NY: Haskell Booksellers, 1970), chs. 9–12, an invaluable sourcebook. On the Susquehanna River see Roger B. Stein, *Susquehanna: Images of the Settled Landscape* (Binghamton, NY: Roberson Center, 1981).

6 Letters 1 April to Macready, 1–4 April to Forster, 4 April to Frederick Dickens and 4 April to Mitton, *Letters*, vol. 3, pp. 173–83, 188–91. For an assessment of Dickens's account of the journey by riverboat, see Dean Hughes, 'Great Expectorations', *Dickensian* (1983), pp. 79, 67–76.

7 Letter 15–17 April 1842 to Forster, *Letters*, vol. 3, pp. 192–202. Forster claimed that he printed this and similar letters 'exactly as they were written'. See Forster, *The Life of Charles Dickens* (London: Chapman and Hall, 1908), vol. 1, p. 235; and pp. 248–57 for the letter. Forster destroyed many of Dickens's letters, including this one. On the circumstances of the destruction, Forster's accuracy, and the editors' policy on punctuation, see *Letters*, vol. 1, pp. xix, xxvii and vol. 3, pp. vii–viii. Edmund Flagg, *The Far West* rpt *Early Western Travels*, ed. Reuben Gold Thwaites (Cleveland, OH: Clark, 1906), vol. 26, p. 252. W. H. Auden, 'Plains', *Collected Poems*, ed. Edward Mendelson (London: Faber and Faber, 1976), p. 432.

8 Dickens, *American Notes*, p. 215; *Martin Chuzzlewit* (Harmondsworth: Penguin, 1968), p. 442. See *Letters*, vol. 3, p. 154 for Forster's 'trust'. See also Harry Stone, 'Dickens' Use of his American Experiences in *Martin Chuzzlewit*', *PMLA*, 72 (1957), 464–78; and Antonello Gerbi, *The Dispute of the New World*, trans. Jeremy Moyle (Pittsburgh: University of Pittsburgh Press, 1973), pp. 497–508.

9 Dickens, *American Notes*, pp. 215–16.

10 Flagg, *The Far West*, in *Early Western Travels*, vol. 26, pp. 93–5. Maximilian, Prince of Wied, *Travels in the Interior of North America*, trans. H. Evans Lloyd, also in *Early Western Travels*, vol. 22, p. 244. *Karl Bodmer's America*,

ed. David C. Hunt and Marsha V. Gallagher (Omaha: Joslyn Art Museum, 1984), pp. 99, 141, 150. John James Audubon, *Audubon and his Journals*, ed. Maria R. Audubon (1897; rpt New York: Dover, 1960), vol. 1, p. 460.

11 Hiram Martin Chittenden, *History of Early Steamboat Navigation on the Missouri River* (Cleveland, OH: Clark, 1903), vol. 1, pp. 74–81. Eliot, 'The Dry Salvages', *Collected Poems, 1909–1962* (London: Faber and Faber, 1963), p. 205. Dickens, *American Notes*, pp. 216–17.

12 Flagg, *The Far West*, in *Early Western Travels*, vol. 26, pp. 52–9. See also Wied in *Early Western Travels*, vol. 22, p. 161; and Audubon, *Audubon and his Journals*, vol. 2, 204–9. Dickens, *American Notes*, p. 205.

13 Dickens, *American Notes*, pp. 188, 153–7.

14 More disturbing collapses, linguistically and psychologically, are to be found in the cases of Meriwether Lewis and John Clare. On Lewis, see Lawson-Peebles, *Landscape and Written Expression in Revolutionary America: The World Turned Upside Down* (Cambridge: Cambridge University Press, 1988), ch. 6. On Clare, see John Barrell, *The Idea of Landscape and the Sense of Place, 1730–1840: An Approach to the Poetry of John Clare* (Cambridge: Cambridge University Press, 1972).

15 Dickens, *The Old Curiosity Shop* (Harmondsworth: Penguin, 1972), pp. 173, 438. Marcus, *Dickens: From Pickwick to Dombey*, pp. 140–5.

16 Dickens, *Martin Chuzzlewit*, pp. 412, 429; *Little Dorrit* (Harmondsworth: Penguin, 1967), p. 118; *Bleak House* (Harmondsworth: Penguin, 1971), pp. 44–5, 47. I would like to thank that fine Dickens scholar, Paul Schlicke, for his advice during the preparation of this essay.

American illustrations

9 ❋ The Old World and the New in the national landscapes of John Neal

FRANCESCA ORESTANO

John Neal was one of the keenest advocates of literary nationalism, yet it was he who induced a Greek god to ramble from the gardens of Parnassus into the primeval wilderness of America. The god Apollo, the father of the Muses, has traditionally been regarded as an icon of classical values; yet he was placed by Neal in a landscape which, as we have seen, had been characterized by negations and absences. Such contradictions seemed to flourish in the new Republic, and from them Neal helped to establish the foundations of an American aesthetic which consisted of a sublime, fictional version of American history transformed into a metaphor in which wilderness itself stood for art and aesthetic principles. I will trace this transformation by examining an early poem, 'The Battle of Niagara'; by considering the landscapes of his fiction; and finally by looking at the Preface to his 'North American Story', *Rachel Dyer*.

Neal was born in 1793 in a Quaker community in Portland, at that time part of the state of Massachusetts. In 1816, while a law student in Baltimore, he joined the Delphian Club, which he called 'a sort of Unitarian efflorescence', and, prompted by their literary debates, became a poet, novelist and critic. This heterodox background produced its first major result in 1818 when, in the space of six days, he wrote the 854-line 'The Battle of Niagara', which was inspired by the Battle of Lundy's Lane. The poem provided the title to his first book, published in that same year, and displayed the contradictions outlined above. The illustration on the book's title page carries the American icons of a bald eagle and the Niagara Falls, while the 'Ode, Delivered before the Delphians' was dedicated to 'the blazing god of Poesy' whose presence is invoked by the literati of Baltimore: 'O, thou of heaven, Apollo, thou shine out upon thy votaries now!'. The first edition was published under the Delphian pseudonym of Jehu O'Cataract.[1]

The name is appropriate. The poems present a cataract of images, allusions and hyperbole. The result in 'The Battle of Niagara' is a battleground blurred and choked by a confused mess of superimposed scenes drawn from the past or the future and set in the sky or among the elements. Influenced, as he openly admits in his prefatory address 'To the Reader', by Byron, Leigh Hunt, Moore's *Lalla Rookh* and Young's *Night Thoughts*, Neal allows these Old World writers to shape his lines with sublime contrasts of obscurity and light, and with sudden shifts in perspective and dramatic changes. Yet Neal manifests his nationalist commitment by placing the American bird right at the beginning of the poem. The eagle first appears 'On the precipice-top – in perpetual snow', and 'On the splintered point of a shivered peak', but then is seen in motion:

> A Bird that is first to worship the sun
> When he gallops in flame – 'till the cloud tides run
> In billows of fire – as his course is done . . .
> Like an imprisoned blaze that is bursting from the night!
>
> (pp. 83–4)

The leader of the American force appears in a similar context. He is seen from a distance, on his horse, 'While he rears o'er the rich-rolling clouds of the height/Like a pageant upraised by the wonders of light'. The troops, in contrast, are given short shrift. They occupy a remote corner of the scene, and are briefly sketched, only to be dismissed:

> And now they have gone! – like a vision of day:
> In a streaming of splendour they came – but they wheeled,
> And instantly all the bright show was concealed!
> As if 'twere a tournament held in the sky,
> Betrayed by some light passing suddenly by . . .
> They came like a cloud that is passing the light,
> That brightens and blazes – and fades from the sight:
> They came like a dream – and as swiftly they fled,
> As the shadows that pass o'er the sun's dying red.   (pp. 86–7)

As Thoreau would later admit, 'We never tire of the drama of sunset.' Here, indeed, the forces engaged on the battleground are essentially the atmospheric agents, pervasively present and endowed with the power to unify the otherwise scattered warfare. The soldiers are portrayed, or rather caught, as if appearing through momentary apertures in the elements. Light controls sight, frames description and ultimately conveys meaning to the landscape. Variously coloured rays of light and clouds in motion dramatically provide a narrative pattern which compensates for the lack of action on the battleground. That icon of the spirit of '76, the eagle, is the winged messenger through which communication and dialogue is established. The bird yokes together story and history, horologicals and chronometricals, inscribing the Battle of Niagara on the destiny of the democratic covenant.[2]

The Battle is brought to life by the generative powers of light. Conversely, Neal asserts that the vision disappears when 'the landscape has less of enchantment and light' (p. 88). This medium, therefore, is endowed with a creative, mythopoetic power and has a moral role. To borrow Barbara Novak's terms, one can consider it 'the spirit of the scene'. One can find many visual counterparts of this literary landscape in early nineteenth-century American painting. Light is used for a similar function in Thomas Cole's landscapes; an instance is 'The Voyage of Life – Youth', with its atmospheric pavilion. There is one substantial difference: Cole's conception of the landscape evolves from religious pietism. Nevertheless, both men try to make the American environment function as a metaphor. Neal's literary landscape aims, above all, at offering a grand version of American history. In this sense, it can be associated with what Novak has called 'the operatically sublime' mode of painting, illustrating the birth process of a new nation with 'a typical mixture of new landscape and old conventions'; that is, 'the "grand style" of history painting popularized into the national landscape'.[3]

Neal's long preface, 'To the Reader', accounts for this complex policy, and for the difficult quest for a national terrain in the treacherous Republic of Letters. Indeed, it contains an open statement of disbelief in the ability of poetry to represent the new nation; a disbelief which is, at once, counterbalanced by a passionate defense of American poets:

We have poets . . . full of the fire and sublimity of genius . . . We have had battles worthy of such bards – and we shall have bards worthy of our battles . . . Our painters are already brightening to the touch of inspiration – and the treasures of American poesy have been discovered, and will yet prove boundless and inexhaustible as our mines. (p. xxiii)

We have here another example of 'the figure of anticipation' discussed by Stephen Fender earlier in this volume, but here it is verified by a geological simile which will assist the process of inspiration and creation. Now, however, that process is under way, for history is in the making. The artist wants 'to leave some proofs of the illumination that an American can experience, when gazing upon the wonders of American history' (pp. xxiii–xxiv).

Yet within two pages Apollo makes his appearance. Neal's poetic creation is attained 'after the manner of another of Apollo's worshippers', Coleridge (p. xxvi). Apollo makes another appearance in 'The Battle of Niagara'. Neal's summary indicates the context of his arrival in Canto II:

Ontario described ... Appearances ... Reflections ... Apostrophe ... Resemblances ... American Indian ... Apollo ... Corruption and Refinement.

(p. 98)

The Canto offers an unexpected digression from the battleground itself and from the history of the Republic, heralded by an appropriate injunction: 'Come, sit thou with me! – we shall both learn to feel,/Like the men of old times' (p. 99). During this hiatus Old Ontario 'sleeps ... in savage Nature's pomp'. The landscape, in other words, takes on what Leo Marx has called 'the sufficiency of nature in its original state'.[4] This is a wild version of the myth of the Garden. It may be no more than a daydream. Certainly, it is an anachronism, and it is threatened, like Virgil's pastoral, with an irruption of history. Neal asserts that the garlands of his Edenic depiction of nature, possessing 'a wild luxuriance ... in their negligence' are under attack and the attack is also a threat to the American Eagle:

> Let but the white man's summons once he heard,
> And gone, for ever, is thy guardian Bird...
> Thy battlements of rocks, and cliffs, and clouds –
> Stripped of their garland flags, and hung with shrouds,
> And bright with glittering spires... (pp. 100–1)

At first sight this fundamental conflict of values seems irreconcileable. But a singular strategy permits the poet to rescue the evanescent values connected with Ontario and to convert the loss (a self-evident fallacy) into an investment for the future. He achieves it by means of an ideal bridge by which the native inhabitant of Ontario, although doomed to extinction, becomes an incarnation of the spirit of the place. There is what we might call a transcendental migration, by which the Indian, variously described as a child of the bow and 'A naked monarch', becomes the American incarnation of the Greek god Apollo. The god, though, must undergo a transformation before he can climb the American Pantheon. In his American version the god must be:

> Not like the airy god of moulded light,
> Just stepping from his chariot on the sight;
> Posing his beauties on a rolling cloud . . .
> But like that angry god, in blazing light
> Bursting from space! and standing in his might:
> Revealed in his omnipotent array –
> Apollo of the skies! and Deity of Day! . . .
> Not like that god, when up in air he springs,
> When heavenly musick murmurs from his strings –
> A buoyant vision – an embodied dream
> Of dainty poesy . . .
> Not that Apollo – not resembling him,
> Of silver bow, and woman's nerveless limb:
> But man! – all man! – the monarch of the wild!
> Not the faint spirit that corrupting smil'd
> On soft, lascivious Greece – but Nature's child, . . .
> Not that Apollo! – not the heavenly one,
> Voluptuous spirit of a setting sun, –
> But this – the offspring of young Solitude,
> Child of the holy spot, where none intrude
> But genii of the torrent – cliff, and wood –
> Nurslings of cloud and storm – the desert's fiery brood.
>
> (pp. 101–4)

As happens with many American pastorals, the landscape depicted here is both Eden and a howling desert. Accordingly, it contains both innovative elements and old conventions. The liminal figure moving from corruption (the setting sun of Greece) to 'refinement' or innocence (the rising sun of the new Republic) is Apollo, whom a momentous transformation sets in a virgin landscape and whose character Neal illustrates by means of a detailed enumeration of old and new qualities.

Formerly a conventional icon of classical values and thence the emblem of dainty poesy, Apollo in these new circumstances becomes the

Francesca Orestano

manly symbol of the American wilderness, which is equated with 'Freedom' and the 'sublime'. This means that, *mutatis mutandis*, Art itself has migrated into the New World, choosing the wilderness as its own domain. Apollo's former companions are forsaken, and he will now share the wilderness with the aboriginal genii. His presence ensures that the raw, native landscape will become the realm most befitting for art and for the American artists. Indeed, one might suggest that Apollo's journey will lead into other landscapes – the landscapes of the mind – and into the wilderness of the human heart, whose boundaries Romanticism lays open to exploration.

The wilderness of Ontario, therefore, does not appear as if teleologically conceived and oriented (a stimulus for the errand, soon to be formalized into the manners of Romantic pietism). Nor is it a *locus amoenus*, chosen in view of its colonization into a rural garden, as Jefferson's Virginia seemed to be. Rather, this wilderness is on the one hand part of a conventional description of a prelapsarian Eden familiar, after Rousseau, for the cult of the Noble Savage; on the other hand the conventional scenery offers a safe bridge for the Grecian immigrant. The strong primitivistic quality of this American pastoral nevertheless confers genuine native strength upon the ancient, decadent god, who is soon transformed and revitalized, in and by the new landscape, into the American Apollo, a wholly native creature, albeit still belonging to the superior spheres of Art. The presence of Apollo in Neal's historical–pastoral poem, therefore, is not due to anachronistic nostalgia for the Golden Age. Apollo, rather, is used here as the cornerstone of a periphrastic construction: as the key-figure of a programme whose ultimate aim is, at one and the same time, to reject classicism and to attain classical status.[5]

In his prefatory remarks 'To the Reader', Neal declares his polemical attitude. He asserts that 'this uniform extravagance and enthusiasm for the ancient classicks, is not the result of judgement – reasoning, or conviction; but of tyranny, conquest and education'. The idea that Homer and Virgil are superior because '*universally* admired' is wrong. 'All the others, who are Homers in their country; the Milton of England, the Tasso of Italy', or Ariosto, who 'has more imagination than Homer and Virgil together', have produced poems as great as either the Iliad and the Aeneid; 'but they are *unlike* them, as *they* are unlike each other' (pp. xv–xvi).

134

The aesthetic evaluations imposed by Greece, and thenceforward by captivated Rome, although still governing 'universal suffrage' are, in Neal's opinion, highly objectionable. The implications of this discourse range beyond a campaign for Romanticism, even though the movement largely inspires Neal's argument and is ultimately favoured by his artistic choices. If other nations such as England or Italy have classics which are by no means inferior to the 'canonized' ones, America too can boast of her classics which, although totally 'unlike' the ancient ones, deserve to be admired and worshipped not only by the nation but by the whole world. The very idea of classic (as expounded, for instance, by Samuel Johnson in his evaluation of Shakespeare's art) as something attaining excellency and universal praise through time and transmission beyond and above its contingent and historical appeal, is here challenged, shaken and turned upside down. Neal defies what is 'hallowed, and embalmed, by the flattery and worship of centuries' and adds, in full awareness of his position: 'This is a subject on which I am not particularly orthodox; I confess it – and glory in it' (p. xvi).[6]

'The Battle of Niagara', then, assists in laying the foundations of American artistic independence. It is as if Neal is trying to replace a 'weak', neoclassical version of classicism – a repetitive, inherited formula defying historical progress and revolutions – with his 'strong' or idealistic conception of it. Against the well-established, formalized and formalist idea of the classic, he maintains that what is classic founds its claim to universal excellency upon freedom from the sweeping rules of the classical tradition and, therefore, upon originality, individuality, particularity and fragmentation; in short, upon a manifest relationship with the American landscape with its social, cultural, and historical meanings.

The image of the new Apollo, therefore, set against the wild terrain of America, becomes a powerful emblem for Neal's artistic enterprise. The symbolic value of this new figure is confirmed by Neal's statements about poetry. He takes care to criticise his own performance, which he thinks altogether fails to do justice to history, to nature and thus to the nation and to his conception of American art. Speaking of the first edition of *The Battle of Niagara* Neal remembers:

I have been villanously criticised . . . for having omitted 'names – dates, &c.' To which I reply thus – the *battle* in the last canto is faithfully represented . . . and . . . I undertook to make a poem, of an event, within arms length of every body. The question was, shall I give an artificial distance to the scenery, or only versify the orderly book and battalion returns? I choose the former – and left out names because, as yet, we have no *names*, except that of Washington, that can give dignity to any poem. (p. xii)

Bitterness for the personal failure is balanced by a degree of critical awareness which determines Neal's rejection of poetry as 'artefact'. His attitude is here expressed in statements that can be seen as the necessary prefiguration of Whitman's achievement:

What is poetry but imagery? And what is imagery but the thought – or rather the *manner* of thinking ... It is not the language of passion. Nor is it the language of nature ... The language of poetry – the descriptions of poetry – are *not* those of nature ... It is all hyperbole – more highly coloured – and better grouped than Nature. So it is in painting. So in statuary. A perfectly *natural* man – sculptured – however perfect the model might be – would excite no such feeling as the Apollo does ... In one word ... poetical description ... is not faithfully natural.

(pp. lviii–lxii)

The old-fashioned Apollo must be forsaken, together with 'old epithets, commonplace similes, and itinerant metaphors', a faded patchwork of ancient mythology with 'a magazine of thunderbolts, and gods and goddesses, and Phoebuses, and Jupiters, and the devil knows what' (pp. liv–lv). The American artist must concentrate instead upon the sensual man, who can move the passions and excite inner feelings, and avoid exacting intellectual admiration for the skillful imitation of nature. The author who avowed, 'I began to scribble from necessity – I continued it from necessity' found that 'scribblers in America' could only 'keep their chins out of water' by renouncing poetry (pp. lxiii–lxiv). Neal heeded his own injunctions in the ensuing years. He began to experiment with the novel and became an advocate of 'colloquial style', which he called 'talk-on-paper' or 'unpremeditated expression'.[7]

Between 1822 and 1823 Neal produced *Logan, A Family History*, *Seventy-six*, *Randolph, A Novel*, and *Errata; or, the Works of Will. Adams*, all novels which give evidence of his experiments and of his awareness that traditional literary forms ought to be replaced, to quote Emory Elliott, 'by structures that could encompass a society of discord and competing voices'. The work was accompanied by a deepening critical awareness of his literary operations:

Logan is a piece of declamation: *Seventy-Six*, a narrative: *Randolph*, epistolary: *Errata, or Will Adams*, colloquial – They are a complete series; a course of experiment, as the author himself declares, upon the forbearance of the age: a multitude of papers thrown off in a sort of transport: amounting to fifteen large English duodecimos – written at the rate of three such volumes a month – while the author was publicly engaged, nearly the whole of each day, in professional business.[8]

Not only does this improvisatory production release the aspirations fettered by poetry; it also draws its strength from Neal's polemical reaction against Sydney Smith's lack of faith in American literature. It flies in the face of the fashion for imported models (Scott, eminently); in the face of the low status of the novel and of novel-writing; in the face of the imitation of canonized English voices (Addison, Johnson, Gold-smith) in American fiction; and in the face of the borrowing of traditional settings or literary landscapes which are transplanted piecemeal onto American soil. In *Randolph*, mixed with a Gothic plot, there are enlightening passages of literary criticism, and a negative catalogue:

We have no old castles – no banditti – no shadow of a thousand years to penetrate – but what of that. We have men and women – creatures that God himself hath fashioned and filled with character . . . Lo! Here is a proof that we want no traditions, no antiquity – nothing but tolerable power, to tell you a tale that shall thrill to your marrow – and that, too, without borrowing from anybody, or imitating anybody. You laugh at my enthusiasm . . . But why need we go back to the past for our heroes? There is no such necessity; and he who shall first dare to grapple with the *present*, will triumph, in this country.[9]

The negative catalogue – that list of Old World phenomena absent from America – would become a common American strategy. It had already been foreshadowed by Neal in his repeated use of the word 'not' when elevating the Indian in 'The Battle of Niagara'. Here he follows Charles Brockden Brown's 'Preface' to *Edgar Huntly* in attempting, as he put it in *The Battle of Niagara*, the 'vindication of the American character' (p. xxxix). The landscapes of his fiction are no longer atmospheric; or artificial, distant scenery; or descriptive passages encased within the plot, representing a fixed stage where action takes place. His characters portray the nation and its present historical time as representatives or fragments of a typically varied social landscape. They tell its history from the limited viewpoint of the individual and they illustrate nationality through spoken language and dialect, characterizing the different regions of America. Neal adopts a principle of individuality also proposed by William Howard Gardiner in 1822. A vision of society hierarchically ordered, substantially neo-classical – and conducive, in fiction, to the adoption of a principle of generalization – is replaced by the idea that in no other country but America can 'a greater variety of specific character' be found. The concept clearly favours the literary trend of regionalism, and there are many critics who have seen Neal's production eminently in this light. Some of his novels, indeed, are largely built upon that principle. In *The Down-Easters*, for instance, a steamboat going from Philadelphia to Baltimore carries a whole gallery of national portraits, such as the New Englander, the Bostonian, the Southerner, the Virginian, the Carolinian, and the Marylander of Irish parentage.[10]

The novel *Brother Jonathan: or, The New Englanders* abounds in local colour, with descriptions of Yankee festivals, husking, raising, and quilting frolicks. Neal defined it as 'altogether American – scenery – incidents – characters'. It consists of a thick, spiced compound of gothicism, local colour, customs carefully described, dialects carefully recorded, glimpses and scenes from the history of the American Revolution. A British critic, however, observed that the novel was remarkable for 'descriptions of scenery, and illustrations of the natural passions of the human heart and soul, worthy of that prodigious continent, whose hills are mountains and whose mountains are immeasurable'.[11] British critics could, at times, be quite perceptive. This one recognizes Neal's intention and traces a connection between a literary microcosm and a geographic macrocosm and sees that the link between literary scenery and the all-encompassing wilderness of hills and mountains is located within the region of the heart.

The sympathetic relationship between heart and landscape recurs throughout Neal's fiction – and directly bears upon his theory of the novel. It is, as I have noted, initially modelled upon the gothic formula of the 'explained supernatural' found in the work of Charles Brockden Brown. In his essays on 'American Writers' Neal rates Brockden Brown 'capital' as a story-teller because he is able to make 'very trifling incidents of importance enough to occupy your whole heart and soul, for many pages'. But although he is a 'story-teller by profession' who has stumbled into some useful native materials, Brown 'has no poetry in his heart – or, at least, nothing that the world mistakes for poetry … but he is altogether compounded of the distinct and earnest; the expressive and terrible in morals'.[12] Brown's recipe for story-telling is adopted by Neal, who introduces the necessary variations: the former's lack of poetry is compensated for by the latter's would-be Byronic impetus (responsible for a number of flaws, but mainly the blurring by unexplained obscurity the strength of several plots) while the gothic formula with its dark, terrific landscapes, acquires unprecedented intensity and reach owing to the influence of the Schlegelian principle of effect.

Wilhelm von Schlegel's lectures were well-known by the Delphians and were discussed in *The Portico* as well as in *Blackwood's*. They helped to establish a hierarchy of the arts according to the effect produced in the reader. Neal used them to formulate his aesthetic theory with its distinctions between poetry or 'artificial' writings (that stimulate either the blood or the brain of the reader), and fiction which, with its natural descriptions, has the positive effect of touching the reader's heart with sympathy (a natural emotion consequently endowed with the powerful force of nature).[13]

Thus Brown's gothic landscape, thick with the 'perils of the Western wilderness', is gradually transformed and 'naturalized' by Neal into familiar settings that are the domain of passions touching the regions of the heart. The gory theatricals and supernatural props of the frontier are ultimately dwarfed by the effect they are wont to provoke; and when they are gradually replaced by the tame, natural, familiar landscape of New England, it becomes clear that the naive gothic mechanism reveals the horror at work in the inner landscape of man. 'Terror is not of Germany but of the soul', observed Poe. Neal adopts a similar tactic, as can be seen in this extract from *Randolph*: 'her dark eyes are fastened upon the face of Molton … with an expression, that is – no, it is not love – it is not tenderness – it is something more terrible … and I go there, I know now why, – perhaps, as I went to the dramas of Germany – to be agitated, and alarmed.'[14]

Wilderness, then, is to be met not only on the frontier, but in everyday life, and often the circumstantial narrowness in which it manifests itself adds breadth and sublimity to the landscape subsequently disclosed. In the novel *Errata* this very strategy is implemented by means of 'the accumulated dust and ashes of a sea coal fire'. 'There is the picture of my life', says the hero to a friend, on a bleak December night, while they sit together and watch the dying fire:

'There it is!... This bleak and desolate place – with only this one, barren, and leafless tree, within the whole circumference of the horizon – its aged branches heavy with snow and ice – standing alone, as it were in the place of the graves.' I followed the blackened point of the cane, as it successively touched along the larger pieces of burnt coal; and disturbed the white ashes, that lay, here and there, upon the larger cinders, like snow upon the rocks and hedges of a wintry landscape.

'I can see the interminable blue Ocean beyond ... and just there' (drawing a line from left to right, across the whole hearth ...) 'where you can perceive the sun setting, the only light that is left ... falls directly upon this poor, worn tree ... Look!'

I shook my head; for I could see only a handful of trodden and crushed cinders...

'Very well – let us proceed. These are tomb-stones, broken and lying about; that one, which is leaning against the old tree, is my own. Behold – it is mouldering and falling, with its own weight ... this grave here, is newly dug – those hills, that you see, of ice and snow – away to your left – are the Glaciers – that Ocean is eternity. The grave is my own.'[15]

Out of a commonplace situation the author extracts a vast, detailed landscape in which natural features stand for those of a bleak, interior waste land. The composition of this landscape is still quite mechanical, insofar as the vision is shaped in the form of an allegory. The Ocean, for instance, is eternity. Nevertheless this passage, written in 1823, is an early maieutic attempt at driving out of a physical reality a landscape of symbolic value, of moral importance. Moreover, it shows already a typical symbolist procedure: namely, the borderline dividing the real from the ideal is very thin, and it can be bridged if the mere act of sight ('I could see', 'I could only see') is replaced by an act of intense perception ('you can perceive', 'behold').

The wintry landscape here represented is akin to many natural landscapes in Hawthorne's fictions, some of which are discussed later in this collection by Bernard Mergen. Both Neal and Hawthorne draw from the natural world and from the lore of provincial New England the outward frames of their inner landscapes; and they both locate the ground of perception in common sights, often at night. Indeed, Neal's technique anticipates in basic procedure and ultimate effect (if not yet in skillful simultaneity of vision) the symbolism that seems to be a prerogative of the literary achievements of the American Renaissance. Issues which are both 'national' and 'spiritual' are compounded together within the vision of the individual.

The artistic process that eventually enables the American artist to rely upon the materials offered by the native landscape and by the history of the new nation is, according to Sacvan Bercovitch, 'the same strategy that directs the symbolist to absorb the materials of history [and] compels him to lift those materials out of history proper into the domain of imagination'.[16] In *Rachel Dyer, A North American Story*, published in 1828, the process can be followed in its making. The novel describes the Salem trials of the 1690s; therefore the incidents which occur, the extraordinary phenomena, the 'unnatural' things, witchcraft, violence and death, are drawn out of the repository of American history. The author emphasizes that Salem is inhabited by wise, religious, learned people. But wilderness now partakes of history and it pervades that small social microcosm, affecting the minds of the learned as well as those of the ignorant, entering the rich homes of the righteous as well as the huts of the squatters. The contagion is apparent in the behaviour of the Fathers, the savages and the Quakers alike. Its destructive operations are to be seen at work in the conscience of George Burroughs, an outcast and a minister, who tries to oppose wilderness but is ultimately defeated. His wisdom and his cogent words in defence of the 'bewitched' seem preternatural. Charged with witchcraft himself, he surrenders to the judges' biased accusations, refusing to speak before he is executed in company with the Quaker outcast woman, Rachel Dyer, who vainly pleads for his innocence. Wilderness in this novel is no longer located within the realms of the pastoral or of the gothic. It swells, from history, into a far-reaching vortex, and a maelstrom, becoming in Bercovitch's terms, a 'metaphor of universal relevance'.[17]

Not only does Hawthorne depend upon the same stored materials for his fiction, but, following Neal's experiments, he argues that by introducing American history into the domain of the novel the latter will be positively enhanced and improved by 'a magic touch that should cause new intellectual and moral shapes to spring up in the reader's mind, peopling with varied life what had hitherto been a barren waste'. With similar concern and in similar words, Neal observes in his 'Unpublished Preface to a North American Story' that the novel should teach (picking up a figure from *Errata*) 'the fire-side biography of nations' while being 'a history of the human heart'. The great American novel should therefore be 'a picture of the present for the future – a picture of human nature not only here, but everywhere'.[18]

Apollo could never be part of the created landscape of fiction, purposefully based upon local and national history and upon provincial particularities. Yet elsewhere, when the landscape described is nothing but the transcription in visual terms of Neal's opinions about the state of American art and letters, and when his aesthetic programme is sketched as a searching itinerary through this very landscape, then his theoretical quest, speculations, and confessed ambitions concerning the future of art in the New World could drive the artist's mind into landscapes of the imagination where pure ideals of classical perfection are revealed to the intellect and, eventually, are made visible through imagined epiphanies.

In the Preface to *Rachel Dyer*, which is set forth as 'another *Declaration of Independence* ... in the great *Republic of Letters*', Neal traces the boundaries of American literature and draws an ideal map in which many contemporary authors appear, cautiously treading the worn paths of imitation. The ancient classics, meanwhile, still keep their position, 'ruling our spirits from their urns'. But Neal argues that since 'the multitude have been steadily advancing both in knowledge and power ... might it not be possible for some improvements to be made, some discoveries, even yet in style and composition, by launching forth into space? ... Islands and planets may still be found ... we should probably encounter some phenomena in the great unvisited moral sky and ocean.'[19]

The American artist envisages a vast 'terra incognita' in which his quest seems to transcend literature and attain the realms and vistas of epistemology. Neal suggests that the destiny of the American artist could be that of another Columbus, to bring forth the discovery of a new world; or like that of Tyho Brahe, the astronomer and explorer of 'a new heaven'. This attitude is shared by Edgar Allan Poe who deals with the same subject in a letter to Neal in which, speaking of his poem 'Al Aaraaf', he reminds our author (then editor of *The Yankee; and Boston Literary Gazette*) that his is 'a tale of another world – the Star discovered by Tyho Brahe'.[20]

Both authors looking for a new world and a 'new system' share the viewpoint of the astronomer who discovers a new star. Al Aaraaf is harmony, beauty, truth, eternal and universal law. It belongs to a distant world, but both artists fix their eyes to its light. It shines upon the American artists, too, because Neal perceives that there are places

barren to all outward appearance ... yet ... if you but lay your ear to the scented ground, you may hear the perpetual gush of innumerable fountains pouring their subterranean melody night and day, among the minerals and rocks, the iron and the gold: places where the way-faring man, the pilgrim or the wanderer through what he may deem the very deserts of literature, the barren places of knowledge, will find the very roots of the withered and blasted shrubbery ... and the very bowels of the earth into which he has torn his way ... heavy with a brightness that may be coined, like the soil about the favorite hiding places of sunny-haired Apollo.[21]

Thus the migration of the god has been accomplished: from the Golden Age and Parnassus, into America and the wilderness, and from thence into classic American literature.

Notes

1 Neal, *Wandering Recollections of a Somewhat Busy Life* (Boston: Roberts Brothers, 1870), pp. 174, 189–92. Neal, *The Battle of Niagara: with Other Poems* 2nd edn (Baltimore: N. G. Maxwell, 1819), title page and p. 230. Future references to this edition will be given parenthetically. Information on Neal has been drawn from: Irving T. Richards, 'John Neal: a Bibliography', *Jahrbuch für Amerikastudien*, 7 (1962), 296–310; Alberta Fabris, 'Il Randolph di John Neal', *Studi Americani*, 12 (1966), 15–44; Donatella Abbate Badin, 'L'opera critica di John Neal', *Studi Americani*, 15 (1969), 7–31; Benjamin Lease, *The Wild Fellow: John Neal and the American Literary Revolution* (Chicago: Chicago University Press, 1972); and Donald A. Sears, *John Neal* (Boston: G. K. Hall, 1978).
2 For American symbolism, see Barbara Novak, *Nature and Culture: American Landscape and Painting, 1825–1875* (New York: Oxford University Press, 1980), pp. 78ff; Clive Bush, *The Dream of Reason: American consciousness and cultural achievement from Independence to the Civil War* (London: Edward Arnold, 1977), pp. 34–5; Sacvan Bercovitch, 'Representing Revolution: The Example of Hester Prynne', *The Early Republic: The Making of a Nation, the Making of a Culture*, ed. Steve Ickringill, Zoltan Abadi-Nagy and Aladar Sarbu, forthcoming; Elinor Lander Horwitz, *The Bird, the Banner and Uncle Sam: Images of America in Folk and Popular Art* (Philadelphia: J. B. Lippincott Co., 1976), pp. 35–9.
3 Barbara Novak, *American Painting of the Nineteenth Century: Realism,*

Francesca Orestano

Idealism and the American Experience (New York: Harper and Row, 1979), pp. 62–3. Novak, *Nature and Culture*, pp. 18–28. Cole's 'Voyage of Life – Youth' is reproduced on p. 21. See also Martin Christadler, 'American Romanticism and the Meanings of Landscape', *Mythos und Aufklärung in Amerikanischen Literatur*, ed. Dieter Meindl, Friedrich W. Horlacher and Martin Christadler (Erlangen: Universitätsbund Erlangen–Nürnberg, 1985), pp. 71–106.

4 Leo Marx, *The Machine in the Garden: Technology and the Pastoral Ideal in America* (1964; rpt New York: Oxford University Press, 1972), p. 42.

5 For a recent discussion of the transformation of one literary mode see Leo Marx, 'Pastoralism in America', *Ideology and Classic American Literature*, ed. Sacvan Bercovitch and Myra Jehlen (Cambridge: Cambridge University Press, 1986), pp. 36–69.

6 Samuel Johnson, *Preface to Shakespeare. E altri scritti Shakespeariani*, ed. Agostino Lombardo (1961; rpt Bari: Adriatica Editrice, 1967), pp. 232–87. Neal, with typical boastfulness, attacked Johnson head on in *American Writers: A Series of Papers Contributed to Blackwood's Magazine (1824–1825)*, ed. Fred Lewis Pattee (Durham, NC: Duke University Press, 1937), p. 162: 'I encountered your English Goliath, Johnson ... overthrew him and his great argument as it appears in the *Preface to Shakespeare*.'

7 See Harold C. Martin, 'The Colloquial Tradition in the Novel: John Neal', *New England Quarterly*, 32 (1959), 455–75; and Richard Bridgman, *The Colloquial Style in America* (New York: Oxford University Press, 1966).

8 Emory Elliott, *Revolutionary Writers: Literature and Authority in the New Republic, 1725–1810* (New York: Oxford University Press, 1982), p. 16. Neal, *American Writers*, p. 168.

9 Neal, *Randolph, A Novel*, 2 vols. (n.p. [Baltimore?]: n.p., 1823), vol. 2, p. 208.

10 Neal, *The Down-Easters* (New York: Harper and Brothers, 1833). For Gardiner, see Sergio Perosa, *American Theories of the Novel: 1793–1903* (New York: New York University Press, 1985), p. 15.

11 Neal, letter to William Blackwood, October 1824, reported in Benjamin Lease, *Anglo-American Encounters: England and the Rise of American Literature* (Cambridge: Cambridge University Press, 1981), p. 58. Anon., review of Neal, *Brother Jonathan*, *Edinburgh Literary Journal*, 1 (1829). See William B. Cairns, *British Criticisms of American Writings, 1815–1833* (Madison, WI: University of Wisconsin Studies in Language and Literature, no. 14), p. 209.

12 Neal, *American Writers*, pp. 56–68, and *Randolph*, vol. 2, pp. 209–13. On the connection between Brown and Neal, see Fritz Fleischmann, *A Right View of the Subject: Feminism in the Works of Charles Brockden Brown and John Neal* (Erlangen: Palm und Enke, 1983).

144

13 Excerpts from Schlegel's *Course of Lectures on Dramatic Art and Literature* appeared in *The Port Folio* and in *Blackwood's Magazine* – Neal contributed to both – and were discussed by the Baltimore Delphians. See Benjamin Lease, 'Yankee Poetics: John Neal's Theory of Poetry and Fiction', *American Literature*, 24 (1956), 505–19; *That Wild Fellow*, pp. 69–80; and 'John Neal and Edgar Allan Poe', *Poe Studies*, 7 (1974), 38–41. See also Sears, *John Neal*, p. 31; and Leon Chai, *The Romantic Foundations of the American Renaissance* (Ithaca, NY: Cornell University Press, 1987).

14 Neal, *Randolph*, vol. 1, p. 70. Poe's remark is to be found in Perosa, *American Theories*, p. 11.

15 Neal, *Errata; or, the Works of Will. Adams*, 2 vols. (New York: for the proprietors, 1823), vol. 1, pp. xi–xii.

16 Sacvan Bercovitch, 'The Image of America: From Hermeneutics to Symbolism', *Early American Literature*, ed. Michael T. Gilmore (Englewood Cliffs, NJ: Prentice-Hall, 1980), p. 165.

17 Bercovitch, 'The Image of America', p. 163. See also Ernest E. Leisy, *The American Historical Novel* (Norman, OK: University of Oklahoma Press, 1950), p. 456.

18 Hawthorne, quoted in Lease, *Anglo-American Encounters*, p. 65. Neal, 'Unpublished Preface to the North American Stories', *Rachel Dyer* (Portland, ME: Shirley and Hyde, 1828), pp. vi-xx.

19 Neal, 'Unpublished Preface', pp. xviii and xiii.

20 Poe, Letter October–November 1829 to Neal, *The Letters of Edgar Allan Poe*, ed. John Ward Ostrom (Cambridge, MA: Harvard University Press, 1948), vol. 1, pp. 32–3.

21 Neal, 'Unpublished Preface', p. xvi. I would like to thank the Italian Ministry of Education for financing the research upon which this essay is based.

10 * Landscape painting and the domestic typology of post-revolutionary America

GRAHAM CLARKE

American painting in the immediate post-revolutionary period is hardly noted for its depiction of the American landscape, especially when one considers the later achievements of the Hudson River school and the Luminists. Certainly, there is no single post-revolutionary painter who matches the major English artists of the time. Yet it is clear that scenes depicting the newly formed Republic were of increasing ideological importance. Matthew Baigell asserts that after the War of Independence, 'a striking new subject matter appeared – the birth of a new country. An instant history and a new set of myths had to be visualized.'[1]

How did the painting of the post-revolutionary period 'visualize' this 'new set of myths'? What, in other words, was its image of the American scene? Leo Marx has situated this image in terms of the pastoral tradition, a 'middle landscape' between wilderness and garden in which the agrarian ideal comes to full articulation.[2] My interest, however, is to suggest ways in which a different symbolic structure emerges in this period. This structure – what I term the *domestic typology* of the post-revolutionary period – does not appropriate its image in the way Marx suggests, although it is dependent in many ways upon the pastoral tradition. Indeed, by looking at the use of domestic images in this period, we can begin to gauge a series of complex debates about the kind of iconography appropriate to an independent America and the way a mythology of independence is depicted in scenes of the land. If an ideal iconography emerges, it does so at the expense of both history and the variety of landscape (as distinct from wilderness) which made up the thirteen states. What we can detect is a domestic typology seeking mythic representation as a social ideal which, in its accumulative

146

meanings, suggests a more problematic image of landscape than Marx's account of pastoral can accommodate.

By 'domestic typology', then, I refer to those elements of what John Stilgoe has called the 'common landscape of America': the images and objects of a local man-made landscape (houses, bridges, barns, roads) which begin to make their appearance in the painting of the period and which increasingly signify a subtle structure of meaning.[3] It suggests both the development of a native tradition to counter the European influence so obvious in such painters as West, Feke, Stuart and Trumbull and a new insistence on landscape as subject rather than background. Flexner tells us that at Charles Willson Peale's Columbianum 1795 exhibition 'landscape vied for popularity with still life'.[4] The 'tradition' had come a long way since West's *Landscape with Cow*.

What was the distinctive American landscape of this time? Crèvecœur's *Letters from an American Farmer* (1782) gives us the quintessential image of a rural American land: 'we daily increase the extent of our settlements . . . We convert huge forests into pleasing fields . . .' exhibiting 'through these thirteen provinces so singular a display of easy subsistence and political felicity'. Everything in America, he continues, is 'modern, peaceful, and benign' and, thus, 'I had rather admire the ample barn of one of the opulent farmers . . . than study the dimensions of the temple of Ceres'.[5]

The distinction between Europe and America is obvious and, indeed, becomes a commonplace in the nineteenth century. There are, however, two aspects here which demand further comment. First, in drawing such a fundamental distinction between the 'barn' and 'Ceres', the speaker not only distances himself from a mythology antipathetic to his own tradition; he insists on a wholly distinctive visual index of symbolic meaning by which to measure the value of *his* landscape. Although Crèvecœur develops his image of America through a language essentially identified with the cultures against which he writes, his position is given immediate focus, and the language a significant context, in terms of the domestic image upon which his eye (and rhetoric) comes to rest: the barn. Thus, while we might identify allusions to Virgil and Theocritus, it is the barn which grounds such allusion, claims them as its own and allows its meaning to emerge in the context of a language which retains its novelty and, in social and cultural terms, its radical difference.

Indeed, it is by this usage of particular domestic images that the *Letters*

147

develops its picture of a rural America; a usage which separates New York, Pennsylvania and New England from the South and the West. Look, for example, at the famous 'scene' from *Letter III*. The 'enlightened Englishman', we are told, will see an America 'discovered and settled'. He will view

Substantial villages, extensive fields, an immense country filled with decent houses, good roads, orchards, meadows and bridges where an hundred years ago all was wild, woody, and uncultivated! What a train of pleasing ideas this fair spectacle must suggest; it is a prospect which must inspire a good citizen with the most heart-felt pleasure. The difficulty consists in viewing so extensive a scene. He is arrived on a new continent: a modern society offers itself to his contemplation, different from what he had hitherto seen. It is not composed, as in Europe, of great lords who possess everything and of a herd of people who have nothing . . . If he travels through our rural districts, he views not the hostile castle with the clay-built hut and miserable cabin, where cattle and men help to keep each other warm and dwell in meanness, smoke, and indigence. A pleasing uniformity of decent competence appears throughout our habitations. The meanest of our log-houses is a dry and comfortable habitation.[6]

The land is viewed as a text to be read – just as an 'enlightened Englishman' of the period would understand the way a landscape painting was to be read. As a text, however, as a prospect and spectacle (basic terms to ways of viewing eighteenth-century English and European landscapes), as a picture the scene refutes the reading (and presumably the assumptions) such an educated eye might bring to it. The difficulty consists, then, not so much in viewing the scene as how to view it, for the Englishman is not confronted with a strange landscape so much as a strange *typology*.[7] This is the cultivated northeast coast, not the western plains or southern swamps. Crèvecœur offers at once both a distinctive iconography and, by implication, an alternative register of meaning in which, once again, social, political and cultural assumptions are given distinctive presence and focus within an ideal visual syntax. The more one separates the elements of this 'scene', the more it is not a description but rather collation of individual cultural counters signifying a localized American landscape in which the idea of an independent, agrarian America is seen to be at work. Thus, as the castle and the mansion are rejected so icons of a different order take the eye's attention. These icons are radical and novel because they deny the picturesque (we are offered log cabins not cottages) and suggest a horizontal rather than a vertical scale of value. Everything (in its energy) builds toward this 'new' nation. The landscape is exemplary to the extent that it offers images of a wholly different order from the 'picture' of an English equivalent. This is an image of the land in which there is no colonial oligarchy nor Tory estates.

What seems remarkable about this passage is the extent to which it declares landscape as an ideological construct: a made text which itself assumes the image of its social and economic bases. If the scene appears a general one, it is surely because its rhetorical insistence hides the degree to which Crèvecœur has identified one type of American landscape as his ideal. This is not so much a 'pastoral' scene as one in which Crèvecœur would have farmed before the Revolution. It is the cultivated farmland of house, barn, fence, and field which he would have viewed in Pennsylvania, New York, and New England. Certainly the local (if widespread) nature of this image is made clear by the way in which Crèvecœur distinguishes it from other American landscapes. In *Sketches of Eighteenth Century America* this 'ideal' land is again given visual credence; in travelling from New Hampshire, 'Everywhere, you saw good houses, well-fenced fields, ample barns, large orchards'.[8] Domestic icons are associated with a moral vocabulary which, in terms of the myth produced, is more akin to the *Declaration of Independence* than Virgilian pastoral; for this sight of beneficence, of peace and plenty, is based upon values in which the moral, economic, and social indexes are seen as a single seam of well-being growing from the results of labour. How different from the South where, says Crèvecœur 'slaves may cultivate the smooth fertile plains'; but 'it is the hands of freemen only that could till this soil'. To look on his rural ideal is thus to assume that an 'honest' industry (in the eighteenth-century sense) is mirrored in what the eye sees: something 'the people of the South cannot boast of' for 'there they labor with slaves; here we do everything ourselves'.[9]

Crèvecœur's ideal scene, then, is a social and moral landscape read through a series of visual tokens. The meaning of the scene as a cultural text distinct from the (commercial and plantation based) South and the (individual and uncultivated) West is sanctioned through a domestic typology which at once informs and confirms the assumed social order; the South presents a vertical visual (and social) order, the West a scene equally inimicable to Crèvecœur's social ideal. Significantly, however, in judging the land as a token of settlement, it is architecture,

149

not cultivation, which is uppermost as a guide to the efficacy of the scene. Thus, the 'original log-house, the cradle of the American, is now gone and has made room for the more elegant framed one'.[10]

We can see a similar insistence on this particular kind of landscape in Timothy Dwight's *Travels in New England* (1821). Here, in remarkable detail, Dwight notes his search for the kind of scene which extols his American (New England) ideal. As such, for example, his use of 'beautiful' has nothing Burkean about it, nothing, that is, that would recommend it to the vocabulary of eighteenth-century landscape painting derived from Claude and Reynolds, or Price and Gilpin. 'Beautiful country', for Dwight, is 'lands suited to the purposes of husbandry' with 'scarcely a remote reference to beauty of landscape', and Dwight's 'beauty' is defined in relation to a series of measurable visual objects: 'In the year 1803, I found these settlements greatly improved. The girdled trees, stumps, and log-houses had in great measure vanished. In their places good farmer's houses ...'[11] This scale of judgment is used consistently in Dwight's *Travels*. He celebrates the house (the farmer's house) and he denigrates the log cabin just as he seeks evidence of advanced and settled cultivation (the fence) rather than new agricultural clearings (girdled trees). Foresters and pioneers are anathema to this ideal. So, too, is the settlement of the South. To him the plantation – socially and economically – is indicative of a hierarchy, antagonistic to what his eye wants. 'Scattered plantations', for example, 'are subject to many serious disadvantages', not least because 'That intelligence and sociability, that softness and refinement which prevail among even the plain people of New England disappear.' New England 'presents a direct contrast to this *picture*': an image, in other words, of community.[12]

Dwight's ideal, like Crèvecœur's, is a New England landscape of farm, village and orchard which signifies an assumed collective energy implicit of post-revolutionary social ideals. Indeed, Dwight offers both a detailed scale of meaning, and a detailed description of those elements which, in their specific presence, add ballast to Crèvecœur's 'national' rhetoric. Thus the *Travels* are full of domestic details – houses, barns, roads, mills, fences, and bridges. All are equated with a larger scale of value. 'Good' buildings are 'neat', 'tidy', and 'thrifty'. They are aspects of the life, liberty, and pursuit of happiness for which Dwight looks, and are distinct as much from the Southern market economy as from the lowliness of the pioneer whose log cabin 'deforms' the land. What

9 Unknown Artist, 'The Plantation', c.1825

emerges is a very particular iconography. It is a domestic index as fundamental to cultural meaning as the lists James and Eliot were to produce as part of *their* alternative cultural register: the farmhouse not the mansion, the barn not the castle.[13] It is a sense of the land of which Cobbett made so much in his visual experience of the barns in Pennsylvania.[14]

We have, then, a series of local landscapes which, through their distinctive domestic typology, extol an ideal landscape emblematic of an assumed national, post-revolutionary myth. It is by looking at this landscape that we can begin both to understand the significance of such typology in the painting of the period and, equally, to measure the painting's use of and relationship to the earlier dominant Claudian structures. This is most obvious in relation to the South. If Dwight sought an ideal New England index signifying 'community', in the South, as Stilgoe tells us, 'A big house objectified the hierarchical order of Southern colonial society, and it spoke forcefully of an economic order as eunomic as those of New Spain and New England'. Thus, 'After a century of colonization, typical Tidewater plantations focused on the big house, slave cabins, and a collection of other structures.'[15] According to L. M. Roth, during the eighteenth century 'the southern planters

10   Claude Lorrain, 'Jacob, Laban and his Daughters', 1654–5

attempted to emulate the high style of English country seats' and established a social landscape which was the image of its economic and cultural base: an élitist rather than democratic landscape made up of separate plantations not communal villages.[16] This was a scene quite opposite to that which Crèvecœur and Dwight found 'beautiful'.

'The Plantation' (pl. 9), for example, an anonymous 'primitive' representation (c. 1825) is wholly suggestive of this hierarchical order; in its (naive) vertical use of space it pictures a Virginian social structure inimical to Crèvecœur's 'new' world. The house is made both dominant and central – settled (seated) upon the 'hill' as it overlooks (and oversees) the scene beneath: a prospect, as it were, of imposed order and control. Beneath lie the lesser buildings: slave huts, working buildings, warehouses etc., and, at the base of the canvas, the waterfront, the final point of significance in a commodity market economy. Yet there is no figure in the picture and certainly no evidence of work. What the artist has done is to construct the plantation symbolically as a social and economic order. The values on which that order establishes its structure have been mapped out for us while simultaneously offering an image of the way in

152

which that order would see itself (as myth); for everything, as it were, flows. The hierarchy, and what it signifies, is encompassed within a border of trees and vines, and all is connected by paths and roads: a circular pattern which suggests a wholly integrated scene: a 'natural' and organic order. Similarly, 'The Washington' (painted before 1820), 'A picture of a country seat in Cincinatti ... on the Ohio'[17] reproduces a parallel structure to that of 'The Plantation': an order in this instance which has been extended to include a garden in the front of the house.

Although these are extreme examples they reveal the extent to which even at this time such domestic typology signified differing Americas and differing values. This use of the house as a central icon should also remind us of the extent to which the New England painter, as inheritor of a fully developed English academic landscape painting, looked upon a classical and pastoral tradition which, like the southern landscape, made the house, and the private estate, its central focus.

In eighteenth-century England the Claudian Italianate structure had established itself as *the* image of a beneficent order (see pl. 10). An ideal classical scene mirrored in park, garden, house and estate signified a different natural 'hierarchy' with the house at the centre (of power, of wealth, and of government). In part the Reynoldsian *beau ideal* buttressed these assumptions in which the myth of an agrarian order was literally pictured as a Claudian canvas. *Humphrey Clinker, Tom Jones, Mansfield Park* and Thomson's *The Seasons* all offer the house and the estate as an emblem at the centre of such a social order. It is a landscape similar to that found time and again in the paintings of Richard Wilson and Gainsborough and, on occasion, in Constable. In Wilson, for example, the Italianate formula is present to a high degree. Solkin has argued that it contains images of 'The Happy Rural Life' based 'within the countryside, or, more specifically, within the confines of a private estate'.[18] Claude was thus used to sanction a mythology of ownership just as the picturesque cultivated a way of handling the landscape beyond the confines of the estate. Cottages become parts of pictures, the Claude glass reflected the land as a picture, gypsies and itinerants are invoked in relation to Salvator Rosa and the sublime.[19]

Surprisingly, it is this Claudian structure we see at work in the early attempts to 'picture' the post-revolutionary landscape of New England and the northeastern seaboard. If it suggested the pastoral order which Marx sees as basic to the American vision, it equally implied – indeed

11 Ralph Earl, 'Daniel Boardman', 1789

invoked at every level – precisely the hierarchy which Crèvecœur dismissed as inimical to his ideal land. If a painter sought to image the land as American ideal, how might its alternative vernacular meaning be suggested within a framework which itself was antagonistic to the very values for which the Revolution spoke? Whereas, for example, William Williams's 'Conversation Piece' (1775) is nothing more than empty pastiche filled with an imaginary landscape; and if, as Flexner remarks, such British born landscapists as William Winstanley and William Groombridge 'painted America as if it were England',[20] can we view the use of landscape in American painting as distinctive in this period? Does it, in other words, offer an American image to match that of Crèvecœur and Dwight?

I think it does. I want briefly to relate the use of Claude within a distinctive American domestic typology to open up, as it were, the distance between a formal, European landscape tradition (with all that implies) and a native vision which ultimately emerges in the primitive and genre painting of the nineteenth century. I want to look at three American examples from the post-revolutionary period and compare them with contemporary equivalents. Two of them are by Ralph Earl, who was much influenced by his English experience, his awareness of the English landscape tradition, and his Tory sympathies. The third is by Samuel Morse. Painted in the 1820s, its single prospect of part of New York State suggests the Crèvecœurian dialectic.

'Daniel Boardman' (1789; pl. 11) is one of two portraits Earl completed of the Boardman brothers in New Milford, Connecticut, on the Connecticut River. Earl had returned to the United States from England in 1785 and this painting clearly shows the influence of eighteenth-century English portraiture. John Wilmerding remarks that 'the formulae of full-length portraiture … [were] grounded in the English academic tradition'.[21] They also extolled, in terms of landscape and the relationship between figure and land, the Claudian *beau ideal* of the kind frequently found in Reynolds and Gainsborough. At first glance this painting appears to follow the tradition: a full-length portrait in which, like any English gentleman, Major Boardman offers his identity to the world. Confident and assured, his relaxed position is a characteristic pose of the eighteenth-century English tradition. Similarly, the painting invokes aspects of a distinctive Claudian structure: the repoussoir trees, the use of water, and the 'smooth' hills of the background.

155

12 Thomas Gainsborough, 'William Woolaston', c.1759

And yet Boardman stands aside and offers for view not a private estate in the English sense, but a Connecticut prospect of New Milford given in extraordinary detail. The distinctive nature of this stance becomes clear if one compares it with an example from Gainsborough which focuses upon a single, full-length figure: 'William Woolaston' (c. 1759; pl. 12). While Boardman moves towards the margin, Woolaston remains central and dominates the painting. Just as he dominates, so his figure controls the space of the painting and of the scene behind, his house and estate. House and figure are, thus, emblems of a single vocabulary of ownership. Earl allows the space in the picture to spread. Boardman associates himself with the scene; he does not dominate. He invites us to share his confidence and establishes the terms on which the eye locates Boardman's America. New Milford is thus offered as the investment of meaning and is pictured in such a way that its value speaks to us through the iconography of its collective image. What we are given, in other words, is a scene of meeting house, farm, village, and fence. It is the ideal of Crèvecœur and Dwight: a settled land of human effort and community. New Milford, as a visual presence, has been 'fixed' in distinction from, rather than deference to, its Claudian counterparts.

There are two further aspects of the detail of New Milford in this painting which would have had a clear significance at this period: the colours of the buildings and the kind of fences in the picture. We may easily forget the importance of particular colours on domestic and public buildings, but their use at the end of the eighteenth century was of special note. They remind us that many of the buildings were built of wood rather than stone or brick. Wood was easily available, and it encouraged vernacular architecture and construction, as in the 'salt box' house. Such colours as red and brown were used to suggest brick. They provided decoration for farm and church to exemplify their symbolic meaning to the community and, of course, they prevented rotting. In particular, because (as John Stilgoe has pointed out) imported paint was taxed under the 1765 Stamp Act, it became a matter of national pride to use locally-manufactured materials.[22]

Some sense of the symbolic importance of colour is conveyed by the use of Spanish brown and white. Spanish brown was both cheap and abundant. It was used essentially as a functional colour, especially on barns, to cover wide surfaces. Its appearance in a landscape at once signified a farm building and suggested its status as a basic, *primary* pigment in the eighteenth-century American scene. For painters it was as far as one could get from the palette of Reynolds and the academy. So too with white, especially in New England. Stilgoe has remarked that white 'was new, completely new, as new as a democratic government free from parliament ... Along with a new flag, new currency, and new ordering of land, white lead paint announced a new country and a political philosophy grounded in liberalism.' It underlined 'the meaning of every farmhouse to the national policy'.[23] White, therefore, assumed a series of distinctive meanings in the home scene. As whitewashing according to Kocher, 'was considered to have a cleansing and sanitary result',[24] its appearance proclaims a dense symbolic vocabulary, whether in a painting or in the land itself. Finally, a painted building once again distinguished the settlement from the temporary and the mobile; they were part of, not distinct from, the setting.[25]

Colour created one kind of native vocabulary. Another kind was made by fences, 'which underwent major transformations on being re-established across the Atlantic'. Hedges were virtually unknown. The stone fence was popular in the north especially as evidence of cleared land. The 'worm' or zig-zag fence was associated with the frontier because of its basic, vernacular construction and easy mobility. In the works of William Sidney Mount, which register development of a fully realized domestic typology, the most unusual building is the barn, and the most usual fence is the worm or zig-zag. By the middle of the nineteenth century a different domestic order is offered. The character-istic native image of this period in New England is, as Zelinsky remarks, the rail and board fence, 'restricted to areas of more intensive culti-vation'; it was 'probably all (in design) of American origin'. The rail fence extolled a level of craftsmanship not to be found in the worm fence. It was confined to more intensively cultivated areas, but was completely American in design.[26] It was an image of *achieved* order: evidence, as Dwight saw, of cultivation and stability. A fence was not so much to keep individuals out as to keep wilderness at bay.

We can see, then, that in addition to an iconography of domestic architecture the landscape had invested in it a subtle and distinctive symbolic structure which signified a land shaped according to national ideals and values. It created a mythology that was rapidly to become as complex as its English equivalent. If we return to the Earl painting we can see how much meaning is invested in the precise colours used and the fences indicated. The dominant colours of the buildings are white and Spanish brown. Fences proliferate around the land and frame New Milford. The effect suggests that, while Earl works within a recognizable academic formula, he situates within the space of the painting an ideological difference which emanates from the careful notation of the native scene. If Boardman, as Flexner puts it, 'serves as doorman for his environment',[27] he does so in order to offer a myth distinct from the visual and cultural vocabulary of Wilson and Claude.

The distinction is made more obvious in Earl's 'Chief Justice and Mrs Oliver Ellsworth' (1792; pl. 13). This is an openly plotted painting in which a series of symbolic motifs offer a portrait of new nationhood. It is worth recalling the extent to which the arrangement of the figures, with the house in the centre, is reminiscent of English estate portraiture. If we compare Earl's painting with Arthur Devis's 'Robert Gwillym and his Family' (1745–7; pl. 14), we can see the degree to which Earl both invokes a typical estate portrait based upon 'a mythology of land-owning'[28] and yet situates the iconographic elements of his painting within an alternative myth of the land. In both paintings the house is central, with the figures of the family arranged on either side. While Devis associates the family *with* the house – and the estate – Earl creates a distinctive American iconography within which his house is to be understood. In addition, the room is significant in domestic and national terms because that is where the sitters received George Wash-ington.[29]

The house calls attention to itself because it is in the centre and, therefore, framed as a portrait. The plotted iconography is funnelled into its presence: it is the arbiter of meaning. As such, and perhaps as we might expect, it is a goodly eighteenth-century New England farm house, significantly white and fronted by a rail and board fence. The scene is given added credence by the way in which the Justice not only holds a copy of the *Constitution* in his hand but does so in a way which makes it parallel to fence and house. House and constitution are brought together just as the 'white' *Constitution* acts as a mirror-image to the house itself: a significant eunomic vocabulary of an assumed collective typology. The 'picture' of the house rests on the *Constitution* – held, in turn, by the hand of the Justice, as the Justice himself is backed by books (of law?) on which he, like the scene, bases his position. The house here,

13   Ralph Earl, 'Chief Justice and Mrs Oliver Ellsworth', 1792

as a symbol of order, has thus gained as much credence as the estate in eighteenth-century English painting, although fed by a distinct iconography and different myths.

Samuel F. B. Morse's 'View from Apple Hill, Cooperstown' (1828–9; pl. 15) suggests ways in which the Claudian structure is, once again, offered in terms of a tension between European and academic formulae and what we might identify as a nascent native vocabulary of the kind found in Earl. However, by the nineteenth century, it has become at once more displaced into a settled west and more mythicized as part of a folk America. A domestic typology is not to be found in the Hudson River painters, but rather in genre painters like Mount and Bingham, and primitive painters who, unaware of the Claudian motif, extol a naive image of the national myth.

Morse's painting exemplifies this tension. He visited the area in the

14 Arthur Devis, 'Arthur Gwillym and his Family', c.1745–7

summer of 1828. Apple Hill, near Cooperstown (the home of his friend, James Fenimore Cooper), was situated at the southern end of Lake Otsego, with the Susquehanna below it, and was purchased by James Adams Dix in 1828. Oliver Larkin tells us that the two female figures in the centre of the foreground represent Morse's 'hostess and her cousin' but these are of importance, it seems to me, not so much because of the artist's personal association with them as the way in which they establish the viewpoint by which we read the scene.[30] They recall, once again, aspects of formal eighteenth-century landscape painting and, more obviously, the use of the foreground figure in Wilson and Claude.

The configuration of landscape elements is clearly Claudian. So, too, is the height, in relation to the figures, from which we view the scene. The progression into the space of the painting is planular – a series of horizontal bends which 'funnel' the eye to its point of rest in the background. As a composition, then, it recalls both Claude and Wilson in its pastoral qualities, its use of figures, and the image of a peaceable

15 Samuel F. B. Morse, 'View from Apple Hill', c.1828–9

kingdom reflected in the composed idyll of the painting: a Claudian *paysage pastoral*.

Indeed, in its use of bridge and figures, Morse's painting creates parallels to specific paintings by both Claude and Wilson. Think, for example, of Claude's 'Landscape with Nymph and Satyr Dancing' (c. 1640–1) or 'Jacob, Laban, and His Daughters' (1654–5; pl. 10) and Wilson's 'Holt Bridge on the River Dee' (c. 1761–2), a painting deeply indebted to Claudian structure and mythology. In the Claude paintings the landscape is read in conjunction with a central narrative, which comprises figures and a bridge (a stock motif in Claude). It is precisely these elements which Wilson takes into his own Claudian version of England, giving to the painting an image of assumed harmony, unity, and control while, equally, as Solkin says, drawing 'upon the classical landscape tradition in order to endow a culturally significant British subject with an aura of venerable antiquity'.[31] Figures and bridge establish a unity of meaning, to which is added a church and ruins to create an image of balance, continuity, and tradition.

Landscape painting and domestic typology

If we look again at the Morse, we see that the figures and the bridge, as in Claude and Wilson, are central, and yet they have no resonance as integers of the scene. Unlike the figures in Claude and Wilson, these possess no narrative content. One is tempted to dismiss 'Apple Hill' as yet another pastiche of eighteenth-century landscape formulae lacking any sense of subject or, even, substance. But the figures in the foreground suggest otherwise. They invoke a tension at the centre of the painting. They exist as active ingredients of the scene, rather than passive motifs: for, as each figure looks in a different direction, so each is associated, janus-like, with different values in the painting. Two distinct 'pictures' emerge.

The figure with the face towards us looks out from a Claudian view; the figure who looks away (and leads our eye away) looks at a series of domestic buildings and a bridge. In these terms, the painting hangs in the balance: two halves, two perspectives, two viewpoints. The figure turned away, like the buildings, punctures the smooth surface of the Claudian mode and, as it does, gives the weight of the painting to the American buildings and the bridge. Lacking any association and value of the kind found in Wilson and Claude, Morse's bridge gains presence through its functional meaning: cutting across the Claudian space as it announces a made vernacular which, like the figure turned to it, will increasingly possess the eye.

'Apple Hill' thus signifies a different direction for the development of a domestic typology in American painting. It makes us aware, as does Earl, of the distinctive place such motifs have as emblems of one kind of America. It equally signifies the use of such motifs, not so much in land-scape painting (which in Luminism, for example, is to *exclude* the evidence of human settlement in favour of a pure moment), as in genre and primitive painting. Barn, house, field, road, and fence make up the 'Peaceful Village' (anonymous 1850): a display of New England motifs of the kind found in Dwight, just as Mount celebrates the barn as the vernacular symbol of a new America. It is worth recalling that the barn, which signified American prosperity to Cobbett, and which was so significant a building for Crèvecœur, becomes, by the time of Charles Sheeler, *the* American form. Like Cobbett, Sheeler was stunned by what he saw in Lancaster, Pennsylvania (see pl. 16). And like his post-revolutionary predecessors, Sheeler develops a domestic typology as *the* subject. But where, in the eighteenth century, Earl moved from history to myth, in the twentieth century, Sheeler has abstracted the myth into colour and space.

163

16 Charles Sheeler, 'Barn Abstraction', 1917

Landscape painting and domestic typology

Notes

1 Matthew Baigell, *A History of American Painting* (London: Thames and Hudson, 1971), p. 63.
2 Leo Marx, *The Machine in the Garden* (New York: Oxford University Press, 1964).
3 John R. Stilgoe, *Common Landscape of America, 1580 to 1845* (New Haven and London: Yale University Press, 1982).
4 James T. Flexner, *History of American Painting* (New York: Dover, 1969), vol. 1, p. 111.
5 Crèvecœur, *Letters from an American Farmer and Sketches of Eighteenth Century America*, ed. and intro. Albert E. Stone (Harmondsworth: Penguin, 1981), pp. 42, 47.
6 *Letters*, p. 67.
7 One thinks, for example, of Richard Payne Knight's poem, *The Landscape* (1749).
8 *Letters*, p. 265.
9 Ibid., pp. 265, 277. And for views of the South, see in particular, *Letter IX: 'Description of Charles Town'*.
10 *Letters*, p. 272.
11 Timothy Dwight, *Travels in New England and New York*, ed. B. M. Solomon with assistance of P. M. King (Cambridge, MA: Harvard University Press, 1965), vol. 4, p. 20; vol. 2, pp. 82–3.
12 Dwight, *Travels*, vol. 2, p. 243, my emphasis.
13 See the very different indices in James's *Hawthorne* and Eliot's *Notes Towards the Definition of Culture*.
14 See *A Year's Residence in the United States* (1830), where Cobbett speaks, for example, of Lancaster having '*Big Barns*, and modest dwelling houses'. They 'are very fine buildings. And then, all about them looks happiness! Such is the country of William Penn's settling!' (Arundel, Sussex: Centaur Press, 1964), p. 47. See also p. 48.
15 Stilgoe, *Common Landscape*, pp. 66, 69.
16 L. M. Roth, *A Concise History of American Architecture* (New York: Harper and Row, 1979), p. 40.
17 Wolfgang Born, *American Landscape Painting* (New Haven: Yale University Press, 1948), p. 126.
18 David H. Solkin, *Richard Wilson: The Landscape of Reaction* (London: Tate Gallery, 1982), p. 24. See also Michael Rosenthal, *Constable the Painter and His Landscape* (New Haven and London: Yale University Press, 1983).
19 In relation to this look at John Barrell, *The Dark Side of the Landscape* (Cambridge: Cambridge University Press, 1980).

20 Flexner, *History of American Painting*, vol. 2, p. 118.
21 John Wilmerding, *American Masterpieces from The National Gallery* (Washington: National Gallery of Art, 1980), p. 60.
22 Stilgoe, *Common Landscape*, p. 167.
23 Ibid., p. 169.
24 A. L. Kocher, 'Color in Early American Architecture', *Architectural Record*, 64 (1928), 287 (but see the whole article – pp. 278–90).
25 Of course, I am giving only a limited context for this New England colour. See what happens to 'white' in Melville, Dickinson, and Frost.
26 Wilbur Zelinsky, 'Walls and Fences', in E. H. and M. J. Zube, eds., *Changing Rural Landscapes* (Amherst, MA: University of Massachusetts Press, 1977), p. 54.
27 Flexner, *History of American Painting*, vol. 3, p. 20.
28 Solkin, *Richard Wilson*, p. 15. See also John Harris, *The Artist and the Country House* (London: Sotheby, Parke Bernet, 1979).
29 See John Wilmerding, *American Art* (Harmondsworth: Penguin, 1976), p. 52.
30 O. W. Larkin, *Samuel Morse and American Democratic Art*, ed. Oscar Handlin (Boston: Little, Brown, 1964), p. 92.
31 Solkin, *Richard Wilson*, p. 208.

11 * Winter landscape in the early Republic: survival and sentimentality

BERNARD MERGEN

'Some people are weatherwise, but most are otherwise', Benjamin Franklin wrote in 1735, in lines with more truth than poetry.[1] Yet the popularity of his own *Poor Richard's Almanac* and similar publications helped to make Americans aware of their climate and the new science of meteorology.[2] By the time the colonies gained their independence there was considerable knowledge of the weather of the eastern United States and strong opinions about it. Early manifestations of the political division of 'frost belt' and 'sun belt' states may be found in essays, poetry, and art dealing with winter, winter landscape, and snow in the years between 1776 and 1866.

Images of General George Washington and his troops crossing the ice-choked Delaware River in 1776, and camped in the snow at Valley Forge, Pennsylvania, in 1778, are forever fixed in the minds of Americans and enshrine the Revolution in terms of fortitude and endurance. Residents of the northern states knew all too well that winter was a test of their hardiness. Citizens of the southern states considered themselves fortunate to be spared the months of snow and ice suffered by their neighbors. The ingenious Yankees made a virtue of necessity, however, by claiming that their ability to survive was proof of their moral as well as physical superiority. Moreover, the long winters provided a time of freedom, creativity, renewal, and recreation in the fullest sense. The contrasts made between winter as a test and as a time of fulfilment created a complex literature filled with paradoxes.

A newcomer's eye helped St John de Crèvecœur to see the paradox of winter weather in 1778. 'A Snow Storm as it Affects the American Farmer', written in English while he was living in Herkimer County, New York, offers a nearly complete analysis of the meanings of winter

167

storms.[3] 'Of all the scenes which this climate offers,' Crèvecœur observes, 'none has struck me with a greater degree of admiration than the ushering in of our winters, and the vehemence with which their first rigour seizes and covers the earth; a rigour which, when once descended, becomes one of the principal favours and blessings this climate has to boast of.'[4]

The explanation of this paradox is that while the farmer and his wife must work hard to be sure that they have stored enough feed for their livestock, repaired their sheds, stables, barn-yards, partitions, racks, and mangers, and prepared 'raiment, fuel, and victuals' for their family and tenants, the farmer learns to be 'prudent', 'vigilant', and 'assiduous'. Thus, the need to provide for a long and hard winter teaches foresight and makes the American farmer superior to 'the wretched of Europe'.

Moral superiority is not the only reward of American winters in the north. Deep snow and frozen lakes bring improved communication among neighbors. The need to clear drifting snow from roads causes communities to work together. Sleighs move more quickly than wagons. This is, Crèvecœur says, 'the season of merriment and mutual visiting. All the labours of the farm are now reduced to those of the barn; to the fetching of fuel and to cleaning their own flax. The fatigues of the preceding summer require now some relaxation.'[5] This idyllic life continues until spring thaws mire the roads and disrupt travel, an irony Crèvecœur savors by contrasting life in the northern states with that in the south where rain kept roads impassable much of the year.

If there is a hint of the beginning of a political debate in this, it is not surprising. In 1785 Thomas Jefferson published his *Notes on the State of Virginia*, a defense of his native land against the criticisms of the Comte de Buffon and others. As Stephen Fender has remarked, Buffon believed that flora and fauna degenerated in America. In part, this occurred because, thought Buffon, America had a cold, damp climate caused by a profusion of trees and wild vegetation.[6] Jefferson's answer went beyond refutation, arguing that, 'Snows are less frequent and less deep. They do not often lie, below the mountains, more than one, two, or three days, and very rarely a week. They are remembered to have been formerly frequent, deep, and of long continuance. The elderly inform me the earth used to be covered with snow about three months in every year.' Although this reply might be dismissed as propaganda, or as faulty use of oral history, it should be added that Jefferson goes on to say that the warming trend has 'produced an unfortunate fluctuation between heat and cold, in the spring of the year, which is very fatal to fruits'.[7] Warmer was better for Jefferson, and his optimism led him to forecast a sunny future for the new nation.

Whatever Jefferson's intentions, his belief in a warming trend was challenged by Noah Webster in a paper read before the Connecticut Academy of Sciences in 1799. Webster offered a sophisticated explanation that modern ecologists confirm:

It appears that all the alternations in a country, in consequence of clearing and cultivation, result only in making a different distribution of heat and cold, moisture and dry weather, among the several seasons. The clearing of lands opens them to the sun, their moisture is exhaled, they are more heated in summer, but more cold in winter near the surface; the temperature becomes unsteady, and the seasons irregular. This is the fact. A smaller degree of cold, if steady, will longer preserve snow and ice, than a greater degree, under frequent changes. Hence we solve the phenomenon, of more constant ice and snow in the early ages; which I believe to have been the case. It is not the degree but the steadiness of the cold which produced this effect. Every forest in America exhibits this phenomenon. We have, in the cultivated districts, deep snow today, and none tomorrow; but the same quantity of snow falling in the woods, lies there till spring. The same fact, on a larger scale, is observed in the ice of our rivers. This will explain all the appearances of the seasons, in ancient and modern times, without resorting to the unphilosophical hypothesis of a general increase of heat.[8]

With that parting blast, Webster turned a discussion of the weather into a political contest, hard winter Federalist against warming trend Republican.

A corollary to these positions on weather is the attitude of the antagonists toward memory as a source of information about changes in climate. While Jefferson accepted the statements of the elderly at face value, the Federalist Timothy Dwight, Webster's mentor, concluded that 'Few persons remember the state of the weather for any length of time.'[9] Dwight elaborated on Crèvecœur's theme in 'Greenfield Hill', a long poem published in 1794, the year before he became President of Yale. For Dwight, winter is a time to enjoy leisure without guilt, a time to meet old friends and remember good times.

> How pleas'd, fond Recollection, with a smile,
> Surveys the varied round of wintery toil . . .
> Yet even stern winter's glooms could joy inspire:

Bernard Mergen

Then social circles grac'd the nutwood fire; . . .
And Hospitality look'd smiling round,
And Leisure told his tale, with gleeful sound.[10]

Winter may be gloomy, but the snow, freshly fallen, contributes to the beauty of the scene in which the tales are told. Webster, ever the champion of New England, allowed himself a personal opinion in his *American Dictionary of the English Language* in 1828, when he concluded his definition of snow with the observation that 'When there is no wind these crystals fall in flakes or unbroken collections, sometimes extremely beautiful.'[11]

Although Americans lagged behind French and British scientists in the study of weather, their almanac writers kept them amused and instructed on the meanings of the weather. Most of the hundreds of almanacs published every year contained calendars with the times of sun rise and sun set, phases of the moon, vague weather predictions, and some random historical facts. Some printed stories and verse. By 1790, few almanac printers were taking themselves or their weather predictions seriously. 'Instead of inserting the *Weather* in the body of it,' wrote the author of *Bickerstaff's Boston Almanack, or Federal Calendar for 1790*, 'I have related some Remarkables that I imagine of equal service; not that I can't fortell the *Weather* to a *Mist* or a *Fog* as well as any man living; but lest some errors mighty escape the *Press*, and should the word *fair* be printed instead of *foul*, numbers might probably agree upon a *frolic* or journey, and be baulk'd, consequently a whole day is lost, for when *Body* and *Mind* too are dress'd in their Pontificalibus, they are seldom or never fit for business upon disappointment; by which the Public would suffer greatly.'[12]

Within this attempt at satire there lies a philosophy of storms, a belief that while the weather is unpredictable, human behavior is not; or, to put it another way, that the one predictable thing about the weather is its variability, a rule that people will use to justify their own unruliness. Note too that it is 'bad' weather, 'mist', 'fog,' and 'foul', that leads to comic misbehavior, a notion carried further by Philip Freneau, Nathaniel Hawthorne, and Henry David Thoreau. It is difficult to say whether the author of *Bickerstaff's* almanac consciously associates meteorological conditions with disorder and irrationality – as did the Romantic poets – but the subtlety of the passage contrasts with other almanac verse of the same year. Most are platitudinous:

170

Winter landscape in the early Republic

> Now Wintry West extends his blast,
> And hail and rain doth blow;
> Or stormy North send driving forth
> The blinding sleet and snow.

Or roughly humorous:

> Now lisps Sir Fopling, tender weed!
> All Shiv'ring like a shaken reed!
> 'How keen the air attacks my back!
> 'John, place some list upon that crack;
> 'Go sand-bag all the sashes round,
> 'And see there's not an air-hole found –
> 'Ah! bless me, now I feel a breath,
> 'Good lack! 'tis the chill of death.'[13]

Both verses, from *Father Hutchins Revived*, an almanac for the year 1790, illustrate the theme of winter as a test of physical and moral strength. Other almanacs of the same year, such as *The New England Almanack* and *Poor Richard Improved*, address this theme with home remedies for frost-bite and exposure.[14] Although almanacs finally lost their central place in American literature, they continued to provide commentary on the weather and the effects of cold and snow throughout the years of the early Republic. By the 1830s and 1840s the almanac writers had created what might be called the frozen traveler motif in writing about the dangers of winter. A variation on this motif, the frozen woman, is developed in both the almanacs and popular songs.

The Improved Farmer's and Scholar's Almanack for 1832, by Dudley Leavitt of Concord, New Hampshire, contains two illustrations of the frozen traveler. The first, in the calendar for February, says simply, 'Keep your roads well broken out that travellers may pass without sticking in a snow drift. Never make a fuss about breaking out the roads.' The second is more complex, being a song supposedly composed about 1630 and written down from memory by a 92-year-old woman in 1791. Called the 'Forefather's Song' by Leavitt, the concluding lines warn:

> Our mountains and hills and our vallies below;
> Being commonly cover'd with ice and with snow;
> And when the north-west wind with violence blows,
> Then every man pulls his cap over his nose;
> But if any's so hardy, and will it withstand,
> He forfeits a finger, a foot or a hand.[15]

171

17 Unknown Artist, illustration in *The People's Almanac*, 1841

Two years later *The People's Almanac* of Boston printed what it called an 'Affective Narrative of a Woman's Sufferings in a Snow Bank', the story of Elizabeth Woodcock who, in February 1799, was riding from Cambridge to Impington, Massachusetts, when she was forced to dismount and then became trapped in a snow bank for eight days. After her rescue her feet had to be amputated and she lived only five months. The almanac writer does not comment, but the incident is described in considerable detail and illustrated with a woodcut, captioned with two stanzas of a ballad that begins:

> She was in prison as you see,
> All in a cave of snow;
> And she could not relieved be
> Though she was frozen so.[16]

This story contains the familiar theme of winter as a test, but it concerns a failed test in the remote past. The pessimistic mood continues in the 1841 edition of the same almanac, where, under the entry for January the anonymous author writes:

Cold as a coy damsel on her first introduction to the man she is destined to marry, commences the new year. On upland and plain, in valley and dell, the bleached bones of the deceased year are found ... The lonely traveller, weary with floundering through the drifted snow, and circumnavigating the treacherous bogs and half hidden springs of water, sits down to rest in the rustling woods, screened from the cold wind by the thick but naked branches of many trees; and here he ponders on his far off home, the quiet fire-side, the hissing tea-urn, and the busy wife, and sighs as he recollects the distance which still lies between him and the centre of his hopes and fears.[17]

The mixture of metaphors, the bleakness of the description, and the woodcut that illustrates the traveler covering his eyes with his hand (pl. 17), all suggest a depth of despair absent in previous winter scenes.

Variations on this maudlin theme may be found in popular songs thought to have been composed in the 1840s. 'Young Charlotte', the best known of these, was composed in 1843 by Seba Smith, a New York journalist and humorist. Versions have been collected by folklorists from the Appalachians to the Ozarks and as far west as Utah. The song tells of a beautiful young woman who lives with her parents fifteen miles from the nearest village. On New Year's Eve she is picked up by her escort in a sleigh, but she refuses to ride under a blanket because she wants everyone to see her ball gown. When they reach the dance, her lover discovers that Charlotte has frozen to death. He returns her body to her parents, then dies of grief.[18] Clearly Charlotte's vanity killed her as much as the cold, but there is a sense in which the frozen woman is a symbol for all lost promises and dashed hopes.

Another ballad of the period, also attributed to Seba Smith, 'She Perished in the Snow', describes the death in a snow storm of a mother and her two children.[19] A third example, collected from a resident of the Outer Banks of North Carolina, admonishes the listener to 'remember the poor' when 'the snow is on the ground' and the icy fingers of death threaten travelers. Reflecting its southern origins, the song indicates that the traveler has more to fear from rising flood waters during a thaw, than from the actual cold, but it contains a number of warnings to both men and animals that give it a kinship with the frozen wanderer stories and songs.[20]

In both 'Young Charlotte' and 'The Snow is on the Ground', there are scenes of pleasure and contentment by warm firesides, the promise of leisure extolled by Crèvecœur and Dwight. The Jeffersonian poet Philip Freneau continued to explore this theme in poems written between 1810 and 1827. In 'The Farmer's Winter Evening', Freneau presents the appeal of long dark winter nights during which young men court rural maids with fanciful tales, and both 'jovial swains' and farmers' daughters listen to 'the hoary headed sage/Recall the days of youthful age'.[21] Winter night is the time for art as well as love, a belief that Freneau maintained despite many personal failures. His last known poem, written in 1827 when he was an embittered alcoholic, is titled simply 'Winter':

> The Sun hangs low! – So much the worse, we say,
> For *those* whose pleasure is a Summer's day;
> Few are the joys which stormy Nature yields
> From blasting winds and desolated fields;
> *Their* only pleasure in that season found
> When orchards bloom and flowers bedeck the ground.
>
> But, are no Joys to these cold mouths assign'd?
> Has winter nothing to delight the Mind?
> No friendly Sun that beams a distant ray,
> No social Moons that light us on our way? –
> Yes, there are Joys that may all storms defy.
> The chill of Nature, and a frozen Sky.
>
> Happy with wine we may indulge an hour;
> The noblest beverage of the mildest power.
> Happy, with Love, to solace every care,
> Happy with sense and wit an hour to share;
> These to the mind a thousand pleasures bring
> And give to winter's frosts the smiles of spring,
> Above all praise pre-eminence they claim
> Nor leave a sting behind – remorse and shame.[22]

Clearly influenced by European Romanticism and his own unhappiness, Freneau is nonetheless making an interesting argument for the reversal of conventional symbols of summer and winter by suggesting that the pleasures of summer are tainted by remorse and shame while those of winter can be indulged in without guilt, perhaps because the delight is more in the mind than the flesh. The association of winter with memory, which in turn inspires imagination and produces art, seems to become stronger as the country grows older. One of Hawthorne's early essays published in *Twice-Told Tales* in 1837, is called simply, 'Snow-flakes', but it is a subtle commentary on the creative process. Hawthorne first remarks on 'The two or three people visible on the side-walks, [who] have an aspect of endurance, a blue-nosed, frosty fortitude, which is evidently assumed in anticipation of a comfortless and blustering day.'[23] After this clear reminder of an earlier interpretation of winter landscape, he comments on the total transformation the snow will bring, covering the earth and preventing it from seeing 'her sister sky'. We also will lose sight of mother earth, causing us to look heavenward more often.

This scene set, Hawthorne becomes a meteorologist of Romantic weather, forecasting hours of inspiration. 'Gloomy as it may seem,' he writes, 'there is an influence productive of cheerfulness and favorable to imaginative thought, in the atmosphere of a snowy day ... Blessed, therefore, and reverently welcomed by me, her trueborn son, be New England's winter, which makes us, one and all, the nurslings of the storm, and sings a familiar lullaby even in the wildest shriek of the December blast.' Looking out of his study window into the storm he sees school-boys having a snowball fight, then he imagines a traveler frozen to death in the snow, and finally he sees a flock of snowbirds, 'playmates of the storm', which cheer his spirit. What can we make of these images? The snowball fight, 'a pretty satire on war and military glory', should, Hawthorne feels, end in the building of a monument of snow of which future observers will ask, 'How came it here?' For Hawthorne, it might jocularly be said, the snowforts of children are the American equivalent of European ruins.

Hawthorne also reflects his ambivalence toward some of the reform movements of his time through a metaphor taken from winter weather. His story 'The Snow Image', published in 1851, tells of two children who build a playmate of snow. The snow girl comes to life and plays with them until their father returns home and insists on bringing her into the house. As she melts, Hawthorne offers two observations: first, 'that it behooves men, and especially men of benevolence, to consider well what they are about, and, before acting on their philanthropic purposes, to be quite sure that they comprehend the nature and all the relations of the business in hand'; second, that 'there is no teaching anything to wise men', because, 'should some phenomenon of nature or Providence transcend their system, they will not recognize it, even if it come to pass under their very noses'.[24] Hawthorne's 'Snow-Image' may be the most complex of the winter images in American literature. Certainly it is one of the most extended metaphors in which snow stands for creativity. Yet the creative playfulness of childhood melts away from the demands of adults and what might have been becomes a puddle for the servant to wipe up.

At one point in the story Hawthorne has a flock of snowbirds flutter around the little snow girl, bestowing on her the life of 'old Winter's grandchildren', and referring to his earlier story on snowflakes. These birds, a type of finch, clearly fascinated writers on the winter landscape. Thoreau refers often to these and other birds that survive the harsh New England winter. Despite the fact that the cold winters at Walden suggest the possible extinction of life, Thoreau also sees winter as a time when nature is simplified, allowing a close examination. In the essay 'A Winter Walk', published in *The Dial* in 1843, he writes: 'In Winter nature is a cabinet of curiosities, full of dried specimens, in their natural order and position.'[25] In *Walden* (1845) he dwells on the metaphor of the ice of Walden pond. 'Why is it', he asks, 'that a bucket of water soon becomes putrid, but frozen remains sweet forever? It is commonly said that this is the difference between the affections and the intellect.' For Thoreau, the winter landscape served as a convenient slate on which to write his personal feelings. Or, to use his own punning metaphor, 'this plain sheet of snow which covers the ice of the pond, is not a blancness as yet unwritten, but such as is unread.'[26]

Thoreau read many signs in the winter landscape, some of them seemingly contradictory. In his journal for the winter of 1840–1, he describes a scene that anticipates the paintings of George Henry Durrie and the lithographs of Haskell and Allen. 'The snow hangs on the trees as the fruit of the season ... The whole tree exhibits a kind of interior and household comfort – a sheltered and covert aspect – It has the snug inviting look of a cottage on the Moors, buried in snow.' A month later he pursues part of this image and discovers visual puns in the snow [that] collects upon the plumes of the pitch pine in the form of a pineapple, which if you divide in the middle will expose three red kernels like the tamarind stone. So does winter with his mock harvest jeer at the sincerity of summer. The tropical fruits which will not bear the rawness of our summer, are imitated in a thousand fantastic shapes by the whimsical genius of winter.[27]

Playfully, Thoreau amuses himself by turning the conventional and sentimental image of the cottage in the snow into a kind of frozen jungle.

Ralph Waldo Emerson also links the theme of survival with the idea of winter as a time of creativity in a suggestive way. The imagery of the first stanza of his poem 'The Snow-Storm' (1841) seems conventionally romantic:

> ... the whited air
> Hides hills and woods, the river, and the heaven,
> And veils the farm-house at the garden's end.
> The sled and traveller stopped, the courier's feet
> Delayed, all friends shut out, the housemates sit
> In a tumultuous privacy of storm.

The snow storm functions as a screen between man and God, man and nature, order and disorder. The second stanza reveals that the storm has blown against trees, fences, and buildings, creating fantastic shapes resembling castles and sculptures, a new and possibly higher order. Works of art that took centuries to construct in the old world are revealed to be mere imitations of 'the mad wind's night-work,/The frolic architecture of the snow'.[28] Thus the American winter landscape is primordial, but it is the creation of a force that is neither rational nor serious.

Changing attitudes toward snow and winter weather, from a test of character to a time of creativity, are clearly seen in the paintings and lithographs of the 1830s and 1840s. One of the first professional artists to paint a winter scene was Thomas Doughty of Philadelphia. After a trip to New England he painted 'Winter Landscape' in 1830, showing a lone driver in a small one-horse sleigh. The road the driver is following disappears into the horizon with just a portion of a roof and chimney suggesting home. Driver and horse are dwarfed by snow-covered trees and a bluff overhung with snow. Although it is not threatening, it suggests a long, cold journey similar to the one taken by the ill-fated Elizabeth Woodcock. Doughty's empty landscape contrasts with those

18 Unknown Artist, 'Winter in the Country', n.d.

of Thomas Birch, done in the 1830s, and of Durrie, done in the 1840s and 1860s, which illustrate the work and leisure routines of winter as described by Crèvecœur. In these paintings the sleigh usually carries four passengers and nearby farm buildings and livestock are arranged in an orderly display. One of Durrie's favorite themes was gathering wood, an activity that he sometimes combined with scenes of celebration, such as the popular 'Home to Thanksgiving', which Currier and Ives made into a lithograph in 1867.[29]

Other lithographers developed such scenes. Two, made by Haskell and Allen in Boston, illustrate the themes of historic struggle and contemporary leisure. 'Winter in the Country' (pl. 18) depicts a family of five walking across a small bridge toward a seventeenth-century-style home. The man carries a load of wood, followed by a boy dragging a stick. The effort to heat their home appears great, but the sense of hardship is relieved by the presence of a woman in a red dress standing in the doorway welcoming the family from its outing. The second litho-

19 Unknown Artist, 'Winter', n.d.

graph, titled simply 'Winter' (pl. 19), shows a sleigh with four persons passing an ox-drawn sled loaded with wood, a substantial house, and eight children sledding and playing in the snow. The children's sleds all have names – 'Gen. Grant', 'Rover', 'Racer', 'Ranger', and 'Clipper'.

One of the most elaborate of the winter lithographs is 'A Home in the Country – Winter', published by Thomas Kelly in New York about 1869 (pl. 20). The landscape appears to be the outskirts of a suburb or small town and contains six pleasure sleighs, an ox-drawn sled piled with wood, and another small work sled pulled by a horse. Adding to the traffic congestion on the roads are several boys sledding and having a snowball fight. A pond filled with skaters, a three-storey Victorian mansion, a farm house, and the inevitable dog complete the scene. 'A Home in the Country – Winter' is the visual equivalent of John Greenleaf Whittier's well-known poem 'Snow-Bound' (1866):

179

A Home in the Country
WINTER

20 Unknown Artist, 'A Home in the Country – Winter' n.d.

We felt the stir of hall and street,
The pulse of life that round us beat:
The chill embargo of the snow
Was melted in the genial glow; ... [30]

Kelly's lithograph and Whittier's poem are good summations of mid-nineteenth-century American attitudes toward winter. Snow storms and snow-covered landscapes no longer symbolized suffering and isolation, but childlike freedom and recreation. In the aftermath of the Civil War the moral superiority of the northern states with severe winters was self-evident. Americans had found a useable past in their memory of the storms of their youth, of well-earned leisure and the means to enjoy it.

Notes

1 *Poor Richard's Almanac*, Dec. 1735, np.
2 Chester Jorgensen, 'The New Science in the Almanacs of Ames and Franklin', *The New England Quarterly*, 8 (1935), 551–61.
3 St John de Crèvecœur, *Sketches of Eighteenth Century America*, eds. Henri L. Bourdin, Ralph H. Gabriel, and Stanley T. Williams (New York: Benjamin Blom, 1972).
4 Ibid., pp. 39–40.
5 Ibid., p. 49.
6 See the essay by Fender in this collection. For an elaboration of this point see also Robert Lawson-Peebles, *Landscape and Written Expression in Revolutionary America: The World Turned Upside Down* (Cambridge: Cambridge University Press, 1988).
7 Thomas Jefferson, *Notes on the State of Virginia*, ed. William Peden (Chapel Hill: University of North Carolina Press, 1955), p. 80.
8 Noah Webster, *A Collection of Papers on Political, Literary, and Moral Subjects* (New York: Webster and Clark, 1843), p. 119. Quoted in David M. Ludlum, *Early American Winters 1604–1820* (Boston: American Meteorological Society, 1966), p. 239.
9 Timothy Dwight, *Travels in New England and New York*, ed. Barbara Miller Solomon (Cambridge, MA: Harvard University Press,1969), 1, 42.
10 Timothy Dwight, *Greenfield Hill: A Poem in Seven Parts* (New York: Childs and Swain, 1794), p. 32.
11 Noah Webster, *An American Dictionary of the English Language* (New York: S. Converse, 1828), np.
12 Benjamin West, *Bickerstaff's Boston Almanack, or Federal Calendar for 1790* (Boston: F. Russell, 1789), np.
13 Father Abraham Hutchins, *Father Hutchins Revived; Being an Almanac and Ephemeris of the Motions of the Sun and Moon ... for the Year of Our Lord 1790* (New York: Hodge, Allen, and Campbell, 1789), np.
14 *Poor Richard Improved: Being an Almanack and Ephemeris for ... 1790* (Philadelphia: Halle and Sellers, 1789), np.; *The New England Almanack and Gentlemen and Ladies Diary ... 1790* (New London, CT: T. Green, 1789), np.
15 Dudley Leavitt, *Leavitt's The Improved Farmer's and Scholar's Almanack, for the Year of Our Lord, 1832* (Concord, NH: Horatio Hill, 1832), np.
16 *The People's Almanac* (Boston: Willard Felt and Co. and Charles Ellms, 1834), pp. 12–15.
17 *The People's Almanac*, 1841, np.
18 Norm Cohen, ed., *Vance Randolph Ozark Folksongs* (Urbana: University of

Illinois Press, 1982), pp. 528–32. I would like to thank Alan Jabbour for this reference.

19 Norman Cazden, Herbert Haufrecht, Norman Studer, eds., *Folk Songs of the Catskills* (Albany: State University of New York Press, 1982), pp. 255–8.

20 Anne Warner, ed., *Traditional American Folk Songs from the Anne and Frank Warner Collection* (Syracuse, NY: Syracuse University Press, 1984), pp. 364–6.

21 Fred Lewis Pattee, ed., *The Poems of Philip Freneau* (Princeton: The University Library, 1907), pp. 394–6.

22 Lewis Leary, ed., *Last Poems of Philip Freneau* (Trenton, NJ: Rutgers University Press,1945), p. 123.

23 Nathaniel Hawthorne, 'Snow-Flakes', in *Twice-Told Tales* (Columbus: Ohio State University Press, 1974), pp. 343–9.

24 Nathaniel Hawthorne, *The Snow-Image and Uncollected Tales* (Columbus: Ohio State University Press, 1974), p. 25.

25 Henry David Thoreau, 'A Winter Walk', *The Dial* (October 1843), p. 233.

26 John C. Broderick, ed., *Henry David Thoreau Journal* (Princeton: Princeton University Press, 1981), vol. 1, p. 207.

27 Thoreau *Journal*, vol. 1, pp. 210, 238.

28 Ralph Waldo Emerson, 'Snow Storm' in *The Complete Essays and Other Writings* (New York: The Modern Library College Editions, 1950), pp. 768–9.

29 The pictures by Doughty and Durrie are reproduced in, respectively, Harold H. Dickson, *Arts of the Young Republic: The Age of William Dunlap* (Chapel Hill, NC: University of North Carolina Press, 1968), plate 103, and J. L. Pratt, ed., *Currier and Ives: Chronicles of America* (Maplewood, NJ: Hammond, 1968), p. 233.

30 John Greenleaf Whittier, *Snow-Bound: A Winter Idyll* (Boston: Ticknor and Fields, 1866), pp. 49–50.

12 * The dark view of things: the isolated figure in the American landscapes of Cole and Bryant

ALLEN J. KOPPENHAVER

From the very first encounter with the American terrain, writers and artists have documented an overpowering feeling of loneliness. As William Bradford noted of the Puritan landfall in 1620:

Being thus passed the vast ocean, and a sea of troubles before in their preparation ... they now had no friends to welcome them nor inns to entertain or refresh their weatherbeaten bodies; no houses or much less towns to repair to; to seek for succor.

Similarly, Mary Rowlandson, taken captive by Indians during the 1676 massacre at Lancaster, Massachusetts, recalled that:

All was gone, my husband gone ... My children gone, my relatives and friends gone, our house and home and all our comforts within door and without, all was gone (except my life); and I knew not but at the next moment that might go too. There remained nothing to me but one poor wounded babe.[1]

What is significant about these extracts, written at different times and in different circumstances, is that they account for distress in terms of absences. Loneliness, of course, is not a uniquely American experience. But a comparison with the German painter Caspar David Friedrich will point up the distinction. Deeply imbued with Romantic solitude, Friedrich's canvasses nevertheless deploy that solitude in terms of presences, the ghosts which are evidence of the generations which have lived on German soil. In contrast, the American landscape is outside history. It does not belong to any group or race recognized within the limited confines of Western 'civilization'. Hence the negations which inform the laments of Bradford and Rowlandson, and which recur throughout American writing, most famously in Henry James's com-

183

plaint that his homeland has 'no shadow, no antiquity, no mystery, no picturesque and gloomy wrong' – in other words none of the 'associations' discussed earlier by Stephen Fender, no sense of the past with memories and ghosts.[2]

There are other factors which contribute to the pervasive sense of loneliness which runs through the American arts. The Puritan religion, of course, demanded isolation; but a sense of alienation was common to most immigrants, no matter their country or origin or religious background. The American continent, too, presented a landmass too large even for the grandest imperial conception. It would only be described in pejorative terms as a 'wilderness' or 'desert'. Yet another element is the awareness that culture, like nature, is transient and fleeting. When Rip Van Winkle awakes from his twenty-year sleep he discovers that everything has changed, and in consequence he has lost his identity: 'God knows', he exclaimed, at his wit's end, 'I'm not myself – I'm somebody else – that's me yonder – no – that's somebody else got into my shoes – I was myself last night, but I fell asleep on the mountain, and they've changed my gun and everything, and I'm changed, and I can't tell what's my name, or who I am!' Likewise, in 'The Legend of Sleepy Hollow' the 'incessant changes' of this 'restless country' comically afflict even the ghosts. They have scarcely finished 'turning over in their graves before all their friends have moved elsewhere'.[3] Loneliness, it seems, pervades the American arts at all times and in all places. Ishmael survives and Huck Finn lights out alone. Loneliness helps to forge Hemingway's strong characters. It is the natural condition even of café habitués in Edward Hopper's paintings. It provides the focal point of one of the first important novels written in the new Republic, Charles Brockden Brown's *Edgar Huntly* (1799). Huntly's recollection of waking in the absolute darkness of a cave, conscious of 'nothing for a time but existence', provides both the severest negation of the constituents of identity and a forerunner of the existential inquisitions of Edgar Allan Poe.[4]

The second quarter of the nineteenth century has often been categorized as a period of expansive optimism producing, on the one hand, the landscape art of the Hudson River school, a celebration of the majestic expanses of wilderness, and, on the other hand, the work of William Sidney Mount and George Caleb Bingham, devoted to portraying the democratic ideals of the community. Yet even in the midst of this period there were artists who expressed a strong sense of loneliness and isolation, who wished to explore the depths of their own humanity rather than reflect the so-called heights of prosperity. They found in the landscape not God, gold and glory, but rather the truth that man is ultimately alone. They often presented this awareness literally by depicting solitary figures in their landscapes. I have in mind here the poet William Cullen Bryant and the painter Thomas Cole, the 'Kindred Spirits' of Asher Durand's justly famous painting.

William Cullen Bryant is rarely read or taught nowadays, largely because he is remembered as a warm, kindly old man of a dreamily Romantic bent who described death in 'Thanatopsis' as simply a gently falling asleep. Instead, it is Poe, Melville and Hawthorne who tend to be regarded as the key figures for their accounts of 'the Power of Blackness'. Yet there is a strong if elusive darker strain in Bryant's work. Influenced by the English school of graveyard poetry, Bryant often dealt with death. Once again, however, the distinction must be made between Europe and America. Gray's graveyard is a populated landscape, a resting place for the dead yet alive with social commentary. In contrast, Bryant's death poems are depictions of solitude, seldom containing more than the mourner and the mourned. It is, rather, the landscape which looms large in these poems. It is not a tamed and comfortable place of repose, but a borderland which disrupts the values of the community by showing how easily the wilderness can triumph. In 'Rizpah', for instance, the protagonist has to drive beasts of prey away from the unburied bodies of her children. Those who are buried soon find, as in 'The Two Graves', that their resting place is quickly overgrown by brambles; or are nameless, forgotten and trampled, as in 'No Man Knoweth his Sepulchre'. At best, as in 'The Burial Place', the graveyard is graced by a briar rose on its broken ground.[5]

The deaths that Bryant describes are often dark, as in 'Earth', 'Massacre at Scio', 'The Murdered Traveller' and others. The speaker of a dramatic monologue, 'An Indian at the Burial-Place of his Fathers', laments the death of his tribe and predicts that the white 'race may vanish, hence like mine / And leave no trace behind'. Similarly, 'A Walk at Sunset' depicts a desolate landscape that is uninhabited, and runs together the present plight of the Red Man with the future fate of 'civilization':

21 Thomas Cole, 'Tornado', 1833

Farewell! but thou shall come again – thy light
 Must shine on other changes, and behold
The place of the thronged city still as night –
 States fallen – new empires built upon the old –
But never shalt thou see these realms again
Darkened by boundless groves, and roamed by savage men.[6]

These last poems bring Bryant close to the concerns of his 'kindred spirit', Thomas Cole, and recall scenes from Cole's series of paintings titled 'The Course of Empire'. Bryant and Cole often drew upon each other for ideas and support. For instance, Cole's 1833 canvas 'Tornado' (pl. 21) depicts a lone figure clinging to a broken tree in left centre foreground, against a backdrop of black, blasted trees and wild, bleak skies. Bryant's 1827 poem 'The Hurricane' seems almost to be a description of the painting. Throughout the poem the language is violent and fearsome, with a 'burning sky', 'heavy gales' and a 'mighty shadow borne along'. And, just as Cole's painting emphasizes the loneliness of the wind-blown refugee from the storm, clutching the tree that dwarfs him, so Bryant's closing lines concentrate upon the narrator who has been describing the terrible effects of the storm:

And I, cut off from the world, remain
Alone with the terrible hurricane.

The sudden shift of focus reveals that the poem is as much a psychological account of alienation as a naturalistic portrait of the storm.[7]

Bryant's 'The African Chief' again depicts the agony of a solitary figure, but this time in a market place where a proud African slave tries to bargain for his freedom, but is scorned by the trader who ultimately drags him 'forth upon the sand, / The foul hyena's prey'. A convinced Abolitionist, Bryant often attacked slavery in his writing. What is important here, however, is that he chooses to underscore the evil done by one person to another by casting the African upon a harsh landscape, to die a victim of a predatory beast.[8]

Bryant's accounts of loneliness are often created by a sudden reversal. In 'A Winter Piece', for instance, he spends most of the poem describing the beauty of the forest, and treats its loneliness as something familiar and positive. It is a poem of the seasons, progressing from Autumn through to Spring. At a surface level, therefore, it anticipates the positive thrust of Thoreau's *Walden*. Yet the superficial optimism is negated in the last six of its 118 lines, in which we see that before Spring can come the hail shall strike the earth and 'the loud North again / Shall buffet the vexed forest in his rage'. The sombre ending contrasts interestingly with Robert Frost's poem 'The Onset'. Frost shows winter burying the landscape in the bleakness of snow. Yet the poem ends with the promise of the renewed freedom of Spring, and blends the landscape with an image of community:

> Nothing will be left white but here a birch,
> And there a clump of houses with a church.[9]

A reversal into a bleak ending occurs again in 'The Prairies', one of Bryant's most famous poems. For the most part, the poem is a reverie about vanished Indian tribes, and therefore returns to the imperial theme. It is set on the 'boundless and beautiful' prairies of Illinois, visited by Bryant in 1832. The Indians have 'long passed away', the sole evidence of their presence being burial mounds. The poem thus treats the pastoral in elegiac mode, sustaining it for 120 lines. The mood is suddenly punctured by the appearance of the narrator on centre stage:

> All at once
> A fresher wind sweeps by, and breaks my dream,
> And I am in the wilderness alone.

The abrupt change, emphasized by the closing adverb, reveals that the reverie is none other than a stereotypical approach to a characteristic American landscape. The dream allows the narrator to be caught off-guard, thus heightening the reversal and underscoring the essential alienation of the narrator from his environment.[10]

In his poem 'To Cole, The Painter, Departing for Europe', Bryant describes the landscapes which Cole had painted in America and which the poet had used for the settings of his own work: 'lone lakes', 'skies, where the desert eagle wheels and screams', and the 'autumn blaze of boundless groves'. In the last line of the poem Bryant appeals to Cole to 'keep that earlier, wilder image bright' before his eyes. 'Brightness' has often been a term associated with Cole's American landscapes. He tends to be regarded as a father of the Hudson River school and his canvasses are usually regarded as optimistic. It is possible, however, to see a different strain in his work if it is examined closely and in the context of his writings.[11]

The isolated figure in the landscapes of Cole and Bryant

In a letter of 1836 to Asher Durand, who had been one of his students, Cole remarked that:

I often think that the dark view of things is perhaps the true one. If such a view were always presented, I doubt whether we could long survive ... Heaven dazzles and deceives, perhaps, that we may live.

Cole thus anticipates T. S. Eliot's remark in 'Burnt Norton' that we 'cannot bear very much reality'. He saw the darker side of humanity. Standing at the Fortress Maschio in Volterra in 1831, he was reminded of the human cruelty that the building symbolized. Wonderful the Medici undoubtedly were, but 'why are we offered such a picture of lights without shadows?' he added. 'Why not at least a few touches of the tyranny and "damned deeds" of these great men?'[12]

Aware, too, of the grandeur of the Colosseum, he nevertheless thought back to the 'awful' spectacles that took place in this 'crater of human passions', that would in the course of time be reduced to 'desolation'. His painting of the 'Interior of the Colosseum' (pl. 22), executed around 1832, emphasizes this perception of the Roman past. It is painted from the point of view of the interior, the sole human presences apparent in the far distance, each barely more than a brush stroke and each standing in one of the arches beyond the structure. The canvas is dominated by the massive, ancient broken wall in the middle-ground and the memorial slabs in the foreground, forbidding reminders of the bloody imperium.[13]

It might be useful to reiterate the distinction between the American and European view of landscape. It is quite normal in Romantic landscape painting to portray human beings as dwarfed by the environment. Yet in European painting humans are endowed with character and identity. In the characteristic Constable landscape humans are identified by their work or leisure pursuits. In the more melodramatic John Martin canvasses – such as 'The Bard' or 'MacBeth and the Witches' – the individuals are identified as famous historical or literary figures. In the typical Cole painting, on the other hand, human beings are anonymous, as in the 'Interior of the Colosseum', or are lost from view. In 'The Oxbow', for instance, we see an artist's equipment, but not the artist. An absence such as this, reminiscent of the complaints of William Bradford and Mary Rowlandson quoted earlier, contrasts not only with European painting but with the social concerns of William Sidney Mount. Mount's

22 Thomas Cole, 'Interior of the Colosseum', c.1832

23 Thomas Cole, 'The Desolation of Empire', 1836

1838 'The Painter's Triumph' is, of course, deeply ironic in its depiction of the artist as hero, but the artist is nevertheless the central controlling presence.[14]

In contrast, the landscape supplied Cole at times with reminders of absent humanity. Hiking in the Catskills, Cole came upon a stone outcropping called 'The Old Man of the Mountain', which he described in his journal as 'a singular crag of some fifteen hundred feet aloft, having the features of a human face'. The meeting was a shock:

Indeed, there was an awfulness in the deep solitude, pent up in the great precipices that was painful . . . features, that bent their severe expression upon me were too dreadful to look upon in my loneliness.[15]

Cole's greatest testament to the tragic fate of humankind is 'The Course of Empire', his series of five paintings for Luman Reed. James Fenimore Cooper described the series as 'the work of the highest genius this country has ever produced . . . one of the noblest works of art that has ever been wrought'. The sequence is well known. The first canvas

191

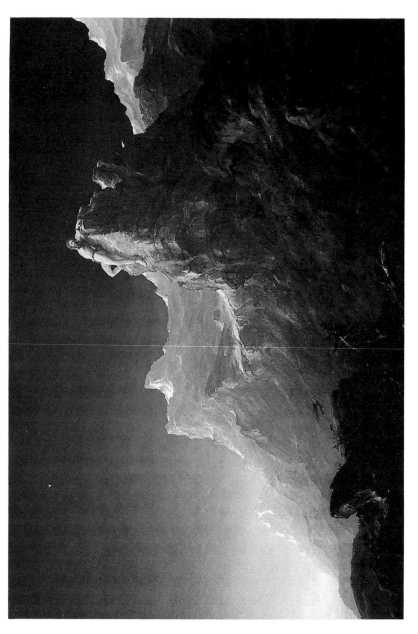

24 Thomas Cole, 'Prometheus Bound', 1846–7

depicts the savage state, while the second and third present a classical arcadia and a Roman city at the height of its power. The fourth shows the same city attacked by Barbarians, and emphasizes the conflagration by the use of purple and dark red background colours. The last canvas, 'The Desolation of Empire' (pl. 23), provides a stark contrast. It is lit solely by the moon, reflected in the empty bay and picking out fragments of architecture covered by vines and bushes. The same physical landscape stands as mute testimony to the rise and inevitable fall of human aspirations. Cole emphasized the absence of humanity in the fifth canvas in a letter to Luman Reed:

no human figure – a solitary bird perhaps: a calm and silent effect. This picture must be as the funeral knell of departed greatness, and may be called the state of desolation.

Cooper regarded it as the capstone of Cole's achievement, proving 'the final nothingness of man'.[16]

The foreboding which informs the early canvasses of 'The Course of Empire' may also be seen in a later painting, 'Prometheus' (pl. 24). The early morning sun just begins to colour the sky and the background hills are a ghostly pale blue and white. The morning star hangs lonely in the sky, a reminder of the night. Prometheus is the only living being in the desolate landscape. The moment is carefully chosen, for it is just before the birds gather to disembowel him. The dread of anticipation and a sense of overwhelming despair is thus captured at the moment before terrifying consummation. The sense of powerlessness and loneliness is heightened by the use of the rock familiar from 'The Course of Empire', jutting high into the mid foreground where Prometheus is tied. At one point during the preparation of the canvas Cole painted out the figure. Fortunately he changed his mind, for all the aspects of the Prometheus myth which he could have painted, he chose the one which fully achieves the overwhelming despair that is mankind's fate.

Cole did not always depict such a despairing state. A short story probably written around 1827 and unpublished in Cole's lifetime both resembles the work of Poe and anticipates the strength of character celebrated by Hemingway. The tale begins in characteristic mood:

I was alone and a stranger in the wilderness. Men in the midst of society and the tumult of cities do not experience those vicissitudes of feeling that result from the mutation of natural objects. But a lone man in the wild is affected by every change.

193

25 Thomas Cole, 'Expulsion from The Garden of Eden', 1828

As the evening imparts a greater gloom to the scene the protagonist climbs a mountain and dives into deep water. He finds a small island on which to rest; and then realizes that there seems to be no escape, for the walls surrounding the lake are sheer. Plunging again into the water, he is filled both with despair and a strange pleasure at 'the fearful sublimity' of his plight. He grasps a floating fragment of a tree and with it floats out into moonlight and freedom. By strength of will he has survived.[17]

Certainly, Cole realized that 'the darker view of things' did not find a ready market. Of his painting 'The Ruined Tower' he remarked, 'there is a stillness, a loneliness about it that may reach the imagination' – but added, 'it is not the kind of work to sell'. He tried therefore to find a balance to set his pessimism in perspective. Indeed, such a balance accorded with the optimistic elements in his character. During an 1837 tour in search of 'the picturesque' he wrote a poem which celebrates both the beauty of the environment and its 'wildness, storm, and flood'; and he concludes with the 'Spirit of Wilderness' singing:

> I spread my shapeless pinions o'er this my calm domain,
> A solitary realm it is, but here I love to reign.

He particularly loved Schroon Lake in the Adirondack Mountains, not only because it was an untamed world unchanged for centuries, 'affected only by the sunshine and the tempest', but because it represented a frontier. 'We stand,' he noted, 'on the border of a civilized plain and look into the heart of nature.'[18]

It was precisely that balance between pessimism and optimism, between 'the heart of nature' and human activity, that Cole sought in a number of his works. He loved to paint paired canvasses depicting success and defeat, a group of knights venturing out to do battle and returning reduced and defeated. His best-known pair is undoubtedly the 1827–8 'The Garden of Eden' and 'Expulsion from the Garden of Eden'. In the first he created, he said, 'a happy spot wherein all the beautiful objects of nature were concentered'. The centrifugal thrust of the second painting (pl. 25) was, Cole added, heightened 'by giving a glimpse of the Garden of Eden in its tranquillity'. The canvas therefore contains its own balance. It is divided almost evenly by a high free-standing arch under which Adam and Eve have just passed. To the left is the world which overwhelms and terrifies the young couple. The landscape is violent, a dark brown with craggy rocks, stormy sky, and in the foreground a wolf devouring a buck it has just killed. The imagery of the open gate gives the obvious clue to the painting's psychological freight: it is a metaphor of birth into the real world from the protection of the womb. Balancing this terrifying vision is a retrospective view of the world they have lost, adding further depth to Cole's tragic vision.[19]

Yet even in attempting to provide a balance in his paintings, Cole did not please the public, as he noted with despair in his journal in 1841:

I am not the painter I should have been had there been a higher taste. Instead of working according to the dictates of feeling and imagination, I have painted to please others in order to exist. Had fortune favored me a little more than she has, even in spite of the taste of the age, and the country in which I live, my imagination should not have been cramped, as it has been; and I would have followed out principles of the beauty and sublimity which have been cast aside, because the result would not have been marketable.[20]

Cole here revealed a further reason why the artist in America depicted states of loneliness and alienation. The public in America did not support the artist. The reasons for this are several and well known: the suspicion of works of the imagination which was the legacy both of Puritanism and Scottish Common Sense, the lack of adequate copyright protection, a subservient preference for the productions of the Old World, and a belief that in a new and growing country it was more noble to plough than to paint or write poetry. The stony soil of American public esteem forced many a painter and writer to give up. Samuel Morse, a pivotal figure in Graham Clarke's essay on early American landscapes, renounced his career as a painter in 1840. Nine years later he still felt bitter about it. Writing to James Fenimore Cooper, he lamented:

The very name of *pictures* produces a sadness of heart I cannot describe. Painting in America has been a smiling mistress to many, but she has been a cruel jilt to me. I did not abandon her; she abandoned me.[21]

Morse is now remembered as the inventor of the telegraph. In contrast, the arts did not abandon Bryant and Cole. Indeed, perhaps the lack of public understanding forced them to become kindred spirits; but then they already had a number of attitudes in common, including the dark view of things.

The isolated figure in the landscapes of Cole and Bryant

Notes

1 Bradford, *Of Plymouth Plantation*, ed. Samuel Eliot Morison (New York: Knopf, 1952), p. 61. Rowlandson, *Narratives of the Indian Wars*, ed. Charles Henry Lincoln (New York: Charles Scribner's Sons, 1913), pp. 121–2. On the theme of loneliness in American literature and culture, see Edwin T. Bowden, *The Dungeon of the Heart: Human Isolation in the American Novel* (New York: Macmillan, 1961); Richard McLanathan, *The American Tradition in the Arts* (New York: Harcourt, Brace, 1968), p. 460; and Philip Slater, *The Pursuit of Loneliness: American Culture at Breaking Point* (1970; rpt Harmondsworth: Penguin, 1975).

2 James, *Hawthorne* (New York: Harper and Brothers, 1894), pp. 42–3. Representative examples of Friedrich's paintings are to be found, for instance, in Barbara Novak, *Nature and Culture: American Landscape and Painting, 1825–1875* (London: Thames and Hudson, 1980), pp. 184–7. For an illuminating discussion of absence in American Literature, see Terence Martin, 'The Negative Structures of American Literature', *American Literature*, 57 (March 1982), 1–22.

3 Washington Irving, *The Sketch-Book of Geoffrey Crayon, Gent* (New York: G.P. Putnam's Sons, 1864), pp. 68, 483–4.

4 Brown, *Edgar Huntly*, ed. David Stineback (New Haven: College and University Press, 1973), p. 154.

5 Bryant, *Poems* (London: Kegan Paul, Trench, Trübner, 1890).

6 Ibid., p. 43.

7 Ibid., p. 133; my emphasis.

8 Ibid., pp. 114–16.

9 Ibid., pp. 32–6. Frost, *Poetry and Prose*, ed. Edward Connery Latham and Lawrance Thompson (New York: Holt, Rinehart and Winston, 1972), p. 92. This theme is further explored in Bernard Mergen's essay, in this collection.

10 Bryant, *Poems*, p. 151. A further reading of this poem is given in Stephen Fender's essay in this collection.

11 Bryant, *Poems*, p. 144. On Cole and his relationship with Bryant see James T. Callow, *Kindred Spirits: Knickerbocker Writers and American Artists, 1807–1855* (Chapel Hill: University of North Carolina Press, 1967); James Thomas Flexner, *The Light of Distant Skies: American Painting 1760–1835* (New York: Dover, 1954) and *That Wilder Image: The Painting of America's Native School* (New York: Bonanza Books, 1962); Oliver Larkin, *Art & Life in America* (New York: Rinehart and Co., 1949); Walter Nathan, *Romanticism in America* (New York: Russell and Russell, 1961); and Charles Sanford, 'The Concept of the Sublime in the Works of Thomas Cole and William Cullen Bryant', *American Literature*, 28 (1957), 435–47.

197

12 Cole, letter 18 Aug. 1836 to Durand and notebook 24 Aug. 1831, in Louis Legrand Noble, *The Life and Works of Thomas Cole*, ed. Elliott S. Vesell (Cambridge, MA: Harvard University Press, 1964), pp. 164, 98. Eliot, 'Burnt Notion', *Collected Poems and Plays* (New York: Harcourt, Brace and World, 1971), p. 118.

13 Noble, *Cole*, p. 116.

14 Mount's 'The Painter's Triumph' may be found in Alfred Frankenstein, *Painter of Rural America: William Sidney Mount* (Washington DC: H.K. Press, 1968), p. 25.

15 Noble, *Cole*, p. 67.

16 Ibid., pp. 137, 130, 174. The series, 'The Course of Empire', is to be found in Novak, *Nature and Culture*, pp. 11–13.

17 Noble, *Cole*, p. 97.

18 Ibid., p. 145.

19 Ibid., p. 64.

20 Cole, journal 30 May 1841, in Noble, *Cole*, p. 220.

21 Morse, quoted in David Tathen, 'Samuel F. B. Morse's *Gallery of the Louvre*: The Figures in the Foreground', *The American Art Journal*, 13 (Autumn 1981), 48.

13 * The figure of the Indian in photographic landscapes

MICK GIDLEY

1

Eadweard J. Muybridge's 'Indian Village, Fort Wrangle, Near Mouth of the Stachine River, Alaska' (1868; pl. 26) includes on its left a huddle of Indians, three women in dark cloaks (or perhaps blankets clasped at the throat) and a man. They are seated on a rocky beach surrounded to the right by luxuriant foliage – firs, bushes, flowers, grasses – so framed as to occupy fully half the picture, almost overwhelming the left side: the Indian figures, the expanse of still water behind them and, in the far distance across the channel, a group of scarcely visible buildings, smoke, a tree-filled ridge and, beyond, a hazy hill. The Native Americans simply sit, all of them looking at the camera, unsmiling, with nothing, apparently, to do. It is impossible to determine why they were included at all – unless their presence in itself was thought to exoticize an otherwise banal scene of water and woods somewhere in the Pacific Northwest, thus justifying it, making it, indeed, an 'Indian Village ...'

By contrast, the Apaches in Timothy O'Sullivan's 'View on Apache Lake, Sierra Blanca Range, Arizona' (1873; pl. 27), although simply sitting on their heels or standing, leaning on their rifles, seem a necessary element in the composition, most notably in that one figure, squatting on a rock in the centre, forms the inevitable focus for the viewer's first gaze. 'View on Apache Lake', with its still, reflecting pool surrounded by cottonwoods is, in effect, an image of Indians at home in, even at one with, their own environment. John C. H. Grabill's 'Villa of Brule' (1891; pl. 28) seems the same kind of image, but out of a more wintry climate. It presents a panoramic vista of tepees spread in all directions across the hillocks of a vast plain, interspersed with groups of small

199

26 Eadweard Muybridge, 'Indian Village, Fort Wrangle, Alaska', 1868

27 Timothy O'Sullivan, 'View on Apache Lake, Arizona', 1873

Mick Gidley

28 John C. H. Grabill, 'Villa of Brule, S. Dakota', 1891

figures going about their business and, in the foreground, some ponies standing in and drinking from a bend in an otherwise frozen stream.

Consider the very title of one of Sumner Matteson's pictures (originally inscribed directly onto the print): 'Ute Indians inspecting the first bicycle track seen in the White River Cañon. "White man heap lazy, sits down to walk" ' (1901).[1] It guides the viewer's thinking about this study of three figures, one kneeling, one standing and one mounted, the sandy cañon floor below them, and the bare, steeply shelving cañon walls rising behind them. The picture is manifestly *about* Indian responses to a new phase of white movement into their land and, sophisticated viewers that we are, we know that the jocular subtitle for

202

29 Francis Harper, 'Tom Hill at his Boat Landing', New York, 1910

the image may well not have represented what the three figures actually believed. There is ample room for other interpretations.

Francis Harper's untitled 1910 picture of Tom Hill at his boat landing in Mastic, Long Island (pl. 29), is both more and less open to interpretation. In some ways it, too, might be taken to be about acculturation, for instance in that the solitary Indian figure looking out over a broad expanse of unruffled sound both holds a very 'traditional' eel spear and wears conventional American shirt, jacket and trousers – what at the time, when assumed by Indians, was called 'citizen's dress'. But in other respects the photograph constitutes a genre study. With its frame encompassing the apparently almost haphazard arrangement of boats, one of them piled with carved bird decoys, the net-drying rack, boxes and other fishing implements, it seems a photographic equivalent to, say, William Sidney Mount's painting 'Eel Spearing at Setauket'

203

(1845),[2] in which the landscape is but the setting for one of mankind's manifold activities.

In counterpoint, there are certain landscapes, Western ones, whose whole *raison d'être* seems to lie in their Indianness. I am thinking of Thomas McKee's views, made in 1900, of Spruce Tree House and other newly discovered ancient Indian ruins in the cañons of Mesa Verde, Colorado, and of the innumerable depictions of inhabited Southwestern pueblos made by such photographers as O'Sullivan, William Henry Jackson, Jack Hillers, Charles Lummis, Matteson, and Joseph Mora.[3] The Hopi pueblo at Walpi, the oldest continuously inhabited community in North America, its stone houses perched atop a steep mesa which rises to the north of Arizona's Painted Desert, seems to have acted as a continuous attraction. The same might be claimed of Taos, northernmost of the Rio Grande pueblos, with its adobe apartment house structures and exterior, mound-like ovens.

Strangely, while the photographers just mentioned were often concerned to capture individual portraits and groups of dancers taking their allotted parts in the celebrated ceremonial life of the pueblos, especially the Hopi Snake Dance, when they composed landscapes in these places they tended to do so without figures, or with figures so static as to appear part of the very masonry on which they stand. Mora's widespread view of Pendenta Kiva in the Tewa village of Hano, taken between 1904 and 1906,[4] with the characteristic kiva ladders pointing skyward from the submerged chamber, stone house wall, some smoking chimneys and, way below First Mesa, little fields and the desert extending to infinity, is typical. Similarly, Lummis's 'Taos Pueblo from the Northeast' (c. 1887–96)[5] clearly shows the two major structures, south and north houses, sage and fields in the foreground, but not a soul in sight.

This initial selection of photographs to exemplify certain trends in the representation of the Indian figure – like, indeed, the slightly larger one constituted by this essay as a whole – is somewhat arbitrary. Although all the images were made by reasonably well-known photographers at different dates, it is virtually impossible to verify the degree to which they are in fact representative. In painting there are numerous depictions of the Indian figure in the landscape, certainly too many for any single person to know them all; but in photography the problem is of such magnitude that it is virtually of a different kind. The very nature of photography as a *mass* medium means that the numbers of potentially relevant images are uncountable. In the archives of the Smithsonian Institution alone there are over 30,000 Indian photographs.[6] Given this problem of plenitude, there are obvious dangers in basing decisive judgments upon a few chosen images, however discussable each one may be. Also, looked at individually, they tend to float free as purely formal constructs. The titles or captions may, as we have seen, limit or expand the viewer's interpretation. Similarly, the images may be contextualized to some degree by the viewer's own range of reference, as in my comparison with genre painting; but fuller contextualization ought to be attainable.

2

One of the many images in *Frank Leslie's Illustrated Newspaper* of 11 December 1886 is a wood engraving titled 'Scene in Glen Cañon, on the Colorado of the West – Photographing a Child of Nature' (pl. 30). It depicts a photographer crouched under his hood taking a picture of a young Indian woman. She stands with her back to a sheer cliff-face. Behind both photographer and woman is a rather foreshortened landscape of cañon walls towering either side of the river which, at the base, flows between them. The image in itself is not particularly memorable. Its composition is relatively conventional and the engraving process has been executed with no appreciable degree of finesse. Nevertheless, if we look at some of the relationships represented here – in the woodcut itself, in its immediate setting within the pages of an illustrated magazine, and in its wider cultural situation – it constitutes, I think, a suggestive text.

The young woman or girl faces the camera and out of the picture towards the viewer. Her stance is virtually that of someone leaning against a surface to the rear. But it is not definitely so. She does not relax against the rock wall, but rather flattens herself against it: her body language, like that of the Indian women in Muybridge's 'Indian Village', seems to speak of at least some degree of discomfort. The photographer, for his part, has his head hidden and his back to the viewer as he faces the Indian woman. And he looks at her through the mechanical eye of his camera. She is the object of his stare and the subject of his picture. He is making an image of her within a chosen environment, part of which forms the background to his composition. He is an anonymous figure

FRANK LESLIE'S
ILLUSTRATED
NEWSPAPER

col
86

No. 1,629.—Vol. LXIII.]   NEW YORK—FOR THE WEEK ENDING DECEMBER 11, 1886.   [Price, 10 Cents.

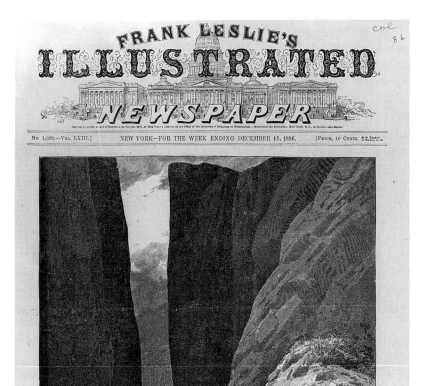

SCENE IN GLEN CAÑON, ON THE COLORADO RIVER OF THE WEST.—PHOTOGRAPHING A CHILD OF NATURE.

30 Engraving, 'Scene in Glen Cañon', 1886

whose position within the picture invites the viewer's gaze inwards. The viewer, in effect, sees both roughly what the photographer sees through his lens and, we are sure, more than the photographer can contain within his frame. The main visual component available to the viewer which would be visible only in part through the photographer's camera is the extent of the landscape, its soaring cañon walls, and these cannot even be contained within the frame of the wood engraving, the 'scene'. The image itself, that is, directly presupposes a viewer in front of it and intimates an expansive landscape beyond it.

The first part of the caption used in *Leslie's*, 'Scene in Glen Cañon, on the Colorado of the West', serves to locate the image topographically. But it does more than just that. It informs the reader that he or she is looking at a depiction of a precisely named place near the Grand Cañon in Arizona; it also inevitably evokes the idea (and aura) of 'the West'. The image, in other words, presents both an area of space and an event in time. The root meaning of the word 'scene' implies that this image proffers an episode in the unfolding drama of the West.

The designation in the remainder of the caption of the young woman as a 'Child of Nature' serves to point up her Indianness, and in specific ways. Her dress in the image is certainly non-white and possibly, to white eyes, exotic. (There is also in her hair-style at least the suggestion of the extravagant squash blossom fashion traditionally adopted by unmarried Hopi women.) She is a 'child' less in terms of age than in those of race. Sometimes, as we have already witnessed in the case of Matteson's image, a caption – in Roland Barthes's formulation – 'invents an entirely new signified which is retroactively projected into the image, so much so as to appear denotated there'.[7] Here the use of the expression 'Child of Nature' especially prompts the viewer not just to be aware of the woman's position in the natural environment in the physical sense, but as closer to the moral category of 'Nature' (with all its associations, good and ill) than to that of 'Civilization'.[8] In this picture it is the photographer to whom she is juxtaposed who implicitly represents Civilization.

'Scene in Glen Cañon' did not begin life as a woodcut but, in accordance with common practice at the time, was itself based on a photograph, possibly by E. O. Beamon, official photographer for John Wesley Powell's 1871 expedition on its descent of the Colorado.[9] This mongrel derivation has a number of ramifications. On the one hand, a photograph, unlike an engraving in itself, possesses a necessary relation-ship, however complex or fraught, with the actual time and place of its making, and is imbued, therefore, with a kind of authority. This one, in its reproduced form in *Leslie's*, is obviously intended for consumption by Eastern folks – why else point to the Colorado as a river 'of the West'? – and conveys information of various sorts to people who, it is assumed, do not know such scenes directly.

On the other hand, photographs of Indians and the West like this one were not seen by most people – unless as stereocards – in actual photographic form; rather, they permeated the culture in various kinds of engraving and were thus inflected by the preconceptions of the West held by engravers and, in some ways, occupied a similar status to actual engravings. That is, they contributed, willy nilly, to the limitation through repetition – indeed, the standardization – of representation of the West and its denizens. This little-known image of an Indian figure in an unmistakably Western landscape has a relationship to countless others – drawn, painted, engraved, or photographed – and all of them contributed to and partook of much discussed ideas and myths of the West.[10] For instance, when Matteson's image of the bicycle tracks was reproduced in 1903, *Leslie's* readers were informed that the leading scout was, in truth, a murderer. This was the *wild* West![11] Those myths and ideas of the West were, in turn, bound up with the actual historical process of white westward expansion. 'The whole imaginative and intellectual life of a culture', as Conor Cruise O'Brien put it, 'is one interacting field of force',[12] and such reciprocities, some of which will be held up for examination here, are tantamount to its moving particles.

3

From its origins, landscape as an artistic genre has often testified to contradictory generative impulses. Clearly, one has been reverence for nature, perhaps nature itself seen as a symbol, even an emanation, of God (as evoked by Philip Stokes in an earlier essay in this book). Another impulse of quite a different order, as John Berger has shown, and as others have affirmed with reference to the American context, has to do with the very acquisition and ownership of land itself.[13] What position could the Native American hold in landscapes thus propelled? One of Currier and Ives's popular allegorical prints actually about white westward expansion and land acquisition, 'Across the Continent' (or 'Westward the Course of Empire Takes its Way') of 1868,[14] placed Indian figures quite straightforwardly. While a settlement, complete with school house, rises on the left and a train prepares to make its way to the horizon on undeviating steel rails, the horses of two mounted Indians baulk at the train smoke which blows in their faces and threatens to obscure them altogether. In the case of photography, the connection between land ownership and landscape was less direct, but essentially just as intimate.

It was no accident that so many aspects of the era of massive white expansion into the trans-Mississippi West came before a camera lens. With the partial exception of the early fur-trading companies, the principal agents of exploration and settlement employed photographers. Government explorers, army surveyors and fort builders, the manufacturers of wagons and railroads, bosses and ranchers: all wanted a record of their activities. Eventually, of course, professional photographers themselves, as individual entrepreneurs, began to set up shop in the new towns of the region and, finally, amateur photographers would arise. As Susan Sontag said, 'Faced with the awesome spread and alienness of a newly settled continent, people wielded cameras as a way of taking possession of the places they visited'.[15]

Thus it was that Muybridge could work as an 'Official Photographer' for a while before striking out on his own; that O'Sullivan could create the range of landscapes mentioned in this book during service with the King and Wheeler surveys; that Hillers could photograph 'all the best scenery' when he took over from Beamon on the second descent of the Colorado with Powell's government party; that E. A. Guernsey could portray a line of wagons climbing a makeshift timber-buttressed road; that Andrew J. Russell, employed by Union Pacific, could celebrate, like other photographers, the driving in of the golden spike when his railroad met the Central Pacific at Promontory Point, Utah; that Laton Huffman, working out of Miles City, Montana, could capture range life; that, in 1861, ten years after its initial settlement, C. A. Clark could take the earliest known photograph of Seattle from outside his newly established log cabin studio; or that Adam Clark Vroman, a Pasadena bookseller by profession, could spend his summer vacations toting his camera through the desert Southwest. This is to reaffirm, of course, that photography was inextricably part and parcel of an economically and politically expansionist movement. The entrepreneurs, for instance, would often not only take individual portraits for newly settled town dwellers to send to their folks back home, but also pictures of their other businesses, perhaps initially housed in tents, then in small stores, then in big ones on main streets complete with wood-planked sidewalks. And these same images would be shown to people in state and federal government to stress how well things were humming along. They were used, that is, as a component in boosting further expansion.[16]

Photographers such as those I have mentioned both recorded aspects of the West and, consciously or unconsciously, helped to create an iconography of it that has retained its potency within the dominant culture, especially as replicated in the Western film. For instance, Jackson's famous image titled 'North from Berthoud Pass' (1874)[17] has little to say about the specific geographical nature of Berthoud Pass, but it *is* a virtually definitive romantic evocation of westering American man. The figure seemingly moving off into the indistinct distant mountains – the unknown – even wears headgear that could be mistaken for a tricorn hat of the Revolutionary War era, as if he is a kind of founding father obeying the injunction of his nation's 'manifest destiny' to subdue the alien and awesome continent.

But what was alien to incoming whites was familiar to those who lived there. As Luther Standing Bear so succinctly put it:

We did not think of the great open plains, the beautiful rolling hills, and winding streams with tangled growth, as 'wild'. Only to the white man was nature a 'wilderness' and only to him was the land 'infested' with 'wild' animals and 'savage' people ... When the very animals of the forest began fleeing from his approach, then it was that for us the 'Wild West' began.[18]

Photography was part of a colonizing movement which not only took possession of land from Native Americans, but also attempted to appropriate their cultures. Indians did not, of course, 'wield cameras' – at least not until relatively recently – and so were almost as powerless to keep control of the images made of them as they were of the land they had inherited. W. H. Illingworth, who was appointed to General Custer's command, actually photographed a specific incursion when, in an ironic adoption of an Indian's eye-view, he depicted the extended line of troops and wagons of Custer's expeditionary force entering the Black Hills in 1874 (one of the events which triggered the Battle of the Little

Big Horn two years later).[19] Indians, despite the earlier specific allocation to a particular tribe of the land in question, are also notably absent in the images Andrew A. Forbes made of the so-called opening up of the Cherokee Strip in April 1889. Even when Indians are present in such photographs this total context must be borne in mind if a better understanding of their images is to be achieved. Whatever the degree to which they comprised the subject of such pictures, they were *always* other, the object of a stare.[20] There is often, in fact, more than an element of ambiguity in the images produced by these expansionist photographers. Consider O'Sullivan's 'Sleeping Mohave Guides' (c. 1871; pl. 31) in which expedition geologist G. K. Gilbert sits pensively in the middleground while three Mojaves lie somnolent on the sandy floor of the desert below him. It is tempting to read this photograph as a kind of sideways prefiguration of his Apache Lake image, a first look at the degree to which Indians were totally at one with their ostensibly hostile environment. But it also speaks graphically of Gilbert's dominance of *his* surroundings, including the Indians. That is, the careful viewer may intuit what was so often the situation: the Indians depicted were merely incidental to the 'real' action and in such images are, literally, marginalized – like the allegorical Indian figures in early maps of the New World.

Sometimes ambiguity arises differently. As cameras were used so bluntly to record everything, we have images, for instance, of the defeated Geronimo and his men sitting on the railroad embankment beside the train which transported them into exile in Florida, far from their own Southwestern border country. Geronimo and his followers were captives, prisoners, and – as photographed by the army lensman – are viewed as objects for our curiosity.[21] A similar objectifying stare is at work in many Native American portraits. Will Soule, who was ostensibly employed by the army to document the construction of Fort Sill in what was to become Oklahoma, went to the lengths of making an actual portrait studio – complete with artificial backdrop of a European lakeland scene – in which to take pictures of both white personnel and such Indian figures as the Kiowa leaders Santanta and Kicking Bird.[22] It is often not appreciated that much of the grave demeanour of such still Indian faces as these – even, paradoxically, their power to intimate tragedy – is attributable to the fact that they are not truly portraits but, rather, mug shots.

31 Timothy O'Sullivan, 'Sleeping Mohave Guides, California', c.1871

It should be expected that images made by self-made entrepreneurial Western photographers will be similarly shot through with ambiguities. It is known, for instance, that Huffman was able to make a living from the constant recycling of his pictures from the 1870s and 1880s – as postcards, hand-tinted enlargements, and so on – right up until his death in 1931.[23] If Huffman acquired a sense of history, Grabill, who made the 'Villa of Brule' image discussed earlier, had it from the start. Realizing that changing times would endow such pictures as 'The Last Run of the

Deadwood Stage' (1890) with enduring interest, he copyrighted them. 'Villa of Brule' itself, in fact, is sometimes subtitled 'The Great Hostile Indian Camp on River Brule near Pine Ridge, South Dakota' and represents not just a large winter landscape with Indian figures, but the final free days of the Sioux. They had fled their reservation in the wake of the notorious army massacre of Big Foot's band at Wounded Knee, but soon afterwards they were rounded up by General Nelson Miles and transported back to the reservation.[24]

Wounded Knee and Miles's subsequent campaign presented for Grabill primarily an opportunity not to be missed; and his Indian images are, for us, a welcome bonus. It was not until the rise of amateur photographers (like Vroman) specifically interested in Native Americans; or of professionals (like Matteson or such Bureau of American Ethnology camera workers as Francis Harper) who would adopt them as dominant subject matter for a period, that images of a different order could emerge. But these, too, especially as exemplified by the life's work of Edward S. Curtis, have their ambiguities.

4

'Landscape', as Denis Cosgrove so concisely put it, 'is not merely the world we see, it is a construction, a composition of the world.'[25] So what of the Indian figure in landscapes impelled by awe of nature, an awe so noticeable in the latter half of the nineteenth century? 'The admiration of mankind is found, in our time, to have passed from men to mountains', wrote Ruskin, 'and from human emotion to natural phenomena.' While Ruskin himself felt that 'all true landscape' nevertheless 'depends for its interest on connection with humanity', in the America of this period, as Barbara Novak has shown, mountains loomed large and the human figure became a small, speculative presence.[26] Allen Koppenhaver is surely right to speak (in his contribution to this book) of 'the *lonely* figure'.

In American painting – and, to a lesser extent, photography – of the time, the figure, according to Novak, was often introduced not to assert humankind's controlling interest in the land, as in 'North from Berthoud Pass' or Andrew Russell's 'Malloy's Cut, near Sherman' (c. 1868), but as a surrogate for the viewer, as a means of inviting contemplation of vast transcendental spaces.[27] Thus, in Novak's opinion, Thomas Cole and

213

William Cullen Bryant as depicted in Asher Durand's 'Kindred Spirits' (1849), while atypical in their recognizability and scale, are 'in dialogue not only with each other as kindred spirits, but with each other *through* the equally kindred spirit of nature itself'.[28] That is, at one end of the spectrum, certain landscapes rendered the desirability and possibility of human consonance with nature. At the opposite end of the spectrum, other landscapes invoked a totally different kind of awe and contemplation: astonishment, terror, uncertainty, an awareness of solitude, silence, and vastness – in short, all the features of the Sublime as defined by Edmund Burke's *A Philosophical Enquiry into the Origin of Our Ideas of the Sublime and the Beautiful* (1757). Thomas Moran's painting 'The Spirit of the Indian' (1869),[29] while professedly an illustration of Hiawatha's conflict with and victory over the malevolent spirit Pearl Feather, encapsulates, to my mind, both ends of the spectrum in an extraordinary manner, with Indian figures representing opposed notions. The figure of Hiawatha is seen in scale, apparently at ease, in a vast wilderness. He is, indeed, consonant with it. But, in the upper right of the painting, among the mountain crags and mists, is another Indian figure: an ethereal, feathered giant whose ghostly rendering allows him simultaneously to advance into the picture and disappear into the mistiness – certainly an evocation of the Sublime.

What seems crucial from our point of view is that at all stages on the much discussed continuum of nature as rendered in landscapes from the picturesque to the Sublime, the figure of the Native American (unlike that of the white American) almost always emerges – in this instance, in whichever guise – as, in the words of *Leslie's* caption, a 'Child of Nature'. Writing of Albert Bierstadt and others, Novak summarized, 'the Indians in ... landscapes represent nature, not culture. Like the forests, the Indian exists in a state of nature, before he is cut down. His tenancy as a natural citizen is premised on his inseparability from nature'. (She also concluded: 'When separated, he dies.')[30] Herein may lie a deeper reason for the inclusion of the huddled Indian figures, surrounded by the profligate flora of nature, in Muybridge's 'Indian Village': seated on rocks, crowded by trees and shrubs, they are photographed not as a cultural group – they literally have nothing to do – but as part of nature.

Thus too, the mere presence of a Native American figure may evoke the past of a particular scene, or perhaps its passing, or, even, its destruction to come. A telling instance of this from painting is Cole's 'A

Distant View of Niagara' (1824) with its two small Indian figures. As Ellwood Parry noted, their inclusion, all wild and befeathered, could not have been based on observation because commercial development of both the Falls and their camp site was already underway at the time of the painting's composition;[31] they serve, rather, as icons of nostalgia. Similarly, in certain photographs dealing with acculturation, the Indian figures inevitably represent a passing era. Matteson's bicycle track image, for instance, records, in mythic terms, 'the taming of the West'. In the case of the image most dwelt upon here, 'Scene in Glen Cañon', that particular landscape has irrevocably gone, transformed by dams on the Colorado and by recreational schemes.

Not surprisingly, it was a powerful sense of nostalgia for the vanishing West as a whole, but also for the Indian, which kept Huffman's work in circulation for so long and which generated many of the artistic photographic landscapes with Indian figures. By the time such self-conscious activity became prevalent, the dominant mode of American art photography was pictorialism. This was a movement which, as contemporary critic Charles Caffin noted, often involved the domination of one tone throughout a composition, avoidance of detail in favour of broad masses, and, most significant of all, 'looking at objects through a great gauze veil'.[32] In the much published work of Edward Curtis and in that of some of his contemporaries, notably Mora, Karl Moon and Roland Reed, such a style was meshed with a profound regard for Native Americans as, in Curtis's adopted phrase, a 'vanishing race'. 'The Vanishing Race' (1904) itself, printed in sepia, its shadows of cañon wall accentuating the evening twilight into which the line of Navahos disappear, is the quintessence of pictorialism. Its indistinctness, to be sure, makes it almost difficult to discern the second rider's head, which is turned to look back, as if in regret, as the party rides, in the words of Curtis's caption, 'into the darkness of an unknown future'.[33]

While it is predominantly Curtis's Indian portraits which are constantly reprinted, it is worth remembering that the first success of his photographic career was as a landscape photographer and the earliest of his Indian pictures to achieve national prominence were landscape-cum-genre studies such as 'The Mussel Gatherer' (1896) or 'Homeward' (1899).[34] They prefigured the kind of photographs Francis Harper was to produce, exemplified here in the view of Tom Hill's boat landing. Also, in the introduction to his monumental *The North American Indian*,

32 Edward S. Curtis, 'A Mountain Fastness, Montana', 1908

published in twenty volumes of illustrated text and twenty portfolios of
photogravures between 1907 and 1930, Curtis spoke quite openly of
'the fact that the Indian and his surroundings lend themselves to artistic
treatment'. 'Indeed,' he continued, 'to overlook those marvellous
touches that Nature has given to the Indian country, and for the origin
of which the native ever has a wonder-tale to relate, would be to neglect a
most important chapter.' This is really another way of saying that his
photographs essentially portrayed Indians as figures in landscapes. *The
North American Indian* would offer, he said, 'a record of the Indian's
relations with ... the phenomena of the universe ... as a broad and
luminous picture.'[35]

Obviously, in an output of such proportions as that of Curtis we once again confront the problem of mass, but if we restrict ourselves to examples among those images which seem most blatantly nostalgic and which also resemble scenes of action akin to those in Frederic Remington paintings – themselves a constituent force in the creation of the iconography of Western movies[36] – the problems are posed in their sharpest form. 'An Ogalala War Party' (1907) depicts a band of Sioux, war lances at the ready, eagle feather headdresses flying in the wind, galloping down a steep hillside.[37] Similarly, 'A Mountain Fastness' (1908; pl. 32) presents a party of mounted Apsaroke or Crow warriors in Pryor Cañon, Montana. While these images represent Indians as a fierce force to be reckoned with – and of the Crows Curtis's caption adds 'nowhere do they seem more at home' – at the time they were taken the Plains Wars had ended, had been ended absolutely in fact by the actions witnessed by Grabill. All the actual figures depicted in such Curtis images were hemmed onto reservations. Their remaining lands were in the process of being allotted in accordance with the Dawes Act to individuals among them in a double effort: to turn them from warriors into tillers of the soil and to extinguish tribal identity.

Interestingly, when Curtis came to defend such images in a letter to his editor, Frederick Webb Hodge, he opposed the position of such anthropologists as James Mooney by arguing for the accuracy of his images precisely *as reconstructions*:

Let us return to the title of the picture in question ['A Cheyenne Warrior']. It does not necessarily imply that the man is engaged in battle, or at the instant of going into the fight. An Indian *of the old days* was a warrior 365 days of the year, a very small part of which would be spent in actual fight ... If a war party were starting out they would ... don all their fine clothing and ride around the camp. A picture made of them then could be titled 'Warriors', and the title be beyond just criticism.[38]

Moreover, there is a curious sense in which a reconstruction cannot leave its objects as mere 'children of nature'. It was, precisely, the *culture* of Indians which was changing under the pressure of events and which had to be reconstituted, composed into, in these cases, landscapes with figures out of a warrior culture. Indeed, all these images, however much or little they seem transcriptions from the physical reality of the world, its people and landscapes, elude anything more than temporary categorization. In retrospect, so to speak, many of Curtis's images cannot fail to

Mick Gidley

evoke in some of us scenes from such John Ford films as *Stagecoach* (1939). The American terrain itself is changed, not just physically by the generations of Indian and white settlers who have worked upon it, but by the multiplicity of vantages and contexts from which it is framed and viewed. The figures in the landscape, however still, fixed there by both the photographer and the action of actual light on chemicals, continue, paradoxically, to move.

Notes

1 Reproduced in Louis B. Casagrande and Phillips Bourns, *Side Trips: The Photography of Sumner W. Matteson, 1898–1908* (Seattle: University of Washington Press for Milwaukee Public Museum and the Science Museum of Minnesota, 1984), p. 53.

2 Mount's painting is reproduced, among other places, in Barbara Novak, *Nature and Culture: American Landscape and Painting, 1825–1875* (London: Thames and Hudson, 1980), p. 262.

3 For McKee, see, for example, Ralph W. Andrews, *Photographers of the Frontier West: Their Lives and Works, 1875–1915* (New York: Bonanza, 1965), pp. 18–29, and for examples by most of the others see Weston J. Naef and James N. Wood, *Era of Exploration: The Rise of Landscape Photography in the American West, 1860–1885* (Boston: New York Graphic Society, 1975) and Karen and William R. Current, *Photography and the Old West* (New York: Harry N. Abrams, 1978).

4 Reproduced in Tyrone Stewart et al., *The Year of the Hopi: Paintings and Photographs by Joseph Mora, 1904–06* (Washington, DC: Smithsonian Institution Traveling Exhibition Service, 1979), pp. 10–11.

5 Reproduced in Patricia Trenton and Patrick Houlihan, *Native Faces: Indian Cultures in American Art* (Los Angeles: Los Angeles Athletic Club and the Southwest Museum, 1984), p. 30.

6 Information from Joanna Cohan Scherer, *Indians: The Great Photographs that Reveal North American Indian Life, 1847–1929, From the Unique Collection of the Smithsonian Institution* (New York: Crown, 1973). This mass of imagery in itself tends to invalidate words like 'great' and 'reveal' as used here.

7 Barthes, *Image, Music, Text*, trans. Stephen Heath (London: Fontana, 1977), p. 27.

8 The idea of Indians as 'children of nature' has a long history and usually embraces both the notion of Indians as innocent and as childlike, *unable* to mature. See Robert E. Bieder, *Science Encounters the Indian, 1820–1880: The Early Years of American Ethnology* (Norman: University of Oklahoma Press, 1986), pp. 5–6.

The figure of the Indian in photographic landscapes

9 Although attributed to Beamon in *Leslie's*, it may have been a mistake; possibly the original photograph was made closer in time to its 1886 publication in engraving form, as would more usually have been the case.

10 For an elaboration of this point, see Mick Gidley, 'Western Photography', in Edward Buscombe, ed., *The BFI Companion to the Western* (London: André Deutsch in association with the British Film Institute, 1988).

11 See Casagrande and Bourns, *Side Trips*, p. 53.

12 O'Brien, in *The New York Review of Books*, 15, No. 8, 5 Nov. 1970, 12.

13 See, among other places, Berger's *Ways of Seeing* (Harmondsworth: Penguin with the BBC, 1972), pp. 104–8; and comments by Bush, Clark, Clarke, Mulvey, and Stokes in their contributions to this book.

14 This print, originally painted by F. F. Palmer, is reproduced, among other places, in J. L. Pratt, ed., *Currier and Ives: Chronicles of America* (Maplewood, NJ: Hammond, 1968), p. 99.

15 Sontag, *On Photography* (Harmondsworth: Penguin, 1979), p. 65.

16 Particular details in this paragraph were culled from such works as Andrews, Naef and Wood, Current and Current, and Robert Taft, *Photography and the American Scene* (1938; New York: Dover, 1964); its point is elaborated somewhat in Gidley, 'Western Photography'.

17 Reproduced, among other places, in Eugene Ostroff, *Western Views and Eastern Visions* (Washington, DC: Smithsonian Institution Traveling Exhibition Service with US Geological Survey, 1981), p. 58. The figure, according to Ostroff, was that of Harry Yount, hunter for the Hayden Survey in 1873 and later the first ranger in Yellowstone Park.

18 Luther Standing Bear, *Land of the Spotted Eagle*, as quoted in T. C. McLuhan, ed., *Touch the Earth: A Self Portrait of Indian Existence* (New York: Pocket Books, 1972), p. 45.

19 Reproduced, among other places, in Martin F. Schmitt and Dee Brown, *Fighting Indians of the West* (New York: Scribner's, 1948), p. 127.

20 For Forbes pictures, see Current and Current, *Photography and the Old West*, pp. 201–5. For an elaboration of the argument here, see Mick Gidley, 'North American Indian Photographs/Images', *American Indian Culture and Research Journal*, 9: 3 (1985), 37–47.

21 Photograph, untitled, reproduced in Schmitt and Brown, *Fighting Indians of the West*, p. 329, who claim it was taken not by an army man, but by an 'enterprising' entrepreneur.

22 See Russell E. Belous and Robert A. Weinstein, *Will Soule: Indian Photographer at Fort Sill, Oklahoma, 1869–74* (Los Angeles: Ward Richie Press, 1969). In Soule's particular case there is a further area of objectification in that he made studies of unnamed Native American women, breasts bared, reclining on skins, often looking more discomforted than the woman in

219

'Scene in Glen Cañon'. They are suspiciously akin to clumsy cheesecake pictures, which some anthropologists have dubbed 'ethnoporn'.

23 See Current and Current, *Photography and the Old West*, p. 166.

24 Grabill also documented these activities: see Current and Current, *Photography and the Old West*, pp. 214–21.

25 Denis E. Cosgrove, *Social Formation and Symbolic Landscape* (London: Croom Helm, 1984), p. 13. Several of the concepts in this interesting work of historical geography could be applied to the American situation in an even fuller manner than Cosgrove, himself, does.

26 Ruskin, *Modern Painters*, as quoted in Estelle Jussim and Elizabeth Lindquist-Cock, *Landscape as Photograph* (New Haven and London: Yale University Press, 1985), p. 29. It is noticeable that very few of the American landscapes assembled in *Landscape as Photograph* contain any figures at all.

27 Novak, *Nature and Culture*, especially pp. 184–96. Russell's 'Malloy's Cut', in which a man surveys the newly laid railroad tracks taking their parallel iron ways almost to infinity, is reproduced on p. 184. See also Philip Stokes's comments on 'contemplators' in this book.

28 Novak, *Nature and Culture*, p. 188.

29 Reproduced in Ellwood Parry, *The Image of the Indian and the Black Man in American Art, 1590–1900* (New York: Braziller, 1974), p. 125.

30 Novak, *Nature and Culture*, p. 189.

31 See Parry, *Indian and Black Man*, who also reproduces the painting, pp. 57–8. Mulvey, in this volume, refers to the concern of other travellers over Niagara's 'development'.

32 Caffin's phrase is quoted in Jussim and Lindquist-Cock, *Landscapes as Photograph*, p. 65. For elaborations of the links between pictorialism and contemporary styles of Indian photography, especially Curtis's, see Beth B. DeWall, 'The Artistic Achievement of Edward Sheriff Curtis' (unpublished MA dissertation, University of Cincinnati, 1980), pp. 49–63.

33 Reproduced, among other places, in Mick Gidley, ed., *The Vanishing Race: Selections from Edward S. Curtis' 'The North American Indian'* (1976; rpt Seattle: University of Washington Press, 1987), p. 12.

34 See Gidley, 'Edward S. Curtis Goes to the Mountain', *Pacific Northwest Quarterly*, 75 (Oct. 1984), 164–70.

35 Curtis, *The North American Indian* (Cambridge, MA: University Press, 1907), vol. 1, pp. xiii–xv.

36 See Edward Buscombe, 'Painting the Legend: Frederic Remington and the Western', *Cinema Journal*, 23 (Summer 1984), 12–27.

37 Reproduced, among other places, in Gidley, *The Vanishing Race*, p. 190.

38 Curtis to Hodge, 14 Jan. 1908, Hodge Papers, Southwest Museum, Los Angeles.

Index

References to page numbers of plates appear in italics.

221

Index

Index

Index

Index

227